On Sidesaddles to Heaven

The Women of the Rocky Mountain Mission

On Sidesaddles to Heaven

The Women of the
Rocky Mountain Mission

Laurie Winn Carlson

CAXTON PRESS ™
Caldwell, Idaho
1998

Library of Congress Cataloging-in-Publication Data

Carlson, Laurie M., 1952 –
  On Sidesaddles to Heaven: the Women of the Rocky
Mountain Mission / Laurie Winn Carlson.
      p. cm.
  Includes bibliographical references and index.
  ISBN 0-87004-384-6
  1. Indians of North America – Missions – Washington (State).
2. Women missionaries – Washington (State) – Biography.   3.
Indians of North America – Missions – Idaho.   4. Women mis-
sionaries – Idaho – Biography. I. Title.
E78.W3C35 1998
979.5'03'082–dc21   98–10199
                                                      CIP

Lithographed and bound in the United States of America by
CAXTON PRESS
A Division of The CAXTON PRINTERS, Ltd.
Caldwell, Idaho
163289

Acknowledgements

I have many thanks to give for the assistance, inspiration, and advice I've received while working on this project. Thanks of course to my husband, Terry, and my parents, Ed and Juanita Winn. You've listened to my "missionary lectures" many times, but you are caring enough to let me continue. Judith Dammel and Linda Rogers, thank you for encouraging me when I needed it. The Idaho Writers League, Coeur d'Alene Chapter gave me much to be thankful for—they listened to chapters several times. Joy Scott, and the Cheney Writers, I appreciate you.

Thank you to Carolyn Bowler, Idaho State Historical Society; Roger Trick, Whitman Mission National Historic Site, Laura Bowler, Stark Museum of Art; Lawrence Dodd, Penrose Memorial Library at Whitman College; Carol Lichtenberg, Holland Library, Washington State University; Jim Darden, saddlemaker, Pine Bluffs, Wyoming; Karen De Seve, Research Library, Cheney Cowles Museum; Nancy Compau, Northwest Room, Spokane Public Library; Marsha Takayanagi Matthews, Oregon Historical Society; Sara Sanders-Buell, National Gallery of Art; Georgia Barnhill, American Antiquarian Society; Richard Rattenbury, National Cowboy Hall of Fame; Mary Rash, Washington State Historical Society; Susan Bushel and Chrisanne Brown, Nez Perce National Historical Park; Research Library, New York State Historical Association in Cooperstown, New York; Martha Asher, Sterling and Francine Clark Art Institute; Glenda Riley, Ball State University; and Robert M. Utley. Thank you to the Spalding family members who were warm and helpful: Joanne Stacy, Thelma Spalding, Diane Spalding and Russ Spalding. Also, thank you to Mike Green, at Eastern Washington University, for advice and assistance, and Wayne Cornell, for putting it all together.

Laurie Winn Carlson
March 1998

Contents

Illustrations

Author's Note

Browsing a used book store in Coeur d'Alene, Idaho, I discovered a thin little volume I couldn't put down. *Memoirs of the West*, was the title, still visible on the faded canvas cover. It was written in 1916 by Eliza Spalding Warren, a daughter of Presbyterian missionaries who went west in 1836. Based on her own recollections (she survived the Whitman Massacre of 1847 as a child and was the only one of the forty-seven hostages who could actually speak the Indians' language) and her mother's diary (Eliza Hart Spalding), the book whet my appetite for more. What were these women's stories?

Narcissa Whitman and Eliza Spalding are mentioned in most histories of the western movement, usually a physical description of Narcissa as a bubbly, fun sort of person, and Eliza as a dark, stick-in-the-mud. Both are lumped together as stiffly self-righteous females with no business in the West. But there were six young women who came to the Oregon country as missionary wives; Eliza and Narcissa were joined by Mary Richardson Walker, Myra Fairbanks Eells, Sarah White Smith, and Mary Dix Gray. They were all from New England, all educated and willing to go anywhere in the world for the mission cause. Beyond stereotypes of women, and the heavier stereotype of missionaries, what was their story?

At a time when a woman's entire fortune and future was tied to the man she married, four of the six mission women married virtual strangers, on short notice, with absolutely no financial security. Why did they take such a gamble? What shaped their lives that allowed them to take such a risk? Was it faith alone?

Apart from the Mormon role, religion in the West has not received the attention it deserves, yet it was one of the shaping influences with a tremendous impact on settlement and politics. Not only western writing, but western art and music, too, show few religious themes. Why? The dominant role of materialism in the settlement of the western United States seems to have crowded out the role idealism played.

The public has ignored religion's role in the West in favor of seeing history as entertainment. Maybe Ferenc Szasz, a scholar of the topic, explains it best by saying that it's difficult for novels and movies to portray a "moral" person; "the dilemmas of rakes and rascals make far more interesting reading, than does a life of righteousness."[1] Perhaps he's right. Maybe the images we hold onto of western do-gooders, Bible-thumpers, and frontier preachers (and their prissy wives) have misled us. As Szasz explains, "In the saga of the mythological West . . . most other characters adapt easily to generalization. The cattleman, cowboy, outlaw, sheriff, and schoolmarm have all achieved a timeless universality. Only the western religious figures cling stubbornly to sectarian boundaries."[2]

Writers who have explored religious themes have usually sung "hymns of praise" rather than analyzing religious figures as complex people. Western movies and novels always portray one preacher per town, never two that interact or compete. In reality, there were many itinerant preachers wandering across the West, staking out "claims" (for souls) and trying to set up churches. We haven't heard about the rivalries, conflicts and sacrifices made by those who came West not to get rich, or build an empire, or fight wars, but to follow a "calling."

Although I had grown up in the area of the Oregon mission stations—Lapwai, Idaho; Walla Walla, Washington; and Spokane, Washington—I knew little about the missionaries' lives. They are out of vogue, and almost an embarrassment to local residents and historians, perhaps because the mission purpose was viewed as a "failure" and now we see the futility of the whole situation. They truly were different from others who came west. They insisted on spreading education, refused to carry arms, and were determined to raise the living conditions and status of Indians at a time when tribes were being forcibly removed from their homelands in the East. The women were more than missionary wives; their goal was to elevate the lives of women through education and spirituality; they were America's first feminists. The real story of their lives shatters all the stereotypes.

And he said unto them, Go ye into all the world, and preach the gospel to every creature.

St. Mark, 16:15
Holy Bible

December 17, 1834
Are females wanted? A Miss Narcissa Prentiss of Amity is very anxious to go to the heathen. Her education is good — piety conspicuous — her influence is good. She will offer herself if needed.

Letter from Rev. Parker to American Board for
Foreign Missions[3]

Notes

[1] Ferenc Morton Szasz, *The Protestant Clergy in the Great Plains and Mountain West*, 1865-1915 (Albuquerque: University of New Mexico Press, 1988), p. 4.

[2] Ibid, p.5.

[3] Clifford Merrill Drury, *Marcus and Narcissa Whitman and the Opening of Old Oregon* (Seattle: Pacific Northwest National Parks and Forests Association, 1986), I, p. 110.

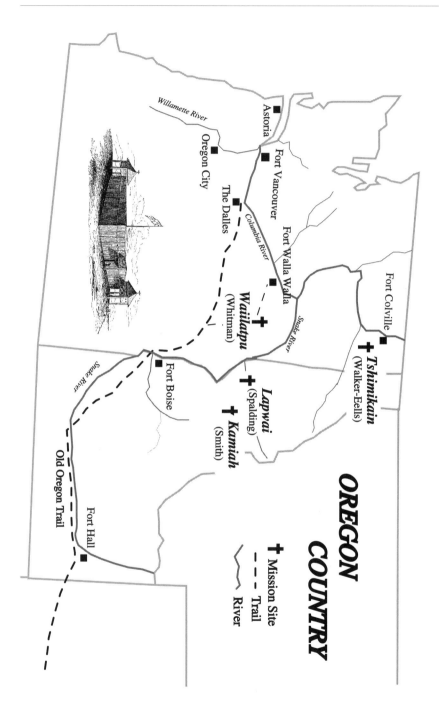

OREGON COUNTRY

✝ Mission Site
– – – Trail
⌒ River

Willamette River

Astoria

Fort Vancouver

Oregon City

The Dalles

Columbia River

Fort Walla Walla

Waiilatpu
(Whitman)

Snake River

Fort Colville

✝ Tshimikain
(Walker-Eells)

✝ Lapwai
(Spalding)

Fort Boise

✝ Kamiah
(Smith)

Snake River

Old Oregon Trail

Fort Hall

Chapter One

A Woman's Place

*May a wise providence direct my way. perhaps I have a
better opinion of myself than I ought to have. Birds that
fly high light low may be true of me yet. But I hope not.*
Mary Richardson (Walker) diary entry, Sept. 1836[1]

Mary Richardson, like any other young woman living in
a rural Maine village in the mid-1830s, faced a future
with hard choices; choices her mother and grandmoth-
er never had to make. They had married young and made their
family and home the mainstay of their lives. But times were
changing.

Mary was a young adult at a time when the country and the
economy were in upheaval. For many, the talk was always of
going farther west; building new communities, clearing new
land, expanding. Surely the West, which was the Ohio Reserve
at that time, was a powerful magnet. But not everyone saw
appeal in forging out away from civilization.

Like nearly all Yankee girls, Mary's social life revolved
around school and church. While seated primly in church, she
would have heard the warnings and worries of clerics who saw
the West, even the far-off Rocky Mountains, as a place where
vile men had gone in order to enjoy "vice and human nature,
even animal nature."[2]

If the West beckoned with financial opportunity, church-
goers were reminded that it was important that civilized people
went West, too, taking their culture with them. Clergymen

warned of "the bowie-knife style of civilization," and the very
real probability that Westerners would descend into anarchy,
with armed bands of ruffians roaming the region at will.[3] With
such dire warnings, it seemed unlikely any properly educated,
upwardly-striving young woman like Mary would ever dream of
going to such a wasteland.

She was practical and a product of her time; she wasn't
flighty or enamored with doing foolish things. When she was a
child she watched swallows building their nests, "Some would
choose a place to build, persevere, and in a few days finish a fine
nest; others would place a few bills full of mud in one spot, a few
in another, & then desert all." She thought the latter "wanting
in good sense."[4]

Mary Richardson wanted to do something with her life.
When she considered her own future, a Spartan New England
cottage filled with children, or the possibility of becoming an
unmarried spinster toiling the rest of her days as an ill-paid
teacher or seamstress, she wasn't enamored with what she
faced. The typical life of the women around her didn't interest
her as much as the potential for taking part in the genuine battle between good and evil that was going on in the West, where
the outcome would determine the fate of the nation. It was a
matter of character; Mary and other missionaries saw themselves as entering a larger arena, and doing something grand
with their lives.

Mrs. Childs, author of a wildly-popular guidebook for
housewives at the time, advised women that "self-denial, in pro-
portion to the narrowness of your income, will eventually be the
happiest and most respectable course for you and yours."[5] If one
were to live in a state of self-denial, as young women were being
advised to do, why not practice self-denial in a situation that
offered the possibility of spiritual salvation? Why not offer one-
self to the missionary cause?

Unmarried, educated young women had real worries about
becoming spinsters. If a girl didn't marry, she would have to
support herself. But how? Teaching was still not entirely acceptable for a young woman. Sunday school, that was alright, but of
course it didn't pay. Otherwise, a girl had to work hard just to
obtain an appointment to her own school. Mary's mother had

been the town's first female teacher, but she'd given it up when she married. Teaching didn't pay much, and the young women were forced to live with students' families and try to collect tuition money from tight-fisted parents.

Mary fretted about a persistent suitor, a neighboring farmer who was always trying to court her. She was frustrated that he took "so much liking," and admitted that she didn't think she "ever could like him much." In fact, she could "find very few" men that interested her. She worried that she might be a "solitary creature," as she could

Historical Photograph Collections, Washington State University Libraries

Mary Richardson Walker

"find few that think and feel as I think & feel."[6]

It was an increasingly complicated world. Young men were waiting longer to marry than their fathers had. In an economy that was changing, they had to make something of themselves in order to someday support a wife and children. It was harder to obtain decent farmland or start new businesses than it had been for the generation before them.

The average age in the United States in the period from 1815 to 1830 was sixteen.[7] That meant by the mid-1830s there were many more young people trying to make a living and start families than there were opportunities. Both men and women were waiting longer to marry, hoping to hit upon a suitable business or profession, often going back to complete their elementary schooling in their twenties in hopes of obtaining a position somewhere. Teaching, military or missionary were often the only choices for young people who wanted to escape their small communities and see the world.

Girls began working while in their teens, and unless they married, they were doomed to a lifetime of genteel poverty due to extremely low wages. And wages were essential in the new, burgeoning industrial economy. Young single women from New England migrated to the mill towns to sign up for work. The jobs demanded twelve to thirteen hours of labor a day, six days a week; and they had to sign a contract committing themselves to one year at the job. Pay was fifty-five cents a week, with piecework rates allowing an energetic worker to make four dollars above their board charges for the week. The average worker earned a little over two dollars a week.

There was no shortage of workers. Women between the ages of sixteen and twenty-five flocked to the mills because living accommodations were furnished and the jobs paid more than teaching, seamstressing and domestic work—the only other jobs available to women. Only Sunday was free from work and mill owners made certain the girls were kept busy that day with church and church-related activities or reading circles. This kept them from organizing labor movements or learning new skills that could lead them away from the mills. With their limited social life revolving around church, stories of foreign missionary women provided them a fantasy life that made their drudgery tolerable.

Knowing her situation, Mary Richardson worried when she turned down a marriage proposal, calling it a "fair sort of an offer," and wondered whether she "ought think of accepting it or not." If only the suitor possessed "knowledge & piety" she would like him. But she was afraid he lacked "a kindred soul." Mary was living during a cusp of change. Marriage, long a business and financial transaction between families, was increasingly becoming romantic. Girls like Mary wanted more than a "fair sort of offer." They wanted romance, and they wanted to marry a hero, someone who was a "kindred soul."[8]

Spring, 1833. Mary Richardson (Walker) had just completed another school term, teaching forty "schoellars":

I have now done my school . . . I am now glad to get through . . . I have a desire to engage in some new enterprise that would call all my energies into exercise.[9]

Obtaining an education was becoming women's salvo. Because churches were the engines of literacy (so necessary to Christian doctrine based on printed text), they also became the launching ground for creating female academies. It became possible, even acceptable, for young girls to be educated beyond elementary school. Obtaining an education became women's hope for a future. It was thrilling, exciting and full of promise; and educated women developed a fervent desire to spread education as a way of helping other females find a better future, too. Knowledge was something precious and new and the opportunity to obtain it far too powerful to waste.

There are beaux that want to call on me full as often as I want to see them. Tell Phebe I didn't come to Readfield (Seminary) to catch beaux.
(Mary Richardson Walker's letter to her brother)[10]

Girls like Mary were eager to learn about all the new ideas swirling around them. When Mary heard her first sermon preached by a black man, at a church in Portland, Maine, she was intrigued. His text was "ye see the distress we are in" and she thought he preached "as well as many white men I have heard." She later heard a lecture about the "colonization society" from the anti-slavery proponents. Mary heard that a colony of about four thousand settlers had been set up in Africa, where one thousand blacks from the U.S. had been relocated. She understood it would put an end to slavery. Hearing all these new ideas intrigued her; she felt she would "burn" herself "under a high degree of excitement" in the stimulating atmosphere of Bowdoin College during a series of lectures and speeches she attended.[11]

While girls like Mary were eager to exercise their abilities, they were warned that they shouldn't expect too much. After all, Mrs. Childs admonished parents that if they were "not prosperous, it would be well for your children that they have not been educated to higher hopes than they will ever realize."[12] Was Mary only setting herself up for disappointment?

Experts warned that young women were being given ideas far above their station in life. "Until sixteen they go to school; sometimes these years are judiciously spent, and sometimes they are half wasted; too often they are spent in acquiring the *elements* of a thousand sciences without being thoroughly acquainted with any; or in a variety of accomplishments of very doubtful value to people of moderate fortune."[13] Attempts for girls to learn music and drawing were "useless and undesirable" unless they had the "taste, talent and time enough to attain excellence."[14] Young women were told to learn "useful things" so they could be "better fitted for the cares" of a family.[15]

The Erie Canal, a giant endeavor into public works as well as the first technological effort to penetrate the West, had just opened. It upset life in nearly every hamlet and home. People could now do something they had never done in the past—they could travel.

Leisure travel was just beginning and it brought interchanges between different social orders. It opened up the isolated, conservative Puritan communities to the cosmopolitan groups that now flooded through. Europeans, notably destitute Catholics from Italy and Ireland, rubbed shoulders with Protestants who had never been out of their own villages. No one knew what to make of it—books admonished people not to waste away their time and money in travel, and people began to distrust the strangers they saw coming through their towns. The rage for traveling was an "extravagance" that would break up "good old home habits of our ancestors" and would result in the loss of "virtue and freedom" next.[16]

Crime began to be a factor, at least in people's minds. With travel, came pickpockets, con artists, thieves and swindlers. All sorts of characters were on the move, and anyone traveling was sure to be too genteel to work and too proud to beg.

Along with the increase in crime, the influx of new people brought disease. Cholera hit New England, and people felt their lives were out of control.

People responded in many ways, but the strongest was through religion. Fervent crowds embraced wildly evangelistic preachers, many who claimed the world was coming to an end. For staid New Englanders facing upheaval in their daily lives, it probably seemed that it might.

Western New York state during the 1830s was a fertile field for itinerant preachers or those who had seen a vision or dreamed of cultivating their own following. Religious revivals spread so quickly and thoroughly through rural New York that the western region was called the, "Burned-Over Area," due to the many revivals that flooded through the communities again and again. It was a hotbed for fresh religious ideas and energetic, enterprising individuals roamed the countryside starting up new religions overnight. All it took was a vision, speaking ability, and a sense of the coming millennium. The world was due to end, and the alarm couldn't be sounded strongly enough.

Women were the audience; the world was changing as men found success in the new trade and industrial world, but their wives and daughters were increasingly being held at home. Men left the home to find success off the farm, and left behind the role they had played as Puritan patriarch. Increasingly out of the house, the father gave up his duty to educate his children to the growing number of schools. Without allowing them into the labor force (where their numbers might take jobs from deserving men) married women were isolated at home and given the task of nurturing and maintaining the family morality. That meant the religious realm of middle class family life was turned over to women, who found identity and solace in religion, as well as a chance to fulfill their own potential. There was little else they were allowed to do.

Advice to young ladies in the 1830s:
I will tell you what will be about the right amusement for you, beyond the garden and field. An occasional ramble with a friend or with a small party in pursuit

*of rare plants, flowers, minerals, insects or birds. And
should you, in your zeal, so far compromise your dignity as to forget the staid snail-like pace, to which, ever
since you entered your teens, society has endeavored to
constrain you, as to walk a little more rapidly, or even
run and clap your hands and shout, 'Eureka', do not
think you have committed the sin unpardonable in
Heaven's Court.*

From a book of the time, *A Gift Book for Young
Ladies*[17]

Women in the past had been charged with creating their
family's clothing. By the 1830s that need was being filled by
American factories, or businesses that imported British factory-
made clothing. A woman's worth was no longer measured in
lengths of homespun, laboriously created from start to finish by
the woman of the house, her elders and her children. Cash now
bought the family's clothing—cash that the husband earned.

With schools educating the children out of the home, and
clothing and many household items purchased with the husband's earnings, married women needed a purpose. That need
was filled by inspirational preachers and close-knit religious
denominations that provided structure, purpose, and a social
life for women who were increasingly finding their field of
dreams limited.

Women filled the small churches and embarked on great
effort to be of some good. Society admonished young ladies to be
"taught that usefulness is happiness, and that all other things
are but incidental."[18]

The idea that women could, through religion, change society and even the world, was gripping. They threw themselves
into Bible study groups, church societies, and hymn singing. But
that was not enough. Women were learning about the outside
world, and they wanted to be involved. The global effort to civilize the "dark" countries held exciting appeal. It was the age of
expansion and settlement, and even housewives in tiny New
England villages wanted to take part.

Women enthusiastically supported mission efforts in the
cities (called home missions) as well as around the globe. They

donated cash, jewelry, and spare time. Missionary societies flourished. During this heyday of mission effort, upright and self-sacrificing Protestant missionaries were sent around the globe to bring the light of Christianity to those who had lived in obscurity long enough.

> *When I reflect upon the wretched condition of those benighted souls who are sitting in the gloom and shadow of death, I actually long to depart and be with them, to tell them the story of a Saviour's dying love.*
> Eliza Hart Spalding's diary[19]

At home, women gathered to thrill to returned missionaries' tales of what life was like in Calcutta, in darkest Africa, or among the exotic Orientals. Educated women who had never left their hometowns devoured accounts and letters published in missionary periodicals. Letters sent home from those in the foreign mission field were read aloud in church meetings and community gatherings or published and distributed. Tracts were widely circulated and mission news filled the front pages. Biographies of the lives of foreign missionaries and their wives were studied with rapt attention by young women who wondered if they would ever be so brave if faced with torture and imprisonment or even exotic disease in a far-off land. The fact that everyone back at home would be singing and praying for you made the fantasy even more attractive.

The women who became missionaries in Oregon were no doubt influenced by a woman whom young girls read about with awe. Ann Judson, considered one of the most remarkable women of her age, was the wife of Adoniram Judson, a missionary-celebrity of the era. One of the first and most famous foreign missionaries, Adoniram and the heroic Ann, wrote letters and diaries that revealed how their days were spent bringing Christianity to heathen people in the magnificent palaces of Burma.[20]

Ann described the richly dressed monarchs, kings, princes, and the viceroy of Rangoon as she traveled by river boat through jungles into a world Americans could only imagine.

Their experiences wowed the audience back home. When Adoniram was imprisoned in Ava after the war between India and Burma broke out, Ann visited him every day, and wrote home about it. The only European in the country not in prison, Ann's courage was admired in Britain and the United States. When she buried her child, 25,000 women in America wept with her. When Ann died a lonely death in a far-off land, women knew she'd gone to her Savior.

Women didn't last long in foreign missions, Adoniram buried three wives. Even that didn't sway young women from wanting to be like Ann, to stand beside a heroic man, fighting the good fight wherever they might be sent by the Mission Board.

The hymns of the era were inspiring to young girls who read about the Judsons and others like them. The words from a missionary hymn of the 1820s seem to focus more on the beautiful and exotic geography than the people:

"From Greenland's icy mountains,
From India's coral strand,
Where Africa's sunny fountains
Roll down their golden sand,
From many an ancient river,
From many a palmy plain,
They call us to deliver
Their land from error's chain.

Can we whose souls are lighted
With wisdom from on high,
Can we to men benighted
The lamp of life deny?
Salvation! O salvation!
The joyful sound proclaim,
Till each remotest nation
Has learned Messiah's Name.

Waft, waft, ye winds, His story,
And you, ye waters, roll,
Till like a sea of glory

It spreads from pole to pole:
Till o'er our ransomed nature
The Lamb for sinners slain,
Redeemer, King, Creator,
In bliss returns to reign. Amen."[21]

If hymns did admit to hardship in the foreign mission field, whatever the missionary endured would be tempered with glory:

"Ye Christian heralds, go proclaim
Salvation through Emmanuel's Name;
To distant climes the tidings bear,
And plant the Rose of Sharon there.

God shield you with a wall of fire,
With flaming zeal your breasts inspire,
Bid raging winds their fury cease,
And hush the tempests into peace.

And when our labors all are o'er,
Then we shall meet to part no more;
Meet with the blood-bought throng to fall,
And crown our Jesus Lord of all. Amen."[22]

. . . I long to be telling the dying heathen the story of the cross. O, how happy I shall be in my laboring for the good of these dear Indians.

Sarah White Smith [23]

While tales of male missionaries in the field were exciting and charismatic, the personal letters and diaries that were published by their wives probably incited the most interest. Women devoured the stories of those heroic females who stood by their missionary husbands when they were imprisoned, who endured privation and torture in foreign lands, or buried their babies far from home. Thousands of sisters, in kitchens or at looms, shed tears along with the women in the field.

These published accounts of mission work and energetic traveling lecturers incited more than just sympathy and admiration, they lit a passion for adventure in young women's minds and hearts.

> *At the age of 9 of 10 my mind first became interested in the cause of the missions, & I determined if ever it were in my power, I would become a missionary. I fixed on the age of 19 as the time when I would engage in the work.*
> Mary Richardson's letter to the American
> Board of Commissioners for Foreign Missions[24]

Educated, independent, and with no opportunities in their tiny home towns, six idealistic young women joined the Rocky Mountain Mission project. It was an experiment, to see if the American Indians living so far from settlement could be brought to Christianity and settled; saved before the encroachment of white civilization destroyed them. The American Board of Commissioners for Foreign Missions, a combined effort of the Presbyterian and Congregational churches, headquartered in Boston, would direct the venture. The innocent heathen were perishing; there was no time to lose. "Who will go?" was the question in church and classroom.

It was intriguing, it was daring, and it was heroic. In the name of Christianity and the United States, six young women married missionary husbands (several were practically strangers before the ceremony) and gave up everything they had known to join the venture into the far West. They'd be going where there were no wagon roads, no towns or way-stations, no government protection. The country didn't even belong to the United States. They didn't hesitate to wonder if it could be done.

This was their chance.

Notes to Chapter One

[1] McKee, *Mary Richardson Walker*, p. 68.

[2] Szasz, *The Protestant Clergy*, p. 13.

[3] Szasz, *The Protestant Clergy*, p. 14.

[4] McKee, *Mary Richardson Walker*, p. 43.

[5] Mrs. Child, *The American Frugal Housewife*, (Boston: Carter and Hendee, 1833) p. 5.

[6] McKee, *Mary Richardson Walker*, p. 61.

[7] Paul Johnson, *The Birth of the Modern: World Society 1815-1830* (New York: Harpercollins, 1991), p. 218.

[8] McKee, *Mary Richardson Walker*, p.68.

[9] Ibid, p. 54.

[10] Ibid, p. 50.

[11] Ibid, p. 57.

[12] Child, *The American Frugal Housewife*, p. 5.

[13] Ibid, p. 93.

[14] Ibid, p. 93.

[15] Ibid, p. 93.

[16] Ibid, p. 93.

[17] Ruth Karr McKee, *Mary Richardson Walker*, p. 33.

[18] Mrs. Child, *The American Frugal Housewife*, p. 92.

[19] Clifford Merrill Drury, *Henry Harmon Spalding* (Caldwell: Caxton Printers, 1936), p. 59.

[20] Francis Wayland, *Memoir of the Life and Labors of the Rev. Adoniram Judson, D.D.* (Boston: Phillips, Sampson and Co., 1853),II, p. 329.

[21] *The Hymnal* (Philadelphia: Presbyterian Board of Christian Education, 1949), p. 385.

[22] Ibid, p. 381.

[23] Clifford Merrill Drury, *First White Women Over the Rockies* (Glendale: Arthur H. Clark, Co., 1963-66), III,p. 87.

[24] Ruth Karr McKee, *Mary Richardson Walker*, p. 44.

Winslow Homer, *Bridle Path, White Mountains,* 1868.
© *Sterling and Francine Clark Art Institute, Williamstown, Mass.*

Chapter Two

Sidesaddle

Husband has got me an excellent sidesaddle, and a very easy horse. He made me a present of a mule to ride, the other day, so I do not know which I shall like best—I have not tried the latter . . .

Narcissa Prentiss Whitman's letter to her sister, Jane, from the steamboat *Chariton*, on the Missouri River, April 7, 1836[1]

A sidesaddle's design (or lack thereof) seems determined to put a woman at complete disadvantage on a horse's back. The high single stirrup makes mounting nearly impossible. With the help of a mounting post and a helpful male, voluminous long skirts must be positioned as a woman swings high to grasp the perch between her thighs.

Once in the saddle, the rider must sit with legs to one side, and shoulders facing forward. The spine twists at an angle, jarring with every forward jerk of the horse's back. A woman's weight is distributed so unevenly that the rider must use the right arm to hold a quirt or parasol simply to balance herself.

If the horse acts up, the rider has only one way to keep her seat. The saddle has no horn to grasp with her hands, no stirrup for the right foot, not even a cantle at the back to hold her in place. She can only push the left foot against the stirrup, left thigh against the leaping horn (a curved piece that juts from the upper left side of the saddle), at the same time pushing down against the leaping horn with her right thigh, pinching the leaping horn between her thighs in an attempt to hold on.

Sidesaddle travel isn't suited for even skilled riders, or cooperative horses. A skittish horse, uneven ground, and an inexperienced rider combine in an equestrian nightmare.

So what compelled six women, educated Yankees all, to travel from New England to far-off Oregon Country in such a manner? They'd spent their days in pews, parlors and class-rooms. They had rarely traveled and were not skilled horse-women—some had never ridden before.

Two of the women were pregnant on the 1,200-mile portion of the journey made on the backs of ill-broke, trading post ponies and mules.

To those women it was a matter of course. In fact, a journey by sidesaddle was somewhat innovative and even liberating, compared to how their mothers had traveled.

Sidesaddles were new "technology." Colonial women rode on pillions, even into the Kentucky and Ohio frontiers. Pillions were small pillows that fastened to a man's saddle. Women on horseback rode on a pillion, either in front or behind a male rider. One sat sideways on the horse's back, feet tucked in a lit-tle wooden swing that hung from the pillion. Pillions were used until the end of the 1700s, particularly in the northern colonies, and weren't completely discarded until the Civil War, when sidesaddles replaced them.

Undoubtedly, for women faced with travel on a pillion, a sidesaddle was indeed freedom. Even though a male (husband or servant) was still needed for mounting the horse and dis-mounting, a woman could ride her own mount, at her own pace. She might even go riding without a man—something unheard of in the past. For women on the frontier, a sidesaddle was def-initely a step in the right direction.

What seems incredibly awkward today—attempting to cross the plains and mountains on a sidesaddle—was logical to the women involved. Compared to how their mothers perched on pillions (if they indeed ever rode), a new sidesaddle was the stylish and independent way for a woman to travel.

The way looks pleasant, notwithstanding we are so near encountering the difficulties of an unheard-of journey for females. — Narcissa Prentiss Whitman[2]

In the spring of 1836, when Eliza Spalding and Narcissa Whitman headed towards the Rockies with their missionary husbands, the very idea of females—American females—going into the Oregon Country, was highly controversial. Indian, Mexican, and *metis* females were considered hardy and insignificant, and they were already there. The fact that these women were educated, cultivated, and from New England, that's what mattered. They were from a completely different world; they were literate. People would pay attention to what they wrote. They would be able to chronicle what it was like in letters and diaries and journals that could be read back home. They would be able to spread literacy to the savages, imperative for Protestant faith based on the written word of the Gospel.

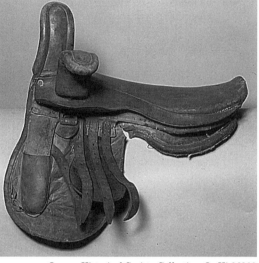

Oregon Historical Society Collection, Or Hi 96908

Mary Walker's sidesaddle

But would these women be able to survive? The Indians weren't Yankees, after all. Would savage passions be ignited by the mere presence of such sacred womanhood? If women *could* make the trip, where only explorers and adventurers had gone before, would there be anything to hold them back? Would they remain putting in long, dark hours of drudgery in the cloth mills of New England?

Critics argued that the husbands were wrong to put their wives in jeopardy. How could anyone expect women to ride horseback so far, to endure the weather and privations such a journey demanded? Some adamantly opposed women going— after all, the West was for hardy adventurers, explorers, traders — *men*.

Rev. Henry Spalding, questioned whether it was a good idea for him and his wife Eliza to go so far—he'd been hoping to receive an appointment to Indians much closer, the Osages, perhaps. He discussed it with the artist, George Catlin, who had just returned from an extensive painting expedition into Indian country.

Catlin was shocked at the very idea of taking American women into the frontier, and urged Henry to reconsider. Henry wrote to the Mission Board expressing his concern about taking Eliza, saying that Catlin warned him he "wouldn't take a white female into that country for the whole continent."[3] Catlin warned that a female would incite the "distant tribes" into "unrestrained passion" which would cause "her ruin" and the "ruin" of the mission. Henry wrote that he had discussed this with Eliza, but she "would trust in God" and "go forward without fear."[4]

Henry was pragmatic about what they would face, asking the Board if it really thought a woman could go so far on horseback; sidesaddle was no easy way to travel, after all. Catlin's opinion was that the physical demands alone would "destroy" women. The physical challenge was enormous: "1,400 miles from the mouth of the Platt, on pack horses, rivers to swim, and every night to be spent in the open air, hot sun and storms, the buffalo meat we can live on doubtless," Henry reminded the Board. Wasn't there an easier way? "I hope we shall be able to take wagons," he suggested.[5]

David Greene, the Secretary for the American Board of Commissioners for Foreign Missions, replied:

"I do not think that you or your wife will find your ride laborious and protracted, to be peculiarly unpleasant or deleterious to your health." Of course he was writing this from the comfort of a comfortable office in Boston. "Nor do I apprehend any danger of the kind Mr. Catlin suggested, from the Indians." How reassuring, particularly since Mr. Greene had not been in the West himself. The Board's motives in sending women on such a dangerous and difficult trek, into a risky situation with no assistance of any kind, shows itself: "The females will, I think, be rather a protection than otherwise," he wrote to Henry.[6]

Ultimately the United States needed to move west; the East was running out of available land in the face of a growing population. People who found themselves landless were being put to work in the emerging factories of New England as the industrial age dawned, and they weren't very happy about it. Bread riots, bank collapses, and strikes were increasing and investors and politicians feared what had happened in France. There was an urgent need to open the West, if only to release the pent up frustrations that were building steam along with industrialism.

The very idea of extending settlement into the Indian Territory appalled those who ran the lucrative fur trade; settlement would wipe out the animals. As if there wasn't enough to contend with already, fur trade rivalries threatened to disrupt business with the natives anyway, and the whole area was a hotbed of political intrigue. Since before Lewis and Clark, small, discreet parties had been sent out by various countries to spy on the fur trade and map the unknown terrain. Settlers would simply add another uncontrollable element.

But some visionaries were eager to see women go into the Rocky Mountains. Where women could go, so could families, and that meant settlement . . . and commerce. The chance to undermine the British fur trade, and a hoped-for base of operations on the Northwest coast, as well as control of the Columbia River, were on the minds of the politicians and financiers. Sending women, even as missionary wives, was a start. Others could soon follow.

It would be nearly a year before anyone back East heard from the women again. It had taken two years for Lewis and Clark to return from the Pacific, and many had thought they perished. The Columbia River drainage, was isolated and difficult to get to, in fact many missionaries had refused to go to the Oregon Country, favoring locations in deepest Africa, China, or the Sandwich Islands, because they were much more accessible. It took a year to get a letter to New England, and another year for the reply, the Oregon Country—for Americans, at least—was about as isolated as one could get. Travel there even required government permission and a passport from the War Department.

Motorists along Idaho's Highway 95, the main link between the northern and southern halves of the state, notice the oasis-like Nez Perce National Historical Park, east of the city of Lewiston. In early autumn it is hot, dry, terrain The naked beige hills rise up starkly from the Snake and Clearwater rivers. Temperatures often are over one-hundred degrees in summer; winters can be harsh. The barren hills are covered in faded, dry grass most of the year.

Just like the Whitman National Park at Walla Walla, Washington, commemorating the early mission at Waiilatpu, the Lapwai site today is a pleasant spot of watered green lawn set amid vast wheat fields and timberless hillsides. Picnickers spread over the grassy expanse, tables overflow with detritus and lunch trash, recreational vehicles line the parking lot. As you walk to the edge of the Clearwater River (Dworshak Dam, thirty miles upstream, holds back some of the once-tumultuous flow), you try to picture this a meadow, what the Nez Perces called, "The Place of the Butterflies." There's no sign of the mission now, the area is part of the Nez Perce Indian Reservation which stretches farther up the Clearwater River to Kamiah, Idaho.

Why would anyone from green, fertile, *civilized* New England villages, come to this isolated, barren spot 150 years ago? What propelled a handful of Americans to settle *here,* so far from trade routes, forts and settlements? There must have been an underlying motive. Was it political? Was it stupidity? Greed? A giant misunderstanding?

When Henry Spalding and Marcus Whitman first visited the Nez Perce homeland, in what is now northern Idaho, looking for a location for the Spaldings' mission station, they were dismayed. The barren landscape "greatly discouraged" them; the spot was "mountainous and broken," the valley "narrow and without soil." Henry was an optimist, but even he was ". . . riding far behind, almost disheartened."[7]

Spalding was looking for farmland; a place where he could settle the Indians, and guide them to prosper. "I thought it was all over with the poor Nez Perces . . ." he worried.[8]

But the Nez Perces were adamant about getting missionaries and teachers; they would do whatever it took to encourage the Godpeople—the *soyappos*—to settle with them. And they had a very good reason.

A tour of the spare yet efficient little museum near Lapwai provides a glimpse into why the intrepid missionaries ventured here in the first place.

Inside the museum, displayed in a glass case, is the innocent reason that people came so far across the continent, braving unknown peril with little protection if things went wrong. A small black book, bound in elkskin. A booklet really. It was printed near where the book is displayed—the first book printed in the Northwest—the first to spring from the Mission Press at the Clear Water Mission station. It was printed on a hand press brought by ship and muleback from Hawaii, handstitched and bound by hand. Printed in the Nez Perce language, its translation and typesetting imperfect, it is the force that propelled the missionaries to leave behind all they had known in order to do something they felt had a larger purpose.

The tiny book was the reason for everything.

Notes on Chapter Two

[1] Narcissa Prentiss Whitman, *The Letters of Narcissa Whitman* (Fairfield, WA: Ye Galleon Press, 1986), p. 14.

[2] Ibid, p. 13.

[3] Clifford Merrill Drury, *Henry Harmon Spalding*, p. 119.

[4] Ibid.

[5] Ibid.

[6] Ibid.

[7] Clifford Merrill Drury, *Henry Harmon Spalding*, p. 159.

[8] Ibid.

Chapter Three

Changing Times

New York, Feb. 20, 1836
*Today we met Dr. Whitman, who has been laboring for
some time to obtain associates to accompany him west
of the Rocky Mountains to establish a mission among
the Nez Perces Indians. These dark minded heathens,
having a few years since learned something about the
Bible, are now very anxious to receive it and to have
missionaries come and live among them . . . He had
failed in every other attempt to obtain some one to go
out with him in the capacity of a minister, and if he did
not succeed in getting Mr. Spalding to engage in this
expedition he should relinquish the idea of going out
this season . . . . Duty seemed to require it, and we are
now with joyful hearts looking for our place of destination west of the Rocky Mountains.*

Eliza Hart Spalding's diary[1]

In 1831 a small band of Indians from the Salish and Nez
Perce tribes traveled all the way from the Pacific Northwest
to St. Louis, to find the white man's Book of Heaven. At least
that's how the story goes. Historians argue over whether the
incident actually happened, or if it was promoted because it
made excellent press for an audience that wanted to save the
world.

The Indians reportedly asked for "The Book," which of
course, to wildly millennial Protestants, meant the Bible.

The incident was published in the *Christian Advocate Journal*, along with woodcuts of Indians, their foreheads grotesquely misshapen by the natives' practice of placing infants in a cradleboard "press." To readers, the distorted forehead symbolized the way women and children were subjugated by heathen practices; the image echoed the abhorrent Chinese practice of binding little girls' feet, which Christian women in Britain and the United States were determined to wipe out through adamant missionary work in efforts to upgrade the lives of females.

Women donated jewelry and meager "mites" to fund mission projects for these extraordinary inquirers after the truth. The images of the Flathead people were so unusual, odd and pathetic, it demanded that good Christians put down whatever worldly goods they were pursuing, and go save them instead.

There was another reason to reach them quickly—it was imperative that Protestant missionaries arrive in the Rocky Mountains before Catholic missionaries. The Jesuits, a Catholic missionary order under the Pope's direction, had been revived in Europe a decade earlier and they were spreading around the globe once again. A hundred years earlier they'd vigorously established missions in Asia and South America, only to be disbanded for political reasons.

It *could* have been that the Indians had traveled to St. Louis (then the headquarters for the western Catholic missions), in order to seek Catholic priests, who were hard at work in the Canadian field. Indians would have known about the Black Robes from the free-roaming traders and trappers who had already taught some of them the rudiments of Christianity.

To Protestant Americans, Catholics equated foreigners; they were *Romans*—Irish, Italians, French, Mexicans, and Canadians. The ultimate foreigners, Jesuits were seldom citizens of the United States and many didn't even speak English. If the Indians were seeking Catholicism, the Protestants needed to hurry the truth to them. Missionaries had to be dispatched, and with Godspeed.

The Indians, incidentally, were on a mission of their own. They had been undergoing a 300-year weather cycle that had made their homeland much colder than normal. Food had been increasingly difficult to obtain. There had been continual war, since horses first arrived in their area between 1730 and 1750. It had been only four generations since their lives and economies had changed completely by the new way of life the horse, and geographic mobility, brought.

Pastoral, wandering people had been turned into wandering, nomadic, warring clans. Warriors were suddenly more important than hunters. No longer did a resourceful hunter steal up on a lone buffalo cow and use skill and handmade

Walker's drawing of a Flathead Indian that appeared in the *New York Christian Advocate and Herald*, March 1, 1833.

tools to bring her down. Fast horses, trade guns, and slaves were a man's hallmark of success.

Women were faced with huge amounts of work, tanning and preparing all the meat that resulted from buffalo hunts. That meant capturing slaves to help with the labor was a necessity. The only way to obtain them was through plunder and theft. The Indian social structure was stretched to the limits. Young men were ignoring old leaders, usurping their right to guide the people. On top of that, a volcano had erupted, bathing the interior Northwest in layers of thick dusty ash, and a comet had streaked across the night sky. Everyone knew something was about to happen.

A common prophecy had circulated among tribes in the Columbia River plateau since 1790, when a man known as the Spokane Prophet, said, "soon there will come from the rising sun a different kind of man from any you have yet seen, who will bring with them a book and will teach you everything, after that the world will fall to pieces," following which a new restored and better world would begin.[2]

So the Indians welcomed whites, because they thought these newcomers might be part of the essential route to a new future. Perhaps that's why the little band of Indians went to St. Louis, to urge white men to come live among them—in order to hasten the coming millennium. Whatever the case, they were met by equally fervent millennial Christians, eager to help out.

Were the Indians asking for the Bible? Who knows. At that time the Spokane Indians had a young man return from attending school at a Hudson's Bay colony in Canada. He'd been chosen to go learn what he could at the British colonial school there, part of a program set up by Canadian Governor Simpson. He was called Spokane Garry and he returned to impress his friends and relatives with skills at reading and writing, and knowledge of white ways. He also brought back a Bible. When the Nez Perces, rivals of the Spokanes, heard about the Bible, they must certainly have thought that it was only right their people, much wealthier and more numerous than the Spokanes, should have one, too. And hearing of it, the Cayuses, neighbors and highly competitive themselves, were not to be outdone. In fact, when the tribes first met the Spalding and Whitman missionary party in the Rocky Mountains in 1836, Nez Perce and Cayuse women fought over who would get to bring the coveted missionaries to their homeland. The argument was settled by reassuring the Indians that there would be two stations, settling one couple with each nation.

Mary Walker arrived with the mission's reinforcement party in 1838 and was well aware of the Indians' efforts to obtain "the Book." Here's what she wrote, in the first letter to her parents after arriving in the Oregon country, published in the *Christian Advocate*:

You have still fresh in mind the story of those Indians who came to St. Louis to try & obtain religious instruction & teachers to come & teach their people. There were if my memory serves seven chiefs some Nez Perce & some Flat Head. They went to the States with the traders of the American Fir Co. & spent the winter at St. Louis I think in the family of Mr. Clark. The same who accompanied Louis in his exploring in this country. By him they were introduced to the Roman Catholics & thus their design in making their long journey had like to have been frustrated. A Methodist Minister however happened by some means to learn something of their intention & published it. And so at length their wishes became known to the publick. This was the origen of all the missions in this western wilderness.[3]

The Indians may have thought "the Book" was endowed with special magic or charms; theirs was a material culture, where objects held deep meanings. A few years later, after the missionaries had printed and passed out small Bibles, Indians often wore them on thongs around their necks, or tucked them in cradleboards with infants for protection and luck. They viewed the object itself as having some meaning or power.

The Book and the efforts to obtain it were the first misunderstandings, in a mission effort that was to be riddled with them. Two very diverse types of people were about to bring their cultures in contact, with very different ideas about how to proceed and the intended goals. While the missionary effort was to save and civilize the Indians before the evils of that very civilization could enfold and corrupt them, the Indians were seeking the technologies of that same civilization in order to enrich their own material culture. They had no intention of changing their own well-entrenched belief system or practices. They were only doing what nations had always done, establishing trade for new and innovative products.

The Indian mission effort was part of a large and energetic mission movement that swept the United States from the early 1800s until the end of the century. A large class of people who were passed over by the technological revolution of the time. The commonly accepted belief that by working hard, delaying gratification and leading an upright life, a farm boy could achieve success in the larger world of trade and commerce didn't always work. Success now meant delaying marriage, living simply, saving one's money, and hoping for a break.

The frontier was closed, and the vast West was Indian Territory or belonged to Spain, Britain, Mexico, and Russia. Agricultural practices had meant continually clearing fresh land, and now they were out of fresh land to put into production. It was not a time of opportunity, and everyone knew it.

It was appalling to see the laboring classes, "drowning in a sea of Sabbath-breaking, laziness, promiscuity, drunkenness, and utter ignorance of the Christian religion."4 The "alarming increase in poverty that accompanied the trade disruptions of the Napoleonic Wars had overwhelmed the alms-giving capacity of the old merchant families."5 While the upper-class had decided these problems were fit for police action, the religious proselytizers felt that appeals to a higher order were needed. Women had already been working long and hard at helping the poor in New York City; the Female Missionary Society began in 1817 as a fund-raising effort to support male missionaries in the city's slums.

The evangelicals preached that poverty and disorder were the result of failed families and bad moral choices. Poverty and its problems weren't the result of God's plan, but of man's willingness to take up vice and ignorance. It was useless to hand out charity to people who drank, avoided work, and sinned. Unable and unwilling to give the poor handouts, the evangelicals gave them preaching and moral instruction. Failure was seen as the result of sin, a common sermon in the early nineteenth century.

Mission stations were built among the boarding houses and waterfront dives. Male missionaries preached at churches established in poor neighborhoods; women, banned from preaching, visited the homes of the poor, taking them prayers, advice and their own notion of what domestic life should be. In doing so, women created the beginnings of the strong female-centered home and family that emerged by the Victorian era. The primary arbiter and teacher of morality in the home was no longer the man.6 Loving mothers praying with their children had overcome the stern father meting out discipline as the central figure in the home and family. The concept was new: no longer would children be clinging to a parent's feet in submission, no longer would the parent mete out discipline and authority. Parenting involved affection, rather than dread and hatred. Power was shifting.

It took courage and confidence to visit the sinful households, but it was much easier for women to gain entry than men. Actively working with the poor children and their "careless" parents, home missionary society women took on a stronger role.[7] They helped the sick, gave out Bibles and religious tracts, urged Sunday School attendance for the children, and invited the mothers and daughters to attend church. As they worked, they gained competence and something else. They gained confidence and saw themselves with a courage they had not found before. They were doing something important, and they were doing good.

"Womanhood as a whole" was being "lifted up and given a position of dignity and influence."[8] Female efforts were also directed towards helping women and their children held prisoner in heathen cultures that despised them. "Heathenism" venerated animals, at the same time it denigrated women.

Heathen homes were "strongholds of Satan" and could only be penetrated by Christian women who were "aglow with gratitude for their elevation through Christ." Deplorable practices in foreign cultures (particularly the Orient and India) made women "unwelcomed at birth, unloved and oppressed in life, and unwept at death." Child marriages, female seclusion, Chinese foot binding, Arab harems—womanhood was "trampled under brutal feet" around the globe.[9]

Not only were females subjugated in the "dark" areas, they were illiterate and "excluded from every avenue for mental culture."[10]

In response to arguments that heathen religions were well-suited to the people who practiced them, proponents of the mission effort asked, "What can be said of religions which doom half of the human race to degradation inconceivable, dwarf aspirations; and stifle sympathies, robbing life of every joy, and the future of every hope?"[11]

Because of their "enviable position" compared to females worldwide, Christian women couldn't "dismiss responsibility without an effort to mitigate a doom incident on heathen birth which but for the grace of God might have been theirs."[12]

It was imperative that courageous women step forward, because "the very first effect of a mission in any . . . pagan community has ever been to force into the minds of men the fact that Christians consider girls and women capable of absorbing book knowledge although they themselves have classed them with cows."[13]

Reforming the poor took a lot of energy but it also took money. Fund-raising became the women's strong suit. Females in that day had practically no money or assets of their own, but response to the appeal was overwhelming. "Cent Societies" were founded, and women and girls were urged to join up and make a weekly donation of pennies. Certainly, no matter how dire one's situation, one cent a week could be found. Women came up with the money by denying themselves small luxuries at home: food, grooming items, entertainments. They were making a personal sacrifice to benefit women and children who were living in worse conditions.

By 1839, there were 688 female religious societies. Much of the success was due to the collective nature of the venture. A Cent Society magazine reminded women that, "The ocean is supplied by rivers, made up of small streams. Remember the widow's two mites."[14] There was a groundswell of interest and copper coins flooded into the mission coffers. In 1813, the American Board received its first legacy, $345.83, from the estate of Sally Thomas, a Cornish, New Hampshire domestic, whose wages had never exceeded fifty cents a week.[15]

But clergymen, supportive of the missions, also realized that it could get out of hand. Dominance and submission, between the sexes, was God's plan. A woman could join mission societies, collect funds, visit the poor, and work for the conversion of her own family; but she also had to be reminded that her true dignity and usefulness consisted in filling that station marked out for her by God. She must remember she should remain satisfied in being an *assistant* of man.[16]

The problem was deeper than women's roles within the home. Something larger was developing. If sinners could be educated and saved, boundaries between sinner and saved, rich and poor, male and female, even, government and governed, might logically disappear. *Was prayer the road to anarchy?* If people felt that sin could be overcome by spiritual rebirth, then what use would hierarchy and government be? The power of laws, husbands, fathers, and ministers, along with prescribed customs and social divisions, might not be heeded.[17]

As if to ward off the possibility that women might actually challenge the old belief system, an ideology of domesticity developed. A rapidly proliferating supply of literature during the early 1800s stressed a return to fundamentalism during a period of religious revivalism.

People, as they always do during periods of change, sought security by reaffirming old beliefs. The immense volume of ladies' periodicals, domestic novels, "manners books" and gift books that appeared in the middle decades of the nineteenth century—attempted to teach (or remind) women about *true womanhood*. The books and magazines were determined to guide them into customary female functions, which points out the fact that they might have needed reminding about the "old-fashioned ways" during a time of growing dissatisfaction with, and questioning of, traditional gender roles by many women.[18]

Called "domestic" writing in that era, novels and magazines directed at a female audience were widely read. Domestic writing focused on a passive or "feminine" ideal, as opposed to the "capitalistic or male standards" that were allied with economic growth, industrial and territorial expansion, and urban development. Partially designed to lend larger meaning to the lives of women, it argued that such women had not become superfluous. Women readers were reminded that they were absolutely crucial as guardians of morality and virtue for an increasingly capitalistic society. Women were important to home and hearth, but they should not interfere in politics, government or anything else that would affect the country's push toward prosperity and power.[19]

The idea that women should remain in their own "spheres" was accepted by even intellectual women of the time. While they sometimes railed against the limitations of being in a "woman's sphere," at the same time some women saw strength in the concept of separate spheres for men and women. In 1814, Abigail Adams, long-time advocate of expanded roles for women in the young nation, wrote: "I believe nature has assigned to each sex its particular duties and sphere of action, and to act well your part, there all the honor lies."[20]

But there were hints that the movement could go much far-ther. The editor of *Godey's Lady's Book*, a popular magazine of the era, believed "that women were the conservators of moral power, which, eventually . . . preserves or destroys the work of the warrior, the statesmen, and the patriot."[21] She wrote of the need for women's education, and the necessity of women as teachers of children, aid to charities for the poor and destitute, "and that the heathen of the world be rescued by women serv-ing as missionaries."[22]

Young Christian women were urged to extend their efforts to help the poor and ignorant by carrying literacy and Christianity to the American frontier. In an era of guilt, what woman would have pursued entrepreneurial or professional ambitions, in face of such overwhelming need?

The women who traveled to the Oregon mission weren't anarchists or rabble rousers. They were young women who had been reared with changing roles for women, been far more edu-cated than their mothers ever dreamed, and then inoculated with admonitions to remain in their proper sphere. Writing in diaries and belting out hymns was about the only recourse they had. Unless they married a missionary. Sent to far-off Siam or to the Zulu tribes of Africa, a woman could really do something. She could travel, see unusual things, teach, promote, raise up a family—all without the watchful eye of those intent on keeping her in a sphere.

It was a life almost too good to be true: along with the excitement of living in foreign lands, being talked about and written about back home, and doing good within the larger world, missioning to the heathen gave a woman a chance to save souls. Women missionaries were praised by poets, and "writers eulogized women missionaries, emphasizing the tal-ents and virtues displayed by such women and even lauding them as more courageous than medieval knights."[23]

There was only one thing an aspiring woman missionary needed.

A husband.

Notes on Chapter Three

[1] Eliza Spalding Warren, *Memoirs of the West* (Portland, OR: Marsh Printing Company, 1916), p. 55.

[2] Robert H. Ruby and John A. Brown, *The Spokane Indians: Children of the Sun* (Norman: University of Oklahoma Press, 1970), p. 32.

[3] Clifford Merrill Drury, Elkanah and Mary Walker: *Pioneers Among the Spokanes* (Caldwell: Caxton Printers, 1940), p. 256.

[4] Paul E. Johnson and Sean Wilentz, *The Kingdom of Mathias* (New York: Oxford University Press, 1994), p. 21.

[5] Ibid, p. 21.

[6] Ibid, p. 22.

[7] Ibid, p. 23.

[8] Rev. Henry Otis Dwight, Rev. H. Allen Tupper, and Rev. Edwin Munsell Bliss, *The Encyclopedia of Missions* (New York: Funk and Wagnalls, 2nd edition, 1950), p. 789.

[9] Ibid, p. 788.

[10] Ibid, p. 789.

[11] Ibid, p. 789.

[12] Ibid.

[13] Ibid.

[14] R. Pierce Beaver, *American Protestant Women in World Mission: History of the First Feminist Movement in North America* (Grand Rapids: W.B. Eerdmans Publishing Company, 1980), p. 20.

[15] Dwight, Tupper, and Bliss, *The Encyclopedia of Missions,* p. 790.

[16] Johnson and Wilentz, *The Kingdom of Mathias*, p. 24.

[17] Ibid, p. 25.

[18] Glenda Riley, *Women and Indians on the Frontier, 1825-1915* (Albuquerque: University of New Mexico Press, 1984), p. 3.

[19] Ibid.

[20] Ibid, p. 4.

[21] Ibid, p. 8.

[22] Ibid.

[23] Ibid, p. 9.

Chapter Four

A Marriage of Convenience

Jane, if you want to be happy, get as good a husband as
I have got, and be a missionary.
                    Narcissa Prentiss Whitman in letter to
                    sister Jane, March, 1836; while traveling
                    by steamboat up the Missouri River[1]

Narcissa Whitman, Mary Gray, and Mary Walker each married men they barely knew at a time when a woman had few options, or even rights related to marriage. In the 1830s women couldn't vote or own property, and had little chance of effecting an acceptable divorce if a marriage was unbearable. Why would they take such a gamble by marrying virtual strangers?

Perhaps the answer relates to young women's emerging literacy and the appearance of a unique type of novel. In 1826, James Fenimore Cooper's novel, *The Last of the Mohicans*, was published to such wide popularity that it was reprinted by thirty German publishers alone (heedless of copyright law!). Like wildfire, the character Hawkeye became a nation's (and the world's) new heroic image. With his stalwart Indian companions, he braved the wilderness like any patriotic Christian Yankee should do. Young women swooned at the romantic vision, and yearned for a frontiersman like Hawkeye. Cooper's message that the Indians were disappearing, reassured rather than dismayed readers as frontier novels began to draw interest to the West like magnets.[2]

Looking for a marriage partner, women were looking beyond the traits so important in the past. Marriage was no longer based on inherited property, the blending of large families, or patriarchal patterns of colonial society. Marriage could now be thought of as a spiritualized union between like-minded partners. When Mary Richardson (Walker) wrote in her diary about her quandary over choosing to marry for what she knew to be lust ("the Devil"), or to wait for something spiritual to come along, she chose to gamble on finding the man who would match her emotionally and spiritually. She was looking for a Hawkeye, who would take her into the wilderness.

To puritanical Protestants, novels were denigrated as wasteful trash. Women were given domestic writing, admonitions to remain in their sphere, and submissive stereotypes, but an undercurrent began to emerge: the capable woman. In 1836, the same year the Whitmans and Spaldings ventured west, a popular women's novel was published which was about a "militantly optimistic heroine who supported a large family and engaged in charitable pursuits including the educating of children while supported by an impossibly small income."[3] A new type of heroine was emerging.

While the capable woman wasn't overwhelmingly accepted by society, or even by very many women, her image did exist. By the 1840s even *Godey's* carried stories about heroic women. Articles began to emphasize health and strength in women—all the more necessary to help them perform their moral duties and responsibilities. *Godey's* even changed their fashion plates. The stiff, pudgy figures were replaced with healthy, graceful figures. The editor, Sarah Hale (a widow with five children), saw the magazine as a way to effect "female improvement" rather than merely catering to fashion.

While rejoicing in this boundless domain, it is well to remember to whom we owe our Western possessions. It is due, not to the sagacity of our statesmen, or the prowess of our arms, but to the courage of American missionaries, that a large part of our western coast is today a part of the United States. How this came to pass, is a story

that ought to be told to the honor of American mission-
aries as well as for the truth of American history.
New York Evangelist, December 29, 1870

The Spaldings, a young couple from upstate New York, were
the original missionaries to the Rocky Mountain Indians. But
before Eliza Hart Spalding even thought of heading to Oregon,
she endured every woman's horror: a painful, debilitating childbirth, and a stillborn baby. Henry and Eliza had been married
two years; Eliza was twenty-eight years old. They buried the
infant daughter named Mary, and Eliza's "sickness was protracted & severe".[4]

The loss of the Spalding's much-awaited baby, and the fact
Henry Spalding was out of college, but without a job, made a difficult winter of 1835-36. The couple had planned to go to the
Osage Presbyterian Mission, but pending the birth of their child
they had postponed their trip west until spring, when travel
with an infant would be easier. They had planned to be missionaries for several years, in fact it was that dream that
brought them together in the first place.

Virtually nothing is known about Eliza's early life. She was
raised on a farm, the eldest of six children. While not wealthy,
her father had enough land to give tracts to her siblings when
they grew up and a horse and wagon as well as cash to Eliza
and Henry when they set out West.

Eliza was a product of the time, educated in local schools,
then sent to a female seminary in Clinton, New York. At the
upper level academy, she undoubtedly received enough training
to do more than an adequate job as a classroom teacher herself.
While she was helping support herself and Henry in their newlywed years she had been asked by "a number of ladies" in "the
society" in Cincinnati to open a "select school." In Eliza's opinion, schools on the Ohio frontier were "in a deplorable condition,
conducted without much order or interest."[5]

New educational philosophies were on the horizon, and
Eliza picked up some of them. She used visual aids in the classroom, making up her own charts and pictures with watercolors
and cardstock. She later took cardstock and paints along to

Reverend Henry Spalding
in later years.

Oregon, where she found them extremely useful when teaching people who spoke another language.

The Hart family was not particularly religious. Eliza's father never could understand why she gave her life to the missionary cause, and when she was in far-off Oregon, promised to give her share of his land to her only if she set foot back on New England soil. He was very opposed to her going to work among the Indians.[6]

While she was pious and obedient to God, she found in religion an independence; it gave her a sense of significance to spread Christ's teachings to foreign lands, and a purpose beyond the home and hearth.

At nineteen, Eliza had joined the Presbyterian church on a confession of faith. She became interested in the missionary movement at about the same time.[7] The freedom Eliza had was unknown to her mother's generation. School, teaching, actively working for the church in various ways, considering traveling to far-off lands to save the heathen—it had been impossible for women earlier. Eliza had even moved away from home to be near Henry Spalding, in order to get to know him better. When they decided to marry, she simply wrote her parents, asking their blessings. Then she had a short, simple ceremony of her own choosing. Even the act of joining a church to which her parents didn't belong, was a liberating move her mother's generation wouldn't have considered.

Women during the evangelical era could act with more independence than ever before. Young women could go to school past the primary grades and participate actively in prayer meetings, revivals, hymn singing, and other church-related activities. Most of the evangelical converts were just like Eliza: young, single, mobile women.[8]

When Eliza was twenty-three years old, a female friend put her in touch with a university student who wanted to write to a "pious young lady.[9] The student was Henry Spalding, twenty-seven years old at the time, and the two began corresponding. Henry went on to Hamilton College but didn't fit in as a charity scholar, so moved on to Western Reserve College in Hudson, Ohio.

He was born in New York state, in Prattsburg, the town where Narcissa Prentiss's family lived. But his childhood was very different from Eliza's or Narcissa's. He was illegitimate; his real mother is unknown, his father evidently didn't want him, either. Reared by a foster family, and "probably physically abused," he was kicked out of the house on his seventeenth birthday.[10] He was taken in by a caring school teacher and began his schooling, but at twenty-one years of age he could barely read and write.[11]

Finding religion, Henry was baptized into the Presbyterian church, then enrolled at Franklin Academy and put himself through school. At twenty-two years, this must have been difficult and humiliating. He was older, bigger, less educated, and destitute. But he was also frugal and single-minded. He read a religious tract that detailed plans to evangelize the world, all 600 million people in twenty-one years; and decided to become a foreign missionary. Henry enrolled in school as a ministerial student (that qualified him for free tuition)— all he needed was a missionary wife.

Many historians have characterized Henry as living with a huge inferiority complex due to his illegitimacy. Looking at his accomplishments, however, and his penchant for public speaking, along with a lack of reticence no matter what situation he found himself in (sometimes endangering himself), that doesn't seem to be the case. Perhaps, like Marcus Whitman (who was thought to be a widower before marrying Narcissa), and Elkanah Walker (who proposed to several women before finding Mary Richardson), he was like any other young man, spurned, but not out of the game for long.

He knew one attractive girl who also wanted to be a missionary, the local judge's daughter, Narcissa Prentiss. He proposed marriage to her but she rebuffed him coldly. After

Narcissa rejected him, he was engaged to another young woman, who was eager to be a bride and a missionary. But she developed tuberculosis and broke off the engagement, urging him to find someone better suited to the foreign field.[12]

After a year away at school in Ohio, Henry proposed, Eliza accepted. Eliza's parents agreed to the match and allowed Eliza to move to Hudson, Ohio for Henry's last year of school. Eliza attended a women's school there, Henry still at Western Reserve. They had planned to wait for marriage, but Henry had two more years at seminary so they decided to marry before he started there. That would allow Eliza to go with him to classes. It was against the rules for her to enroll or take examinations (she *was* a woman, after all), but as a *married* female, she could attend classes along with Henry. She would enjoy educational challenges otherwise unavailable to her as a female. They were a perfect match: true soulmates, intellectuals, and would-be missionaries.

Eliza, independent spirit that she was, had followed a man she barely knew to a city almost four hundred miles from home. Now she wrote to her parents about their decision to get married immediately, Henry adding a note to them reassuring that Eliza's "health" was just fine, a euphemism that let them know she wasn't pregnant. October 13, 1833, they were married in a quiet ceremony after the Sunday evening service in the college's chapel.

Now their financial situation, always precarious, needed to be addressed. Two more resourceful people would be hard to find. They rented a house and took in six male students as boarders, which Eliza cooked and cleaned for. Henry worked for a printer when not in class. He took up "the axe" to make ends meet, hiring out at splitting wood.

Eliza wanted to take a teaching position, too, but Henry felt she wouldn't have any time for her own studies. She tutored students on the side to bring in a little more money. She wrote to her sister that she was happy, and that their mother worried too much.[13] Henry wrote to Eliza's sister that she, "does much work in a short time, as probably you already know."[14]

In that era, Cincinnati provided a very stimulating atmosphere. Henry's professor was Lyman Beecher, and two of his classmates were Charles and Henry Ward Beecher. Sister Catherine Beecher, educator, feminist and reformer, was no doubt in attendance as well, made to sit alongside the men without getting credit.

Eliza studied astronomy, algebra, Greek, Hebrew, and theology. She belonged to a prayer group, a sewing club and a female missionary society.[15] Henry was working on the theological degree which would see him ordained in the Presbyterian church. They picked up whatever money-making jobs they could find, and in spite of their hand-to-mouth existence, were able to donate generously to charity and build a decent book collection of their own, the seeds of a future "library" in some far-off land. They made many friends in Cincinnati, and kept a full social life.

After two years' study, the Spaldings applied to the ABCFM to go into a foreign mission immediately. Henry was through with school and had been ordained. In light of the company they had been keeping, and the vigor they had put into study and prayer, they simply *had* to go on a foreign mission. It had become the focus of their lives.

Henry's recommendations were somewhat weak. His professor wrote the Board that he wasn't particularly brilliant, but decent, and that he didn't have much judgment or common sense. He also noted that Henry was quick to criticize anyone who appeared to be less zealous than himself in spreading the word of the Lord.[16]

Eliza, on the other hand, was recommended heartily by the same professor, as being "very highly respected and beloved by a large circle of friends" in Cincinnati. "She is one of the best women for a missionary's wife with whom I am acquainted."[17]

Their long-awaited assignment came by letter, from David Greene, secretary of the American Board for Foreign Missions. They were to go to the Osage nation, in the present state of Missouri. It was August, 1835, and there was one minor detail. Eliza was about to have a baby. An infant would make travel and opening a mission impossible. The Spaldings cancelled their plans. Henry began applying at small churches and government schools for any position available.

After Eliza recovered from the stillborn birth and subsequent poor health, her thoughts turned back to the Indian mission again. The Lord had punished them by taking their infant, but that was past now. Perhaps they could obtain another appointment to the Osage.

By early February, 1836, the Board agreed and the Spaldings were headed towards the Osage mission. In a Dearborn wagon, painted bright blue and yellow, (a gift from Eliza's parents) loaded with their supplies and books, they headed west.

One man heard about their plans and hurried to catch up with them. Marcus Whitman, a single country doctor, accompanied by two Nez Perce Indian youths he'd brought back from the Rocky Mountains the year before, hastened after them. Whitman hoped to become a mission doctor in the far-off mountain West. He had already cleared one hurdle set up by the ABCFM Board—his poor health, due to a continuing pain in his side—had improved. Only two things stood in his way: one was a wife, the other was a preacher.

Whitman had already approached several would-be missionaries, who all turned him down because of where he intended to settle—the Oregon country—which they considered too remote and unsettled. He had one last chance. He could convince the Spaldings to go farther west than the Osage.

He hurried to catch up with them and pleaded the case for the Flatheads, who of course the Spaldings had read about in the *Advocate*. With the smiling faces of the two Nez Perce youths, he pressed his case.

The Spaldings considered the idea, but Eliza's health was doubtful. Henry certainly couldn't expect her to travel so far. Beyond where any white woman had ever gone before—-vast deserts, wild animals, immense mountains—it held little appeal to the couple.

Whitman persisted. Without the Spaldings, he had nothing. Without missionaries along, the entire venture was ended before it began. He must have used powerful persuasion, reminding the Spaldings that unless they went with him, the entire tribes of the Rocky Mountains would be abandoned to the devil. The Osage were already enjoying the benefits of a struggling mission, but the poor natives farther west had nothing.

There could be no hesitating. Travel cross-country, relying on animals, meant careful planning to coincide with the growth of grass; too early into the mountains, or too late, and the animals would starve, stranding travelers. If they were to go that summer, they had to begin now.

Henry was caught in a dilemma. He wasn't impressed much with Whitman, but if this *was* the will of the Lord, who was he to stand in the way? He was told that Narcissa Prentiss was to go along, as Whitman's wife, and he didn't want to go into a mission with her at all. He questioned her judgment; after all she *had* rejected him as a suitor in the past.

He did what came naturally, he left it up to Eliza. He trusted her judgment and relied on her for guidance and advice.

But Eliza wasn't eager to step into the situation, either. A drastic change of plans forced on them by a rough fellow who was clearly their inferior; who intended on bringing a wife her husband had once wanted to marry, on an arduous trek that was unheard of—the whole thing must have seemed so unreal that it could only be the will of the Lord; a mortal couldn't have dreamed up such a strange adventure.

Eliza retreated to pray alone. She had but "a short time to decide the question, whether to change . . . course or not." She announced to the two men, "I have made up my mind to go."[18] To Eliza, "duty seemed to require it . . ." and she would try to be optimistic about what was to come. "We are now with joyful hearts looking for our place of destination west of the Rocky Mountains," she told herself.[19]

Decision made, the Spaldings agreed to wait for Whitman to return to Prattsburg, marry Narcissa Prentiss and meet them in Cincinnati. They spent several weeks in Cincinnati, visiting old school friends and saying goodbyes.

While in Cincinnati, they must have listened to Catherine Beecher's plans to improve female education, and to expand teacher education in order to fill the educational void in the growing Western regions. Another educator that Eliza would have met and listened to was a young man who had just printed up his own textbooks: the first school readers. His name was

William McGuffey, and he'd written simple books to help children learn to read, and was attempting to sell them all over the country. He had spent his career teaching elementary school teachers better methods. He maintained a model school for neighborhood children in his own home, and in 1836 he was president of Cincinnati College. He'd begun teaching in frontier schools at age thirteen, and would have delighted in sharing expertise and ideas with the Spaldings.

Eliza (and Henry, too, being an experienced printer) would have been very interested in this new tool for teaching literacy. It was something they could do, too. Once they were settled with the Indians, who were after all seeking books, they could provide them. All they needed was a huge, bulky printing press, and reams of paper, and barrels of ink, and . . . and it would be next to impossible in the Rocky Mountains . . . or would it?

Notes on Chapter Four

[1] Whitman, *The Letters of Narcissa Whitman*, p. 13.

[2] Paul Johnson, *The Birth of the Modern: World Society 1815-1830*. (New York: Harper Collins, 1991), p. 218.

[3] Riley, *Women and Indians on the Frontier*, p. 27.

[4] Drury, *First White Women Over the Rockies*, p. 180.

[5] Ibid, p. 176.

[6] Deborah Lynn Dawson, *Laboring in My Savior's Vineyard: the Mission of Eliza Hart Spalding* (Ann Arbor: University Microfilms, 1988), p. 19.

[7] Ibid.

[8] Ibid, p. 21.

[9] Drury, *First White Women*, I, p. 174.

[10] Dawson, *Laboring in My Savior's Vineyard*, p. 25.

[11] Drury, *Henry Harmon Spalding*, p. 23.

[12] Dawson, *Laboring in My Savior's Vineyard*, p. 27.

[13] Ibid, p. 29.

[14] Drury, *Henry Harmon Spalding*, p. 58.

[15] Ibid, p. 57.

[16] Ibid, p. 64.

[17] Ibid.

[18] Drury, *First White Women*, p. 184.

[19] Ibid.

Chapter Five

Departure

The Presbyterian Church is a Missionary Society, the object of which is to aid in the conversion of the world, and every member of this Church is a member for life of said Society, and bound to do all in his power for the Accomplishment of this object.

Presbyterian General Assembly, 1847[1]

While Henry and Eliza were chatting it up with the intellectuals, artists, and visionaries of the day in Cincinnati, back in Prattsburg, New York, Marcus Whitman rushed to the altar to claim his bride. It had been a courtship more practical than passionate.

After the *Advocate* article about the pathetic Indians searching for the Bible was published, a Methodist volunteer, Jason Lee, was quick to heed the call. He and his nephew immediately went west with a fur trade caravan from St. Louis. In Oregon, they'd diverted their mission from the Indians to choice farmland in the Willamette Valley, and the chance to save the souls of retired Hudson Bay Company employees there, mostly French and half-breeds.

On Lee's heels was the American Board's man sent to scope out the possibilities for Presbyterian and Congregationalist missions in Oregon: fifty-six-year-old Reverend Samuel Parker, a preacher, scholar and former headmaster of a girls' school. He and two companions headed west to catch up with a fur caravan out of St. Louis, too, but missed them. Parker's two companions set up a mission to the Pawnees in eastern Kansas and he

Reverend Samuel Parker

returned to New England to drum up volunteers and donations. He went to small church meetings where he met a thirty-two year old country doctor and would-be missionary, Marcus Whitman.

Whitman was practicing in a small town, but for some reason wanted to move on. He'd tried setting up a practice in Canada and had returned. He had little money and no property. Riding rounds as a country doctor was no way to get rich or to get respect. Medications weren't usually effective and amputations were about all one could do, but that was done without painkillers or sterilization. A cholera epidemic had passed through the area, wiping out families and leaving misery behind, which may have added to his frustration. Whatever the reason, Marcus Whitman wanted to go elsewhere.

He'd taken two sixteen-week sessions at a medical college and ridden with a country doctor for training. He'd become active in the local church, and decided to go into the mission field. Unmarried, he'd applied to the Board the year before and been denied due to "poor health." He'd sought an appointment to a warm climate, where he thought his health would improve. But the Board was reluctant about his health and his lack of education. When he was finally offered Oregon, he accepted.

Rev. Parker had also met another potential missionary—Narcissa Prentiss—daughter of a distillery owner/builder/judge in the small town of Prattsburg, who attended one of his promotional talks. Narcissa asked him if unmarried females could go, too. He was stymied. It wasn't something he could answer, but he was determined not to let a volunteer get away. If Narcissa Prentiss was willing to go, he had at least two volunteers.

He mentioned her to Dr. Whitman, who wasted no time calling on Narcissa at the Prentiss home. He spent one weekend visiting and they were engaged immediately, with Narcissa's stipulation that the marriage had to wait until the feasibility of the Rocky Mountain mission had been determined. She wasn't willing to marry Whitman unless he had a solid mission appointment.

Narcissa has been described by many writers; large eyes, golden red hair, buxom or "full-bodied," with a lovely singing voice she enjoyed using. She was sparkling, vivacious, and delighted in being the center of attention. At twenty-six, she had not married, but did not lack admirers. Perhaps she was fickle or perhaps she too, was waiting for a "Hawkeye" of her own.

Since Whitman and Parker still needed to investigate the possiblities of an Oregon mission (neither had a clue what lay out West—but neither did anyone else), Marcus hurried off after the two-day visit. However, after leaving the Prentiss home, he spent six weeks making a trip that took Parker two weeks. He hadn't been compelled to spend any extra time visiting his new bride-to-be. Marcus, during the Whitman's eleven years of marriage, often left Narcissa alone with little concern or caring. She tried to put up a good front, but she was a romantic and his negligence bothered her deeply.

The two men caught up with a fur caravan, and made it to the rendezvous in the Rocky Mountains. They weren't well-liked or even tolerated by the fur trade men, except for Marcus's medical skills during a bout of cholera and when Jim Bridger needed a three-inch iron arrow tip cut out of his back. At the rendezvous they decided that Parker would continue on to Fort Vancouver, on the Pacific Coast near the mouth of the Columbia River, scouting the way and setting everything up for the missionary party that Whitman would bring back the next summer. Whitman hurried back eastward with the fur caravan, Parker continued exploring with a party of Indians.

Marcus took two Nez Perce youths back East with him as interpreters and to use in appeals for financial donations and missionary volunteers.

National Park Service,
Whitman Mission National Park

Narcissa Whitman
Painting by Drury Haight from a
sketch done from life by Paul Kane.

After a year's engagement, Narcissa and Marcus had actually been in each other's presence only a handful of days. And Narcissa hadn't been happy waiting for Marcus to return from the exploring tour with Parker. She'd been impatient with the delay in starting her missionary career, and besides, she had been determined to go with them immediately. Marcus's urgent proposal of marriage—well, she'd accepted it without hesitation the year before, being caught up in the desire to set out immediately. Narcissa was a romantic, and that's what had appealed to her in the first place: the urgency, a man appearing at her door proposing she accompany him into the wilderness, the excitement of the whole thing.

But of course the men didn't take her seriously. They knew the Board wouldn't ever approve a single woman traveling with them. And Narcissa realized that if she married Whitman before he had a concrete mission appointment, she might be making the mistake of a lifetime. So she'd spent the year waiting, unable to make plans, not knowing when or where her wedding might take place, or even when Marcus would return.

During his months in the West, Narcissa threw herself into local church revivals, happy because the minister, a "radical reformer," favored the "stimulating and arousing methods" that were so popular at drawing excited crowds.

But even revivals couldn't fill the anxious void Narcissa felt. What had she gotten herself into? The waiting and insecurity of her own situation overwhelmed her with "clouds of darkness" as a deep depression made it difficult for her to even pray.

Perhaps the choice of a black wedding gown points up the depressed mood she was wrapped in.

Narcissa Prentiss, in a strange form of decorum, outfitted herself in a wedding dress of black bombazine. In that day, wedding dresses were not always white, but were usually soft and flattering. Black bombazine, a silk and wool fabric, was commonly used for funerals, or widow's "weeds." At least she could take it on the journey; certainly the fabric and color would wear well while traveling. She had been engaged for a year, but had never been able to set a date for the wedding. Marcus arrived at the Prentiss home, accompanied by one of the Nez Perce youths, and insisted they be married that weekend. There could be no delay, as they had to leave immediately in order to get to St. Louis to travel with a fur caravan. Without definite wedding plans that would have allowed suitable time and opportunity to make or have made a new dress, Narcissa had to choose from her existing wardrobe; her choice was black.

Her family is reported to have worn black, as well, apparently the chosen theme for Narcissa's nuptial celebration. The wedding followed an evening church service at which her father was ordained as a church elder. At the close, all sang a somber missionary hymn. Listeners were said to have been moved to tears as Narcissa's soprano voice finished the last few stanzas in solo, ". . . let me hasten, For in heathen lands to dwell."[2]

It was terribly dramatic, a young missionary wife leaving for a foreign land to "never return." We don't know if she thought she would return to her family and friends or not. She had never traveled away from home before. She had been teaching Sunday school and kindergarten with her sister, and had led a very sheltered life. But she was twenty-seven years old and had waited long enough.

After the ceremony, a collection was taken and the Whitmans received twenty-six dollars towards their "outfit." An outfit consisted of supplies, clothing, and tools—everything a couple would need, plus traveling items. It was up to each missionary to secure their own outfit for going out in the field. Narcissa and Marcus sought donations from the community and church, just as the Spaldings had done in the same community only weeks before.

The newlyweds stopped to visit the Whitman family in Rushville, New York, where Marcus's brother, a cobbler, made a proper pair of men's boots for Narcissa to wear on the journey. The Rushville church ladies sewed shirts for Marcus and donated two hundred dollars.

The newlywed Whitmans and the two Nez Perce Indian youths set out for Pennsylvania, and Cincinnati, where the Spaldings waited for them. In Pennsylvania, they joined three missionaries heading to a Pawnee mission under direction of the American Board: Dr. and Mrs. Satterlee (he to be a mission doctor), and Emeline Parker (a single woman engaged to marry a missionary already in the field).[3]

The group went by riverboat to Cincinnati to meet the Spaldings. It was during that boat trip that Narcissa wrote the first letters to friends and family and began a journal. Her mother had urged her to make a trip diary, but she hadn't been very interested, protesting that it was too difficult to write while traveling by land. Indeed it must have been because writing then was not a simple matter.

She wrote with a metal pen point, and mixed ink from powder as she needed it. The paper was thin, yet her handwriting was extremely controlled and beautiful, and easy to read. Narcissa's diaries and letters are fun to read; she seems to take the reader into consideration, writing on topics she knows will be of general interest. She always mentions people at home by name, and carefully details the foods and meals eaten (something that would interest her mother and sisters). At times she describes the terrain, flora and fauna, comparing it to that of New York that the readers know so well.

Narcissa wrote for an audience. She knew her diary would be read and passed around back home, and her letters read aloud at church gatherings. Her sister had one of her diaries published, and after that Narcissa wrote even more expansively. Although she wasn't keen on writing when the trip began, she found release and joy in writing and during the rest of her life wrote copiously.

Eliza Spalding wrote quite differently. Her diary is not as lucid or interesting. She wrote with a more serious, less personal, tone and often remarked about the soil and whether or not it might be suited to farming. She wasn't writing to interest settlers, just from her frame of reference as a farm girl. She wrote what we now call "positive affirmations;" when faced with difficult or dangerous situations she wrote that she was unafraid and that things would turn out for the best, and then she put it in the hands of the Lord.

The women's writings include many references that sometimes are difficult to understand. America in the 1830s and 1840s was in a state of cultural confusion: new versus old, new technology versus the past. The language of the era shows how confused people were. They tried to talk about new ideas and freedoms, with wording from a bygone age. Writings were thick with weak words and prudery. It was dubbed the "Golden Age of Euphemism." Nothing was called by its proper name, and everything was masked in symbolism. Reading the writings of the Oregon mission women one ferrets out their fears, horrors and confusion, only by looking through the words they put on paper. Perhaps even they didn't know how to express their fears and problems to themselves.[4]

Once they met in Cincinnati, the two couples purchased supplies for the trip. Narcissa and Eliza sewed a large conical tent out of blue and white-striped bedticking. The two couples would sleep in it while traveling, separated by a hanging curtain between them. They took along heavy blankets, sidesaddles for the women, India rubber life preservers to inflate and wear during river crossings, traveling boots and dinnerware for each person. Each wore a knife and tin cup on their belt.

Another man joined them, William Gray, "a good teacher, cabinet maker and housejoiner."[5] Another missionary volunteer had agreed to go along but was rejected by the Board as being "too deficient" in the "elements of knowledge" to justify sending along. Gray was hired by the Board to go as a "mechanic" (handyman) for a one-year term. The party that left Cincinnati on March 22, 1836, included the Whitmans, Spaldings, the two Nez Perce youths, William Gray, and the three missionaries to the Pawnees. They changed boats two more times, going by the Ohio River, then the Mississippi, to St. Louis.

Eliza realized how far they'd already traveled, and the unlikelihood of ever returning. As they watched civilization along the riverbank dwindle into wilderness, she wrote, "The waters of the grand Ohio are rapidly bearing me away from all I hold dear in this life. Yet I am happy; the hope of spending the remnant of my life among the heathen . . . affords me much happiness." For her sacrifice, there would be some sort of gain, "surely the consolations of God are neither few nor small."[6]

St. Louis was a culture shock for the New Englanders in many ways. The jumping off place for the rest of the continent, it was filled with French Creoles, Canadian fur traders, Kentucky hunters, and eager merchants. The city reeked of Catholicism; a grand cathedral had just been completed. Eliza wrote about St. Louis: "Arrived at this city last evening—am not plesed with its appearance, particularly that part which is occupied by the French. The buildings are not splendid, many of them are uncouthly constructed, and it has the appearance of a city going to decay."[7]

The missionaries walked around the town, glad to not be traveling on a Sabbath, when they heard the bells of the Cathedral and saw the people entering. Eliza wrote in her diary, "Our curiosity was excited to call, but the unpleasant sensations we experienced on witnessing their heartless forms and ceremonies, induced us soon to leave, rejoicing that we had never been left to embrace such delusions."[8] It was their first opportunity to see first-hand what a Catholic church, clergy and Mass were like. They had heard of the evils of "Popism" all their adult lives and had extolled its horrors, but they had never set foot inside a Catholic church, and knew nothing of the sacraments or ceremony.

Narcissa wasn't as upset over the tour of the cathedral as Eiza. In a letter she simply said they left the cathedral, after staying an hour or so, "it was a highmass day." Contrasting with Eliza's disparaging remarks about the looks of St. Louis, Narcissa noted "many delightful residences in Missouri," as they left the town. She described the scenery, the majestic rivers coming together, and her rambles along the riverbank whenever they stopped for the boat to take on wood. She described how interesting her first prickly pear was—how she got the plant's needles in her hands, and Marcus bit into one and got them in his lip, and how they were glad to "render mutual assistance in a case of extermination."[9]

The Whitmans were clearly on a honeymoon trip; they stood on the top deck in the evening, watching the scenery in the moonlight, and reluctantly went inside for Brother Spalding's prayer service. Moonlit nights, rambles along the shore in April weather—it must have been romantic.

Tragedies and dangers began to show themselves. The steamboat *Siam's* wrecked hulk loomed in the river, "She ran upon a snag and sank, last winter. No lives lost." Narcissa wrote. Eliza noted that Mrs. Satterlee's illness was getting very serious, "Mrs. S.'s health continues to decline, the symptoms of her disease appear somewhat alarming."[10]

Narcissa was always quick to wipe away insecurities with bravado. She maintained that Mrs. Satterlee only had, "a very bad cough and cold which has kept her feeble." And she reassurred herself in a letter to her sister that the rest of the party had been feeling very well, except for the problems caused by drinking the dirty river water. "I am an exception, however My health was never better than since I have been on the river. I was weighed last week, and came up to 136 pounds. I think I shall endure the journey well—perhaps better than any of the rest of us. Mrs. Spalding does not look nor feel quite healthy enough for our enterprise."[11]

Narcissa judged that Eliza was not as able to ride as she was, and that everyone complimented her for her ability to endure the trip ahead of them. During the same time period, Eliza noted in her diary that she hadn't paid much attention to the scenery, she had been absorbed with her books. Eliza's intellectual superiority may have made Narcissa feel a bit inadequate, and her many references to her suitability (physically) for the trip were compensation for the worries she was having about how suitable intellectually she was for the challenges ahead.

In her letter home, Narcissa adds a few polite thoughts about poor Mrs. Spalding, saying she was certainly suitable for Mr. Spalding, with the right temperament to match him. Not wanting others at home to think things weren't going well, she added, "I think we shall get along very well together; we have so far. I have such a good place to shelter—under my husband's wings. He is so excellent." She must have made herself feel better, by regarding Marcus as quite a catch compared to poor Eliza's inferior husband.

It was Narcissa's wedding trip, but perhaps things weren't as smooth between herself and Marcus. She writes in the same letter to her sister that her husband, "is just like mother in telling me my failings. He does it in such a way that I like to have him, for it gives me a chance to improve." She urges her sister to get as good a husband, "as I have," and be a missionary, too. The difficulties and life of being a missionary are only alluded to the journey, "the way looks pleasant," and the impending dangers to come, "so near encountering the difficulties of an unheard-of journey for females."[12]

Narcissa wrote for whoever back home would read her letters, calling them, "free plunder," with the knowledge (and perhaps hope) that they would be widely shared and read. She wrote for an audience. She tried to write colorful, descriptive passages, and her letters and journals are warm and witty. In a different circumstance, she might have been a successful writer.

The writing style of the day was one of formality. In all written references, Narcissa refers to Marcus as "husband" or "the Doctor." Eliza Spalding makes few references to Henry, but he always refers to her as "Mrs. Spalding." It was the same with the missionary reinforcements that arrived the next year. It was proper etiquette during that era, among contemporaries, especially when writing about someone else, such as in letters and diaries. In letters, siblings back home were called by first names, but members of the mission referred to each other formally, as "Sister" Spalding or "Brother" Walker.

The group was forced to wait for a fur company steamboat to take them on the next leg of the journey, and while they waited, the men (Henry Spalding, the two Nez Perce youths, William Gray and another young man named Hinds, whom they'd hired as a laborer) went ahead with the animals, planning to meet them upstream. Eliza, Narcissa and Marcus, and the missionaries to the Pawnees, remained on the steamboat traveling upstream. Mrs. Satterlee's health rapidly deteriorated and it became clear she was dying. The others realized it, and Eliza noted that the woman herself knew what was happening; ". . . she had not apprehended her case so dangerous, but had thought she should recover." When told of her "situation," she appeared "reconciled."[13] The twenty-three year old woman died two nights later. While they were taking her body ashore for burial, the fur company's steamboat they had planned to board passed them by, refusing any more cargo or passengers. They were stranded and had just witnessed a young woman like themselves die quickly without aid. Marcus and Dr. Satterlee, both trained medical men, had not been able to help her. Marcus determined she'd died of a lung problem (tuberculosis, probably). They buried a sister missionary's "lifeless remains,"[14] beside a lonely river in a lawless, godless land.

Marcus had not been able to obtain passage for the next leg of the journey; Spalding and Gray were far ahead with all the possessions except light luggage, and now they stood on the riverbank as the water rushed by.

No doubt Eliza felt exasperated if not resentful that the situation had deteriorated so badly. Wasn't the entire mission to have been planned thoroughly by Whitman, who begged them to accompany him? He was supposed to have made the trip to the Rockies the previous summer in order to arrange everything. Why wasn't everything going as planned? Or, had there been no planning at all?

Eliza's worries show up in her journal, "May we go to the right source for guidance and direction in this and every other pursuit, that we may indeed glorify God, our Savior in whose cause *we hope we have embarked*."[15] (Italics added.) Eliza is tough, but definitely worried and apprehensive. Narcissa made no note of the incident.

One feels this antagonism between Eliza and the Whitmans, because Whitman writes in a letter to Greene telling the Board about Mrs. Satterlee's death that he worries Mrs. Spalding will not be up to enduring the journey ahead. He notes that Mrs. Whitman is "very well and in good spirits."[16] Unable to do anything to save Mrs. Satterlee's life, he may have been trying to protect himself in case Eliza weakened next.

Was Eliza truly as weak as he portrayed? In her diary, a few days later, she wrote that, "Camping out at night has not been

so disagreeable and uncomfortable as I anticipated. Traveling
on horseback has appeared to benefit my health . . ."[17]

After much confusion, the missionaries reunited and
reached the Otoe Mission, still attempting to catch up with the
overland caravan of trade goods on its way to the Rocky
Mountain rendezvous. Henry was ailing; he'd been sick with the
"consequence of taking cold after taking calomel."[18] Calomel—
mercurous chloride—was used as a purgative and was a popular remedy; it's effects were laxative. It was dangerous, but a
widely popular medicine. Obviously, not traveling with Dr.
Whitman at the time, Henry had dosed himself.

Catching up with the fur caravan was no small object, and
they had to do it before reaching the first of the Mandan villages, where they had been warned the Indians would be difficult to deal with. A hired guide got them lost, they had to cross
the swollen Platte River with overloaded wagons, and they had
the inevitable breakdowns—the party considered they might
have to turn back in defeat.

By traveling on Sunday (something they tried not to do, but
often were forced to do), crossing rivers in bullboats (round
boats made of skins stretched over pole frames) and pressing on
in marches of up to sixty miles in one day, they hurried on. The
party had two wagons, Eliza's light Dearborn, which the
Whitmans and Spaldings rode in, and a larger freight wagon,
which Gray drove. The Indian youths herded the cattle, and
Dulin and Goodyear (two young hired men) moved the horses.[19]

Unable to stop for anything but rest or feeding the animals,
supper was only fresh milk from the cows (they had four milk
cows along), drunk from a common tin cup. After several more
days of grueling travel, which even Marcus admitted, "tested
the abilities of our ladies to journey in this way,"[20] they caught
up with the caravan.

Miraculously, the caravan's movement had been slowed
because they ran out of axle grease. During the several days
needed to butcher animals and boil down the necessary grease,
the missionary party was able to catch them. Now all would be
well. They would follow the huge moving cavalcade across the
plains and into the mountains.

The missionaries would travel behind the long line of the American Fur Company's caravan. Captain Fitzpatrick and the pilot were in front, followed by four hundred animals and seventy people that made up the entourage: seven wagons drawn by six mules each and strings of pack mules all laden with trade goods. The missionary party followed at the rear, women riding in the Dearborn, while Gray drove the other wagon. Spalding and Whitman were behind, bringing up their herd of horses and cows, along with the hired youths and Nez Perce boys. The dust must have been tremendous, and riding drag after such a caravan would have been pure misery. The only time the women would have been able to visit with their husbands was during the rest break at mid-day, or at night.

Fitzpatrick traveled from six until eleven each day, then there was a complete stop for rest and feeding animals from eleven until two. Called "nooning," it was the only break until camp was set up again for the night at about six. Breakfast and supper were eaten in the missionary tent. During the noonday rest period the tent wasn't set up; the women were shielded from the burning prairie sun by a piece of canvas or blanket draped on sticks. Without chairs, they sat on their saddles or napped on folded apishimores (saddle blankets).

They spread an India rubber mat on the ground, and sat around, in the style of "the Turks," as Narcissa described it. They sipped tea with plenty of warm milk from tin bowls, ate meat from forks fashioned from twigs, and bread baked over an open fire. The bread lasted only as long as the flour supply, which wasn't enough for long. Planning on living off buffalo once they reached the plains, they hadn't taken food supplies for the entire journey.[21]

"When we left Liberty we expected to take bread to last us part of the way, but could not get enough to carry us any distance," so Narcissa and Eliza did "all our cooking." It was "awkward work to bake out of doors at first, but we have become so accustomed to it now we do it very easily."[22]

The milk from the cows was "a luxury in this country." The milk "assisted" them with breadmaking and was a "great service" to them. The mission entourage numbered ten, with the hired men they picked up along the way, and that meant "considerable work" for the women to "supply ten people with bread three times a day." But the flour supply dwindled, until there was only enough for "thickening . . . broth, which is excellent."

Narcissa "never saw anything like buffalo meat to satisfy hunger," which was fortunate for her, as there was nothing else to eat.[23]

Notes on Chapter Five

1 Robert Speer, *Presbyterian Foreign Missions* (Philadelphia: Presbyterian Board of Publications and Sabbath School Work, 1901), p. 18.

2 Julie Roy Jeffrey, *Converting the West: a Biography of Narcissa Whitman* (Norman: University of Oklahoma Press, 1991), p. 61.

3 Ibid, p. 61.

4 Cathy Luchetti, *I Do! Courtship, Love and Marriage on the American Frontier* (New York: Crown Publishers, 1996) p. 232.

5 Clifford Merrill Drury, *Marcus and Narcissa Whitman and the Opening of Old Oregon* (Seattle: Pacific Northwest National Parks and Forests Association, 1986) I, p. 173.

6 Eliza Spalding Warren, *Memoirs of the West* (Portland: Marsh Printing Company, 1916), p. 56.

7 Ibid, p. 57.

8 Ibid.

9 Whitman, Letters, p. 13.

10 Warren, Memoirs, p. 58.

11 Whitman, Letters, p. 13.

12 Ibid.

13 Warren, *Memoirs*, p. 59.

14 Ibid, p. 60.

15 Ibid.

16 Drury, *First White Women*, p. 189.

17 Warren, *Memoirs*, p. 61.

18 Ibid, p. 60.

19 Drury, *Marcus and Narcissa Whitman*, 180.

20 Whitman, Letters, p. 19.

21 Ibid, p. 16.

22 Ibid.

23 Ibid, p. 17.

Fort Boise. The last haven on the road to Oregon.

Chapter Six

Rendevous

It was the first of June, and the long caravan was passing over the "plains of the Platte." Eliza thought it was "beautiful country," with "majestic sand bluffs on either side" and "extensive plains" between the bluffs and river. It was warm, and the plains were "covered with beautiful flowers and roses," creating "delightful scenery to the eye of the traveler."

Along with the pleasing terrain, came relief that they had, ". . . met with but few Indians." Eliza reasoned that ". . . the natives who once roamed over these vast and delightful plains are fast fading away, as is the Buffalo and the other game which once in vast herds ranged throughout this country."[1] It's the first mention by either woman of the people they were to save. Eliza's words reveal her opinion that the Indians were indeed desperate in the face of advancing settlement.

Fresh buffalo became the caravan's chief diet. Narcissa and Eliza didn't indulge in a lot of cooking—the flour supply was being saved to thicken broth.

Narcissa liked it, ". . . I have eaten three meals of it and it relishes well." They had nothing but tea and buffalo, buffalo and tea, for weeks. Narcissa welcomed it, but noticed that ". . . Sister Spaulding is affected by it considerably—has been quite sick."[2]

Marcus had been doing the cooking, delighting Narcissa with the way he could cook buffalo meat cuts in so many different ways over the campfire. It's the first glimpse of Marcus, the mountain man. He was eager to leave behind the trappings of civilization, and ready to fit in with the wildly raw men around him. Shortly, he decided to sell all his eastern clothing (including the shirts made by the church ladies back home) in order to adopt the breeches and skin clothing the fur men wore. Narcissa put up a fight, appalled at his decision and threatening to abandon her clothes, as well. She threatened to write back to people at home about his actions, so he kept the clothing, but didn't wear it. Her delight at winning this round showed in the letter she wrote to Marcus' sister detailing the entire scene.

Narcissa described her first sight of buffalo, "We have seen wonders this forenoon. Herds of buffalo hove in sight; one, a bull, crossed our trail and ran upon the bluffs near the rear of the camp." Oblivious to danger, the two women got out of the wagon and ran up on the bluff to see him better. Excited to be traveling through country so beautiful and grand, with immense herds of exotic animals, Narcissa began to think about the "dear Indians" they were going to, and wrote sensitively about the Nez Perce boys that had been with Marcus for so many months.

She had become very attached to Richard, who attended their wedding with Marcus. "He calls me mother," she wrote, pleased that he saw her in the supreme womanly role. "I love to teach him—to take care of him, and hear them talk." There were five Nez Perces in the group, the two with the missionaries and three others in the fur company caravan.

The youths were kept busy herding and caring for the mission's band of cattle and horses. While excited at the novel prospect of traveling with white women, and the interesting entourage, they were obviously being used as laborers on the trip—something they had never been accustomed to. Narcissa wrote in a letter home that occasionally, "husband and myself would ride with them as company and encouragement."[3]

The caravan, still moving towards the mountains, was met by a man on his way back to civilization. He agreed to take letters with him, so the missionaries halted their wagon to write, posted the letters with him, then scurried to catch up with the rest of the company.

Narcissa closed her letter to her sister and brother, "Tell mother that if I had looked the world over I could not have found one more careful and better qualified to transport a

Pages from Eliza Spalding's diary, February, 1836.

female such a distance." But her enjoyable letter-writing stint was ended when, "Husband says, 'stop.'" She quickly signed the letter, *Narcissa Prentiss*.[4] During their years of marriage, she always glossed over his poor treatment of her, always writing of him in a romantic manner, although his behavior seldom warranted it.

Narcissa and Eliza usually rode in the wagon from the time they met up with the fur caravan until they reached the Black Hills. When they reached Fort William (now Fort Laramie, Wyoming), the party stopped. This was the last leg of the fur caravan's journey and goods were taken off the wagons and packed on mules for the rest of the way to the rendezvous. The missionaries left behind their large wagon, packing what they could in the Dearborn and on mules. The women would ride on sidesaddles the rest of the way.

The stop gave the women the first opportunity to wash clothing. Personal hygiene for Eliza and Narcissa, something that would always be difficult for women making the western journey was difficult at best, awkward no matter what. On the treeless plains, how were they to relieve themselves, or attend to personal hygiene? Female travelers who came later in groups, held blankets to create privacy screens for one another. With only one other woman, it must have been very difficult.

No mention is made by either woman regarding personal matters pertaining to "health." Narcissa became pregnant on the journey, probably during the month of June, and would have noticed when she didn't menstruate. Eliza, still reeling from giving birth the past autumn, referred to her own poor health several times. Was she menstruating, and found it difficult to perform the hygiene practices common to women of the day; soaking and laundering menstrual rags and hanging them out to dry? How would she take charge of menstrual flow, with a party of men, in the wide-open spaces? Perhaps "riding in the wagon" was simply the only way to deal with it.

Contraceptive practices of the day included douching with a variety of folk remedies for "all obstructions" such as yellow dock sarsaparilla, or hot water, ice water, alcohol or sulfate of zinc. Tansy root, rue root, pulverized ergot, aloe and rusty-nail-tea were all used to prevent or end pregnancy. A male sheath, and a rubber cap for the uterus were sold, but ovulation timing and withdrawal were the most popular contraceptive practices. No matter to the women missionaries, limiting childbearing was not something they were interested in at this time. They were intent on raising families, and doing it among the Indians, where the benighted heathen could see exactly how a civilized Christian family lived. Caring for children, and raising them up as Christians was one of their goals.

The mentions of Eliza's health could be that she had endured a miscarriage on the journey. Later, in her years at Lapwai, she had at least one, maybe more, miscarriages. She could very well have been sick not only with diarrahea from the all-red meat diet she was now eating (the Spalding's frugal student lifestyle wouldn't have included much fresh meat), but morning sickness as well. Neither would have been mentioned in a woman's diary of the time.

Eliza wrote on the day they left the fort, ". . . we have no resting place in view, till we reach Rendevoux, 400 miles distant. We are now 2,800 miles from my dear parents' dwelling, expecting in a few days to commence ascending the Rocky Mountains."[5]

On July 4, they crossed the South Pass on the Continental Divide. They were the first white women to do so, and it was later considered a great feat in political circles back East. But in the Rockies, it wasn't mentioned. Neither woman wrote about the day having any significance. Eliza noted briefly in her diary that they had "crossed a ridge of land today called the divide; which separated the waters that flow into the Atlantic from those that flow into the Pacific."[6]

When they finally neared the rendezvous location, along a branch of the Green River in what's now Wyoming, dusk was coming on when the party was suddenly disturbed by a loud, raucous party of Indians. The welcoming committee, a band of Nez Perces and some trappers dressed in the wild clothing of the mountains, gave the group a loud welcome. Shots rang out, screams and shouts echoed, and the group thundered past on horseback. Terrified it was an attack, the missionaries were relieved to learn that it was a friendly welcome, even though the first meeting necessitated four translations: English, Iroquois, Salish, and Nez Perce. "All appear happy to see us," Eliza wrote, and the entire group headed towards the huge encampment to settle for the night.

What an effect the women's appearance must have made as they rode through the hundreds of Indians who turned out to see them. It was a stunning and amazing sight: the two white women were, "hung on the sides of their horses," as the Nez Perces described it, in a way the Indians could never have imagined.[7]

Big medicine had arrived in the Rockies.

As soon as the women had "alighted" from their horses, they were "met by a company of matrons, native women one after another shaking hands, and saluting" them with a practice they'd learned from the fur traders: ". . . a most hearty kiss." This was "unexpected" and "affected" Narcissa "very much."[8]

The native women, dark eyes snapping with excitement, hovered around Eliza and Narcissa, eager for a glimpse of the strange women's clothing, and a touch of their pale skin or the soft fabric of their garments.

Swathed head-to-toe in traveling clothes, the Bostons (as the natives referred to Americans) were exotic creatures to the Indians. Eliza and Narcissa were draped in fabric as protection from the sun: long skirts, long sleeves, high collars. Topped with wide-brimmed hats draped with thick veils to shelter their delicate faces from sun and wind, they sported tinted traveling goggles, too. Parasols, too, which by that time had been torn and bent—useless except to effect a balance on a sidesaddle. Hands wrapped in gloves and ample India rubber aprons with pockets to protect their clothing from rain and soil, they were unusual—and absolutely unlike anything the native women had ever imagined.

The Indians were equally fascinating to the missionaries. It was rendezvous, and there were as many as a thousand Nez Perce, Salish, Snake and Bannock Indians gathered along the Green River. They paraded in a magnificent procession for the new teachers, dressed in full regalia, paint and elaborate horse trappings. Rendezvous was a trading event, and there were hundreds of buckskin-suited trappers, Mexican traders, Hudson's Bay Company deserters (Iroquois or French-Canadian), and anyone else who could make the trek to the mountains.

Anyone, except the Hudson's Bay Company. This was a rendezvous of the *American* Fur Company, an upstart competitor seen by the HBC as an interloper in its fur domain. The annual rendezvous's location was always at a secret place and time, so one trading company wouldn't get there ahead of the other. The first competitor to reach the trade got the pick of the furs, at top prices. To arrive a week too late for rendezvous was financial disaster; even the watered-down whiskey was worthless if there were no furs left to barter for.

Horse racing, gambling, drinking, wrestling and at times even jousting in medieval armor, took place. Sir William Drummond Stewart, a wandering nobleman from Britain on a grand adventure had come just to enjoy the revelry. But those things happened every year. The special titillation at this rendezvous were the white women. For some of the mountain trappers, it had been over a decade since they had last seen a white woman.

The Indian women were the most fascinated by the two female "teachers." All day, they passed by the blue and white striped missionary tent, staring at Eliza and Narcissa. They wanted to examine their cooking uten-

Historical Photograph Collections, Washington State University Libraries

This trunk held Mary Richardson Walker's belongings on the trip across the continent.

sils, and clothing, their possessions and especially, the books they had brought.

Narcissa was delighted with the attention; it suited her just fine to be surrounded by adoring, appreciative men. And they were. Men flocked to her, hoping to get a smile, or even better, a chance to receive a missionary tract from her delicate hand. Narcissa passed out so many of the cheap Bibles they had brought for the Indians, that Henry ordered her to stop. Arguments ensued; he reminded her they had come to serve the Indians, not lawless, whiskey-drinking mountain men.

Eliza, sick in the tent at first, was the center of the Indian women's attention. They flocked around her, caring for her, examining her sewing supplies, watching her dress and groom. She made the most of their attention, setting right to work attempting to create a small dictionary of native languages. By the end of the rendezvous, Eliza could speak haltingly with the women in their own tongue.

William Gray, the lay assistant hired to help with the mission, was a difficult man to get along with. He was jealous of Henry and Marcus, the two official missionaries, and felt himself undervalued and inadequate. Gaining little attention from the Indians, because he had no wife along, he brooded. He was-

n't well-educated and had no official standing. Being the hired
help was a position that began to gnaw on him. Eliza, and her
quick study of the natives, seemed to hit the ground running as
far as missionary work went. Narcissa, on the other hand, was
distracted by what Gray called, "gentlemen callers,"—the mountain men, but also the Fur Company's leader, Fitzpatrick.
Several times Fitzpatrick had "tea," with the ladies, and
Narcissa described him in glowing terms. Gray thought highly
of Eliza, but criticized Narcissa, saying she was "too busy flirt-
ing with dazzled and savage mountain men to pay much attention to her charges."[9] One of the mountain men, Joe Meek,
thought Narcissa had far too much refinement and education to
be "thrown away on the Indians."

Gray also described how the men reacted to Eliza. The men
thought (so Gray wrote) Eliza was "a first-rate woman," with no
"starch" in her. She would "do first-rate to teach the Indians," or
anyone. She had "good common sense" and didn't put on "any
frills."[10] Most couldn't stand her husband, calling him a "green-
horn," or worse. As a minister, Henry would have reminded
them of the rules and society they'd turned their backs on by
leaving civilization. To do as they pleased was the prime reason
for living in the mountains in the first place. It's unlikely they
would have responded warmly to *any* preacher, especially one so
inexperienced and intently serious as Henry Spalding.

The mountain men knew the missionaries had overcome
immense obstacles in making the journey this far. If they could
overcome the Hudson's Bay Company, and the Indians—well,
who could know what would come after that? They must have
chuckled, knowing that Dr. John McLoughlin, Chief Factor at
Fort Vancouver, and head of the entire Columbia Department
for the Hudson's Bay Company would be extremely upset to
hear about these two delicate, innocent missionary wives. They
were more threatening to the HBC's control of the fur domain,
than a regiment of U.S. soldiers.

What did the missionary women forsee? They weren't quite
as confident. Eliza noted in her diary, after several days at rendezvous, ". . . health a little improved. We feel that we soon shall
be situated, *if we live,* where opportunities for communicating

with our friends will be few, but I hope it will be where we shall be useful in our Master's service." (Italics added)[11]

"If we live" is a fairly revealing phrase. The trip had been hard on all of them. They'd brought the Spalding's Dearborn wagon this far, and the women had ridden in it much of the time from when they joined the fur caravan until they reached the Black Hills. They'd spent many hours on horseback, too. Their husbands' assessment of the trip differed: Marcus Whitman wrote to the Board, "I see no reason to regret our choice of a journey by land." Henry Spalding, always more sensitive to his wife's needs, warned the Board, "Never send another mission over these mountains if you value life . . ." That particular line was omitted when the Board later printed the letter in the *Missionary Herald.*[12]

What the missionaries didn't know was that the tribes they sought to serve—the Cayuses, Nez Perce and Spokanes—had quite a bit of experience with white men's ways already. And it hadn't always been positive.

By 1836 the fur trade era in the far West was in decline. For decades the French Canadian trappers and their brigades of Iroquois and Delaware Indian laborers had plied the waterways trapping the most valuable animal in the hemisphere, an unobtrusive rodent—the beaver. Demand for beaver had exploded when fashion decreed the beaver hat to be the only suitable headpiece for gentlemen in Europe and the United States. From the east coast of Canada, the trade spread to the Great Lakes, then westward to the Columbia River. One giant company had eliminated all competitors, either by destroying them in bloody battles over territory or absorbing them, until the British Hudson's Bay Company ruled the area unchallenged.

But hadn't Lewis and Clark made their epic journey to claim the Pacific Northwest for the United States? The United States claimed territory north to Alaska, but the British claimed south to California. In 1818 a joint occupation treaty was signed giving citizens of both countries equal rights of trade or settlement for the next ten years.

Why didn't the United States push its claim? Congress wasn't interested in the matter, and there didn't seem to be a worthwhile reason to pursue taking possession of the area. The British East India Company controlled and restricted the trade into Canton, so a United States presence on the Pacific coast wasn't very desirable to Boston-based sea traders. Situated between the Russians to the north and the Spanish to the south in California, the Pacific Northwest was of no real importance to the rest of the country. Besides, it was considered impossible to travel across the continent to the Pacific; the vast deserts and difficult mountain ranges made it impractical if not unrealistic.

Potential profits did lie in the Northwest fur trade and the area crawled with opportunists set on beating out competitors while coercing the Indians to trap. Cut-throat business practices and total disregard for the natives set the tone for the whites who came later.

Just prior to the outbreak of the War of 1812, American financier John Jacob Astor ordered fur trade houses built near the British North West Company trade houses. At Spokane House, in the heart of the Spokane Indians' land, the two rival trading groups taunted and challenged each other. Rivalry ensued with each undercutting the other's trade goods prices. A duel broke out between clerks of the rival houses. Another eager Astorian, Donald McKenzie had been sent to establish a trading post along the Clearwater River, where it empties into the Snake River, but he couldn't get the Nez Perces to trap beaver for him. These ill-fated houses were near the very spots the missionaries would build Tshimikain and Clear Water missions only twenty-six years later.

When the Astorians heard about the war with Britain in 1812, they abandoned their enterprise and tried to rush back to St. Louis with their fur inventory. But they needed nearly 400 horses to get the huge cavalcade to St. Louis. They set a rendezvous for June 1, at the mouth of the Walla Walla River on the Columbia. (This was near the later Waiilatpu mission location.) The Indians refused to barter for the supplies and horses McKenzie needed. When he discovered that supplies had been pilfered he stalked through the village, slashing Indian property in response.

Desperate for supplies and fearing the British were upon them, McKenzie pointed to horses he wanted and offered a fair price. When the Indians refused to sell, he ordered the animals shot dead. He paid the Indians, and the men ate the carcasses, but the Indians found it a disconcerting way to do business.

Back at Spokane House, John Clarke, the Astorian in charge there, caused more problems. On his way to the rendezvous with McKenzie, he discovered an Indian had stolen a silver goblet. He retaliated by hanging the culprit in front of his shocked tribesmen. Word of such unprecedented punishment flashed from village to village, and when the trappers finally gathered together at their rendezvous, so did a crowd of threatening natives. A worried chief warned the whites, who broke camp in the middle of a meal, abandoned their horses for canoes and paddled away unscathed. Natives along the Columbia plateau wouldn't soon forget the summer of 1813.

Meanwhile a fur trade war raged in Canada between the two giant British fur companies: the North West Company and the Hudson's Bay Company. The best *voyageurs* (French boatmen and laborers) were kept busy in the East; the Columbia River Department was sent more and more Iroquois and Abenaki Indian employees. They were wanton, trigger-happy horse thieves who robbed and raped the local tribes when sent to the Willamette River to trap. The fur trade continued to leave its mark on the natives' lives along the Columbia.

The Nez Perce Indians along the Snake River had always refused to trap for the fur companies. They were horsemen who traversed the plains and mountains freely; stooping midstream to bait a rodent was work fit only for slaves. But the beaver must be gotten out, so the North West Company sent out brigades to trap instead. The Iroquois who made up a large portion of each brigade were not reliable; they tried to murder McKenzie, and once traded off guns, horses and traps for women obtained from a party of Snake Indians.

The North West Company set up a base of operations for the area in the midst of Cayuse country, called Fort Nez Perce. McKenzie, now working for the North West Company, was back. This time he built an impregnable fort, protected by an outer wall nearly twenty feet high and reinforced with an inner wall twelve feet tall. It held bastions, galleries, loopholes and balustrades. Two large water tanks guarded against assault by fire. Except for special councils, Indians weren't allowed inside; trade was conducted through a wicket cut in the ponderous outer gate. A hefty building project, it was built for protection against a formidable foe. McKenzie wrote that it would be a "new post at the mouth of the Walla Walla River, surrounded by the most unfriendly of the inland natives."[13]

The people he was so terrified of were the Cayuses, the very same people to whom Narcissa and Marcus Whitman would attempt to teach the Gospel.

Notes on Chapter Six

[1] *Warren, Memoirs*, p. 62.

[2] Whitman, Letters, p. 21.

[3] Ibid, p. 20.

[4] Ibid, p. 17.

[5] *Warren, Memoirs*, p. 63.

[6] Ibid, p. 64.

[7] William Drummond Stewart, *Edward Warren* (London: G. Walker, 1854, reprint, Missoula: Mountain Press Publishing Company, 1986), p. 2.

[8] Whitman, Letters, p. 22.

[9] DeVoto, *Across the Wide Missouri*, p. 255.

[10] Ibid, p. 129.

[11] Warren, Memoirs, p. 65.

[12] Drury, *Henry Harmon Spalding*, p. 143.

[13] David Lavender, *Land of Giants: The Drive to the Pacific Northwest*, 1750-1950 (Lincoln: University of Nebraska Press, 1956), p. 111.

Chapter Seven

"This Adventurous Journey"

. . . they are very independent of us requiring but few of our supplies and it is not until absolutely in need of an essential article of finery such as Guns & Beads that they will take the trouble of hunting.

Governor Simpson of Canada on
the Hudson's Bay Company's failure to
enlist the Nez Perces in trapping furs[1]

Grasping at whatever might motivate the Indians to trap, Governor Simpson even considered using the growing missionary movement in England. Missionaries would encourage the Indians to adopt European "manners and customs: and they'd want to "imitate" the British in "dress." That desire for material goods would mean the HBC's "supplies would thus become necessary to them" which would increase the consumption of European trade goods. The Indians would then find it "requisite to become more industrious" and they would have to trap furs.[2]

But until English missionaries could be obtained, brigades were the easiest solution.

Brigades, wandering bands of trappers with their wives and children and near-wild herds of horses, were sent out into the mountains to get the furs. They weren't the most desirable agents, but who else could do the job?

Governor Simpson of Canada called them ". . . the most unruly and troublesom gang to deal with in this or any other part of the world . . ."[3] The problem was the so-called freemen.

Half-breeds, Iroquois, and French-Canadian laborers, they had worked out their term of service with the company and preferred to remain in the wilderness with their native families, rather than return East. To survive, they bought a few overpriced supplies on company credit, went into the fur country under the direction of a company *bourgeois*, or boss, then paid off their bills by bringing in their fur take at the end of the season and earning scanty prices the company decided to pay.

The brigades were known to be utterly irresponsible, and prey to explosive resentments. Every bourgeois sentenced to work with them seethed at their indolence and lack of loyalty. They frequently traded with American fur companies if they could get a better deal, sometimes deserted, and preyed on whatever native villages they encountered.

About 1825, American trappers reached the Salt Lake region in swarms, and were furious to discover the HBC brigades had been trapping in what was supposed to be virgin country; in a region popularly considered belonging to the U.S. Neither side stopped bickering long enough to realize they were on land that technically belonged to Mexico.

Historically, the HBC had practiced conservation of the game to keep a region profitable over time But to keep the Americans out they trapped out the drainages completely, creating a fur desert. Nothing could be left to lure the Americans westward.

In four years, the HBC brigades had completely trapped out the regions south of the Columbia, from a base at Fort Nez Perce (the impregnable fortress on Cayuse land). It kept the Americans out. What it did for long-term Indian attitudes wasn't considered.

Along with their other woes, Columbia River natives were decimated by a plague that broke out in 1830 along the lower Columbia River. Ninety percent of the Indians died from fever. Some Chinooks blamed the recent arrival of American ships for bringing "bad water." Others (whites, included) believed it was due to a miasma arising from newly plowed ground near burgeoning Fort Vancouver. Seventy-five Fort employees were sick, too, but it had passed by 1831.[4]

The rest of the world was embroiled in controversy over African slave trading, Barbary pirates, Canton trade battles — and the expansion of industrialism and commerce. Except to a handful of fur trade investors, the Pacific Northwest was a bit inconsequential. But there was always the possibility . . .

Dr. John McLoughlin, Chief Factor at Fort Vancouver and overall administrator for the Columbia River Department of the HBC, was wary of what was coming. He studied American newspapers brought by each ship that rounded the Horn. When he read about, "a plan which I see in a Boston newspaper of March, 1831 to colonize the Willamette . . ."[5] he grew concerned.

United States government aid had been sought for Oregon colonization several times. A company from Virginia (1819); eighty enterprising farmers from Maryland (1823); and Hall Kelly, a promoter from Massachusetts had applied to Congress for support in settlement schemes. Kelley proposed that he lead a group of 3,000 settlers to Oregon, with government financing and protection. While Congress considered it, he threw himself into writing and publishing articles and pamphlets, trying to drum up the 3,000. As he generated more publicity for his scheme, fear grew that he might lure workers from the already tight labor markets of New England. Boston newspapers opened their columns to counter-arguments, attempting to dissuade anyone from joining up. Kelly garnered no more than three dozen potential pilgrims; Congress dropped the matter.

Kelley proposed missionaries be sent to Oregon, after all, since 1820, the American Board for Foreign Missions, a combined effort of the Presbyterian and Congregational churches, had supported a mission station in the Sandwich Islands, why not the Rocky Mountains?

There hadn't been a dramatic reason to go. Indians were too common, too close to everyday life. It was easier to get volunteers to go to places like the Islands, where they could fight the sinful sailors, or to China, where little girls' feet were bound to disfigurement and women kept in near bondage. Indians were unglamorous and serving them simply didn't stir the imagination, like missions to Constantinople, the Zulus and Pacific Islands.

But interest was sparked when the Walker letter was published in the *Christian Advocate*, and attention was given to the plight of the pitiful Indian visitors to St. Louis who desperately sought the white man's religion. The lost, mutilated, souls deserved to be saved. And, as Methodist minister on the ground, Jason Lee, wrote back, "send no more single men, but families." He wanted, "pious, industrious, intelligent females." White women were needed to exert "influence over Indian families."[6]

Women were needed, but how would they be received? Missionaries and settlers welcomed women, to do the work and settle the land, but what about fur trappers and traders? And the Indian families they sought to save?

A look at western Canadian history, where the fur trade dominated social and economic life since the Hudson's Bay Company was founded in 1670, shows that women had always been an integral part of the fur trade business. Following the lead of the early French, men in the North West Company, and later the Hudson's Bay Company, saw the value of marrying Indian wives. Wives of trappers did their own trapping as well as preparing the furs and taking part in the trade for European goods. Women wanted the kettles, cloth, knives, needles and axes; technology that made their work easier. Without Indian women as customers, the Europeans would have been unable to buy pelts.

Incoming Canadian traders married Cree, Ojibwa and Chipewyan women, who were indispensable to the men at all levels. Women married to top officials were excellent in the role of peacemakers and interpreters, as well as cementing alliances with the tribes. Women were integral to the success of the fur trade, but because they were unpaid, they were largely ignored. White women were forbidden entry to the Canadian domain, because their coming meant settlement along European patterns. In fact, the few British women who did go to western Canada in the mid-nineteenth century, returned to Europe. It wasn't until the 1870s when European women coming with farm families began to settle and stay.

The Hudson's Bay Company was a business, first and foremost. Investors in London expected high returns on their capital. Dividends from 1828-1838 ran between twenty to twenty-five percent annually (but after 1846 they dwindled to ten percent), and with such significant profits, nothing could be allowed to get in the way.[7] White women, with no economic role to play in the fur trade, could only bring settlement and farms, and that meant wild animals would dwindle. Abhorrent to settlement within their fur preserve, the HBC didn't allow any families to take up land and farm except in designated colonies set up for retired Company employees.

The news that two white women, Americans besides, were on their way over the Rockies, was not what the Hudson's Bay men wanted to hear.

We are now at the Rocky Mountains, at the encampment of Messrs. McLeod and McKay, expecting to leave on Monday morning for Walla Walla. It seems a special favor that that company has come to Rendezvous this season: for otherwise we would have had to have gone with the Indians a difficult route, and so slow that we should have been late at Walla Walla and not have had the time we wanted to make preparations for winter.

Narcissa's letter to Marcus's sister and brother[8]

John McLeod and Tom McKay were Hudson's Bay Company "gentlemen" who had come to the rendezvous to see if what they had heard was true, if indeed white women had appeared in the Rockies. So it was, but there were only two of them, and McKay's stepfather, Dr. John McLoughlin back at Fort Vancouver, would be able to handle them. Tom McKay must have grinned, eager to take the news back to Fort Vancouver's dining room full of gentlemen himself.

Henry Spalding, writing years later, remembered what McKay had said upon meeting the mission party; something that hadn't seemed important at the time: "There is something that Doctor McLoughlin cannot ship out of the country so easy," referring to the white women.[9]

But at Rendezvous, the missionaries had more immediate problems. Narcissa lamented that they "did not meet the party they expected." Where was Reverend Parker? Hadn't he agreed to meet Marcus and the rest of the party here? Hadn't they come this far, endured so much, in order to get his expert advice on where to go next, and with whom?

Parker had not kept his promises, it seemed. They had no way of knowing he'd trekked up and down the mountain ranges and rivers, living with the Indians for a year, before heading to Fort Vancouver, and wending his way home via an English ship to London. To the nervous, exhausted and disappointed travelers at rendezvous, he'd "neglected even to write a single letter containing any information concerning the country, company, Indians, prospects, or advice of any kind whatever."[10] Anger became frustration, as they decided he'd not been able to send a letter to them with the HBC gentlemen. After all, if his advice had been read by the HBC men, the whole mission endeavor might have been nipped in the bud. It was a consolation of sorts.

The Indians were no help sorting out the situation. A rivalry had developed between the Cayuses and Nez Perces, each demanding the missionaries go home with them. Neither of the competitive tribes was willing to let the prize go to the other. "All appear very anxious to have us locate in their country, that they may be taught about God, and be instructed in the habits of civilized life," Eliza thought.

Arguments broke out between the Indian women, who had to be restrained. Much great medicine would accrue to the people who got the *Soyappos*, or "crowned ones" (because they wore big hats), to live with them and share the white man's secrets. Diplomacy and restraint was in order.

The trading fair wrapped up, the whiskey was gone, the trade goods all bartered away, the American Fur Company mules headed back eastward laden with precious pelts. The missionaries had no idea where to go next. Marcus hadn't gone farther west than rendezvous the year before—he had no idea which direction to head. The Indians planned to head north to the plains for their buffalo hunting season—they begged the missionaries to go with them. That would take months of their schedule, and the mission had to be started before winter. What could they do?

John McLeod solved the problem by inviting them to go with him and his party, taking the southern route through the mountains to Fort Walla Walla. That way he could keep an eye on the Americans, and know where they intended to go and what their plans were.

How could he be sure of their "missionary" status? It was quite common to meet up with spies in the interior. Everyone wanted to know where the furs were being trapped, and where unknown drainages existed. Spies were always in the field in the guise of being botanists, painters, or even aristocrats on outings. One had to be wise to them, show them what you wanted them to see, and keep you mouth shut about the rest. McLeod had not risen to his rank without merit, and he'd been trained at McLoughlin's knee.

The trail ahead would be a rugged one, difficult for hardy trappers, let alone a band of greenhorns from the East. The Americans had to abandon much of their baggage, as they were overloaded and overburdened for the trail ahead. Iron, tools, kettles, and many supplies were left behind. The Indians were delighted, and McLeod reassured them they could purchase what they needed from the Fort Vancouver stores.

They still had the little Dearborn wagon, though, and although it belonged to the Spaldings, Whitman began to think he would be the first to take a wagon over the Rockies. Historians have discussed the wagon issue in depth, attributing the wagon to Whitman's belief that he was pioneering the way for the wagon trains that would follow. How he could have thought that is inconceivable; wagon trains hadn't been significant on the frontier of Kentucky and Missouri, where settlers were streaming in. Traders' wagon trains made the trek to Santa Fe, but he wouldn't have known much about them.

The reason he grabbed onto the wagon, determined to wrest it through, was because at rendezvous he'd been upstaged by the women; natives had swarmed around them and they had garnered all the attention. Even Henry Spalding had more going for him—he was an actual preacher—and held services for crowds of Indians with the help of interpreters. No, Marcus Whitman was relegated to nearly the same status as William Gray, and he didn't like it. When he realized how much attention the natives were giving the wagon, the "land canoe" that they'd never imagined before, he'd found his place. He would persist in hauling the wagon over whatever terrain was ahead so that once he was in Oregon, he could use it to garner a bit of attention of his own.

McLeod's arrival at Rendezvous, and his offer to take them west with him, saved the mission. The missionaries felt their prayers were answered; Narcissa wrote in a letter home, "It seems a special favor of Providence that that Company has come to Rendezvous this season."[11] Otherwise they had nowhere to turn.

A small group of Nez Perces, led by a chief named Isholholhoatshoats, or the Lawyer, went along, too. Henry tried to dissuade them, knowing the Nez Perces needed to go on the buffalo hunt to obtain food for the winter. But they wouldn't hear of it. Lawyer spoke English quite ably, and told Henry, "I shall go no more with my people, but with you; where you settle I shall settle."[12]

Chief Lawyer had met Marcus and Samuel Parker the previous summer, and he was not about to let these precious teachers, purveyors of secrets leading to everything the Nez Perces needed to best their enemies, out of his sight. What Marcus didn't know was that Parker, during his extensive tourings through the mountain areas, promised the tribes that white people would come bringing them many gifts. While that allusion must have helped Parker garner favor during his tour, and guaranteed a warm welcome at the rendezvous in 1836, it set the stage for the myriad problems the missionaries would generate (usually without even being aware of it) with the Indians.

Along with the "land canoe," the Indians also kept their eyes on the boxes full of the very important books the teachers had brought. Hadn't they passed them out to the the mountain men, who had clasped them to their chests with joy? Surely such valuable items were big medicine. When would the Nez Perce people get theirs?

The next leg of the journey was over seemingly endless desert (now southern Idaho), It was rugged, rocky terrain, under blazing sun. A span of thirty-six hours was spent without water; twenty-six hours of it in the saddle. William Gray collapsed once, laying down in the sand to die. He argued that the others should go on without him, but Chief Lawyer helped him to his horse and rode behind him, supporting his limp body until they reached camp. No matter what, the Hudson's Bay men didn't stop or slow for anything or anyone. Perhaps they needed to travel that fast and hard (they were in Blackfoot territory). More likely they were trying to dissuade the mission party from sending word back east that the passage was an easy one. Certainly McLeod and McKay were irritated by Whitman who continued to haul the Dearborn along.

At Fort Hall there was trouble. McLeod suggested Whitman take the wagon apart until on the other side of the mountains where it could be reassembled. He refused. It would take several men to lift, push and pry the wagon over the mountains. Disgusted and worn out, Miles Goodyear, a young man hired to help the mission party and their animals, quit. Whitman took off the front axle and turned it into a two-wheeled cart. The little Dearborn, still sporting patches of blue and yellow paint, refused to die.

Narcissa's writings reveal how disgusted she was with Whitman's vehement refusal to abandon the wagon. She was mad that he was wearing himself out with the silly thing. No one wanted it along. Couldn't he see that? Obstinate, determined to achieve a goal he'd put his mind to, it was a key glimpse into the sort of mindset he had. Years later, when the Cayuses begged then demanded he leave their land, he would refuse to give it up, over and over again.

Eliza and Henry seemed to have little interest in getting a wagon over the trail. They held the belief that the Indians were diminishing because settlement was crowding them out too fast. Their whole purpose in creating a mission was to protect the people from the settlers who had ruined so many tribes in the past. Breaking a trail for emigrants would have been anathema to them.

The going got no easier. Days later, Eliza's horse tripped into a hornet's nest, jumped aside and she was thrown from the sidesaddle. Her size-five booted foot "remained a moment in the stirrup," and her "body was dragged some distance" until the frightened horse could be stopped. She "received no serious injury,"[13] but after being dragged over rough sand, lava rocks and sage brush, she was lucky to be alive. After Doctor Whitman's ministrations, she was even more fortunate. Heroic medicine of the day meant using the lancet, bleeding a patient until their body's inner balance could be "equalized." He stopped long enough to bleed her extensively, before they moved along.

She wrote about it the next day, "suffered but little inconvenience in riding today in consequence of being thrown from my horse yesterday." Although there really was no way to turn back now, she vowed she would continue on "this adventurous journey."[14]

The cattle's feet were sore, the mosquitoes unbearable, but they pushed on. McLeod was a gentleman, and Narcissa mentions him often during this passage. The ladies had "tea" with him several times, and he frequently sent his cook back with gifts of rice or fish, for the missionaries' meals. Narcissa described how to make the fried cakes he had fixed for them: ". . . taking a little flour and water, make some dough, and roll it thin, cut it into square blocks, then take some beef fat and fry them."[15] They were delicious, especially after so many days of so little. Near Fort Boise, the going was so rough Whitman had to finally abandon the wagon-cart, but he determined to come back for it the next spring. The animals were not doing well, and the loads had to be lightened. Narcissa's little trunk, what must have been her hope chest, was chosen for discard. It had been carried in the cart and now that the contents had to be loaded on the pack animals, Whitman chose to abandon it (along with other items, no doubt). She hated to part with it, and wrote a farewell soliloquoy to it in a letter to her sister.

She realized she would do things differently if making the trip again, "It would have been better for me not to have attempted to bring any baggage whatever, only what was necessary to use on the way . . . If I were to make the journey again I would make quite different preparations."[16] McLeod must have felt sorry for the woman's situation, because he retrieved the little trunk from along the trail and asked her if he could take it along on one of his animals. She agreed.

The Snake River was high, the crossing treacherous. The women were taken across by Indians on rafts woven from bulrushes and grass ropes. Ahead was the Blue Mountain range: steep, dark and rugged. McKay had stayed behind at one of the trading posts (Snake Fort) and McLeod, needing to travel faster than the missionary entourage was capable, had gone on to Fort Vancouver (no doubt eager to spill the beans about the missionary venture to McLoughlin). The missionaries were on their own, under the guidance of the Nez Perces who led them through.

The Whitmans and Gray decided to hurry ahead to Fort Vancouver, too, where they could get supplies and hopefully catch up with Parker who they hoped might still be there. They took along Richard, one of the Nez Perce youths, and left behind the Spaldings with "the hired men with the most of our baggage, & the Nez Perce Chief Rottenbelly," who would "pilot them in."[17] The herd did need to move slower, they were by now worn-out, two mules and a horse had just given out.

Whether it was the right decision for the time and place or not, one can't help but think the Whitmans and Gray were abandoning the Spaldings in the most difficult terrain they'd come across yet. Obviously, it was easier and more comfortable traveling with gentlemen of the HBC than a band of Indians. Hurrying to continue in the protective cover of the HBC party, they even took the tent, leaving the Spaldings to sleep under the stars.

McLeod, always the gentleman, offered to lend Narcissa his tent. She had taken the blue and white striped tent for her and Marcus, and now abandoned it beside a tree for "Mrs. Spalding . . . as she might be out many [nights]."[18]

It's easy to see that the couples were not getting along. Things were not going well at all; no Reverend Parker, no wagon, no mission location. The Spaldings had no doubt chewed Whitman out for his misleading them into a venture that had no planning at all. Tempers must certainly have flared, as nerves frazzled.

Narcissa wrote a letter to her mother about how beautiful the Grand Ronde Valley was, and how McLeod had given them nine wild ducks, and that Richard (who must have been taken along to do the fire-tending and cooking) had caught fresh salmon and made them up for a delicious supper. She detailed how they camped with no furniture (they hadn't sat in a chair for months); husband, "one of the best the world ever knew"[19] spread the saddle blankets over forked willow sticks pushed in the ground to make a canopy, and they lay on the saddles and other blankets under the shade, where they rested "until dinner is ready."

Cooking on the trip was difficult; and the men did most of it. The fur caravans always used hired male cooks; McLeod certainly had one along who often sent back dinner items to share with the missionaries. Whether Narcissa was inexperienced at cooking (a newlywed), too exhausted to try, or simply a product of her class—domestics did that sort of thing, and after all, wasn't Richard their "boy?"

During this part of the journey, the Whitmans were finally able to have some privacy. Sleeping in the communal tent for months must have been frustrating to a newly-married couple. Now, they lagged behind the smaller party, stopping to pick berries or admire the scenery. They felt they were past the "dangerous country"[20] and could safely wander out of sight of the camp and the other travelers. Riding together, the Whitmans had an opportunity to discuss personal matters, something they were reluctant to do in front of the Spaldings or the others. "I always enjoy riding alone with him, especially when we talk about home friends. It is then the tedious hours are sweetly decoyed away," Narcissa wrote.[21]

There was another reason for optimistic spirits; the countryside had changed. Suddenly they were out of the vast, hot, barren desert that must have been like a foreign country or different planet to the New Englanders. As they entered the Blue Mountains they saw big timber again, wild berries, hills covered with greenery, flowers, and birds singing. "The scenery reminded me of the hills in my native county of Steuben," Narcissa wrote.[22] The trail grew rugged but they made it through the passes to find McLeod with camp set up, Narcissa's tent readied, and tea waiting. It cheered her considerably.

They were near Fort Walla Walla, a HBC trading post, and a messenger was sent to alert the post that visitors were on the way: "It is the custom of the country to send heralds ahead to announce the arrival of a party and prepare for their reception." The anticipation of ending the long, hard journey must have been incredible. Narcissa wrote that they hurried to get ready in the morning to go in. Up at first light, quick sips of coffee and

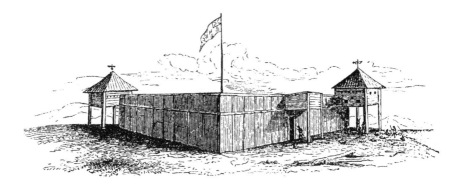

Wilkes, *The United States Exploring Expedition, 1838-1842, Vol. IV*

Fort Walla Walla

bites of the cold duck from the night before, then dressing for the Fort. ". . . both man and beast appeared alike propelled by the same force," she wrote. "The whole company galloped almost the whole way to the Fort. The fatigues of the long journey seemed to be forgotten in the excitement of being so near the close."[23]

As they rode up to the Fort, McLeod, Pierre Pambrun (the fort's head factor), and John Kirk Townsend, a traveling American naturalist passing through, greeted them. Narcissa was delighted by the reception, quickly sinking into "cushioned armed chairs." She detailed the breakfast they settled into with gusto: fresh salmon, potatoes, tea, bread and butter. "What a variety, thought I," she wrote. "You cannot imagine what an appetite these rides in the mountains give a person."[24]

The fort had other comforts of home: hens, turkeys, pigeons, cows, goats, and pigs. They were shown their room, where Pambrun had already set up beds; it was the "west bastion of the fort full of port holes in the sides, but no windows & filled with fire arms. A large cannon, allway loaded stood behind the door, by one of the holes." The armaments didn't alert her to any danger, in fact they "didn't move" Narcissa at all. She was so glad to have the "possession of a room" for shelter from the elements that she "scarcely Noticed them." She ignored the defense weaponry (and the need for it) in her delight over sleeping within walls once again. She did a little unpacking, then they were invited to a melon feast. Another meal at four o'clock: pork, cabbage, turnips, tea, bread and butter.

The next day she unpacked her trunk and began arranging things to take to Fort Vancouver. It was another three hundred miles, but this would be by water; not on horseback. She felt refreshed, eager to move on. "I feel as vigorous and as well able to engage in any domestic employment as I ever did in my life."[25] She refers to housework, not the mission. Whether she had thought much about what she would do as a missionary once in the field, it's hard to tell. Now that she was in a house again, she was in high spirits.

The Pambruns were not rugged fur trappers. Pierre Pambrun had risen within the HBC, something that took skill and finesse. His wife, of mixed Indian-Scotch blood, was refined and quite "English" in her ways, although she spoke only French and the native tongues. Their dining room was furnished with the cushioned arm chairs Narcissa mentions, also polished wood table, lace tablecloths, fine English bone china (in a blue and white pattern), with silver utensils. There were several servants to do the household chores: all men from the Sandwich Islands (Hawaii) or French-Canadians in employ of the Company.

"Mr. Pambrun is from Canada, and much of the gentlemen in his appearance," is how Narcissa described the Fort's manager. Noticing the sophistication of the Pambruns, she "covered a stock," (a neck-tie) for her "first work here for Husband."[26] She must have thanked the Lord she made Marcus keep his eastern clothing when he tried to sell it. Here, appearances counted for much more. The Canadian and British fur trade gentlemen and their families dressed in style and elegance, receiving shipments by sea directly from London. Decent society was a pleasant, even exciting prospect to a woman who had been living for months like a mountain man.

Three days after the Whitmans' arrival, the Spaldings and their entourage dragged up to the fort. In spite of the rugged pass and the lagging animals, they'd arrived sooner than the Whitmans expected. Suddenly, Narcissa's writing mentions her missionary effort (something she'd left out of her writings while traveling without the Spaldings). "Surely my heart is ready to leap for joy at the thought of being so near the long-desired work of teaching the benighted ones the knowledge of a Savior . . ."[27]

The arrival of the Spaldings seemed to remind her why she had come. Not to enjoy "domestic" employment, but to save souls.

Notes on Chapter 7

[1] Christopher L. Miller, *Prophetic Worlds: Indians and Whites on the Columbia Plateau* (New Jersey: Rutgers University Press, 1985), p. 55.

[2] Ibid, p. 56.

[3] Lavender, *Land of Giants*, p. 123.

[4] Ibid, p. 137.

[5] Ibid, p. 139.

[6] Ibid, p. 170.

[7] Peter C. Newman, *Company of Adventurers: the Story of the Hudson's Bay Company* (New York: Penguin Books, 1985), p. 471.

[8] *Whitman, Letters*, p. 22.

[9] Drury, *Marcus and Narcissa Whitman*, p. 198.

[10] Drury, *Henry Harmon Spalding*, p. 141.

[11] *Whitman, Letters*, p. 22.

[12] Drury, *Henry Harmon Spalding*, p. 147.

[13] *Warren, Memoirs*, p. 65.

[14] Ibid, p. 66.

[15] *Whitman, Letters*, p. 26.

[16] *Whitman, Letters*, p. 27.

[17] Narcissa Prentiss Whitman, *My Journal, 1836* (Fairfield, Wash: Ye Galleon Press, 1994), p. 33.

[18] *Whitman, Letters*, p. 29.

[19] Ibid, p. 30.

[20] Ibid.

[21] Ibid.

[22] Ibid.

[23] Ibid, p. 32.

[24] Ibid.

[25] Ibid, p. 33.

[26] Ibid, p. 33.

[27] Ibid, p. 34.

Chapter Eight

"This Desirable Spot"

S paldings, Whitmans and Gray decided to make the trip to
Vancouver together, to get supplies and in search of the
elusive Parker who was said to be staying there. Pambrun
was going downriver on business anyway, and the group tucked
into the Company's large open sail boat manned with six oars-
men and a steersman; nearly all Iroquois from Montreal, "men
accustomed to the water from their childhood, and well
acquainted with the dangers of the river."[1]

The Columbia River was unlike anything they'd ever seen.
There was no timber and the banks soared sharply up from the
water's edge. The river was, "clear as crystal and smooth as a
sea of glass," but very different from the Ohio. The riverbanks
were barren, "perpendicular banks of rocks" with "rugged bluffs
and plains of sand."[2]

They camped in tents on the riverbank, and Pambrun's
cook took charge of the meals. When resting, Narcissa wrote in
her journal or letters to be posted with HBC couriers who
passed up and down the river. Never again would women journey west with such royal treatment. Later, as wagons plied the
Oregon Trail's ruts, women would be exceedingly overworked
and exhausted. For the first two, however, there were servants
to help.

One incident on the downriver trip marred the experience
for Narcissa. While stopped along shore, she discovered her
clothing was crawling with lice. She felt the creatures on her
neck, then examined her cape and dress and saw it was crawling with the black vermin, "making all possible speed to lay

seige to my neck and ears." She became "frantic." She raced up a hill for Marcus, and he helped her brush them off her clothing "for an hour" until they had been removed from all the gathers and plaits of her skirt. In the boat once more, filled with both missionaries and Indians, "everyone in the boat was alike troubled . . ." by the "miserable companions."[3]

As the party sailed downriver, they encountered Indians unlike those they had met in the mountains. These were the river tribes, people who lived and looked very different from any they had met so far. Narcissa saw natives with flattened heads, the first time she'd been "near enough to be able to examine them. Their eyes have a dull and heavy expression."[4] The Americans were astounded that the Indian women were actually showing off their infants in the "pressing machine," as if they were proud of their distorted craniums.

Narcissa described the practice: "I saw an infant here whose head was in the pressing machine. This was a pitiful sight. Its mother took great satisfaction in unbinding and showing its naked head to us. The child lay upon a board between which and its head was a squirrel skin. On its forehead lay a small square cushion, over which was a bandage drawn tight around, pressing its head against the board. In this position it is kept three or four months or longer, until the head becomes a fashionable shape."[5] It was a dying practice, just as the Chinook upper-class was fading fast, "we are told that this custom is wearing away very fast. There are only a few tribes of this river who practice it."

Unknown to the missionaries, flattened foreheads were a mark of the upper caste among the Columbia River peoples. Only aristocrats were allowed to perform the practice on their infants. A flattened head meant you were a member of the ruling class, not a slave. To be allowed to flatten your infant's head was very important in class conscious Chinook life. Years before, when the first Indian women had joined with the British fur traders in marriages, they had been so distraught when their husbands wouldn't allow them to flatten their infant's heads that they killed the babies. They chose to destroy their infants, rather than force them to go though life with the sign of slavery and lower classes: normal foreheads.

Author's Photo

Home of Hudson's Bay Company Chief Factor,
Dr. McLoughlin, Fort Vancouver.

When the travelers arrived in Fort Vancouver, they described it as the "New York of the Pacific Ocean." There were two ships in harbor, fresh from London and the Sandwich Islands. Suddenly they were propelled from the backwoods journey into a vibrant, cosmopolitan society. People spoke a variety of languages; French mainly, some English, Chinook, and the island tongue of the Kanaka laborers from the Sandwich Islands. Everything was salted heavily with Scottish brogue.

Mr. Townsend was there, as well as the chief Factor, Dr. McLoughlin. There were several gentlemen of the fort who welcomed them, and McLoughlin ushered them into his personal residence and "seated us on a sofa." Mrs. McLoughlin and Mrs. Douglas, "both natives of the country—half breeds . . ."[6] were introduced. This was nothing like Fort William or Fort Walla Walla. They were in the "midst of civilization" where an awed Eliza thought "the luxuries of life seem to abound."[7]

There were two ladies from England, the McLoughlins' polished young daughter, a Church of England minister and his wife just arrived from London, the sea captains, and the gentlemen of the Company. "This is more than we expected when we left home—that we should be privileged with the acquaintance and society of two English ladies. Indeed we seem to be nearly allied to Old England, for most of the gentlemen of the Company are from there or Scotland,"[8] Narcissa observed.

Everyone was there, it seemed, except Reverend Parker. He'd gone on a ship to the Sandwich Islands a few weeks earlier, leaving them furious and disappointed. He was supposed to tell them where to build the mission, to give them advice about the Indians and the country, to tell them what to do now that the harrowing trek was over. They "mourned about it considerably," but there was nothing they could do.[9]

They would have to establish the mission stations themselves. The men—Spalding, Whitman and Gray—would go back upriver to "explore the Cayuse and Nez Perce countries," the women waiting in the McLoughlin home "until they can select a location and return for us."[10]

Winter was on its way, and the rainy season would slow any building or travel. Narcissa was three months pregnant, and must have been nervous about watching her husband disappear upriver to unknown territory, "when it seems to be least desirable."[11] She took consolation by the fact that the men were unwilling to leave them behind and only did so because it was impossible to take the women and the building supplies in the same boat. Again, Narcissa was left with uncertainty about her (and her baby's) future, ". . . we are sure that they will make every effort to return for us soon."[12]

The women busied themselves with touring the fort, studying how things were done, and ordering some household supplies made up by HBC craftsmen. There was a school with fifty-one students: mixed blood children of Indian mothers and French fathers, in employ of the Company. The Yankees were in a foreign land; few of the fort residents spoke English, and Eliza and Narcissa no French or Chinook.

Etiquette and customs were different, the gentlemen even ate meals separate from their wives in the "custom of the country."[13] All the domestic labor was performed by Kanaka laborers hired from the Sandwich Islands.

Narcissa and Eliza dined on coffee and cocoa, and sat through meals served one course after another by excellent cooks and servants. They went riding once a week with the ladies of the Fort at Mrs. McLoughlin's invitation. The women may have been gentle mannered in the ladies' dining room, but on horseback they were hellions. They rode all afternoon, up to fifteen miles at a time, and the pace was fast. Mrs. McLoughlin "keeps her old fashion of riding gentleman fashion," rather than having a ladies' saddle as Eliza and Narcissa did. "This is the universal custom of Indian women, and they have saddles with high backs and fronts." The Americans were urged to adopt the "more easy way of riding," but declined; ". . . we have never seen the necessity of changing our fashion."[14]

The women of the fort were very well-dressed in the current London styles, but they all wore skin leggings, a custom they adapted from their native culture. They were women between two cultures, who skillfully adopted whatever worked for them. They spent hours doing embroidery and playing cribbage, just like Englishwomen across the seas, but they were embroidering and beading skin leggings and betting on cards just as their mothers had on stick games.

The Americans began to adapt, too. Narcissa noted that Dr. McLoughlin gave Marcus a pair of leather pantaloons. "All gentlemen here wear them for riding for economy. Riding horseback and carrying a gun is very destructive to cloth pantaloons."[15] She and Eliza, with the help of ladies of the Fort, made themselves feather ticks, from soft deerskin filled with wild bird feathers.

When Henry returned to take the women upriver less than a month after leaving them—"so soon"—they almost had to pull themselves away from comfortable fort life. It was harvest season in the fields at the fort, two ships in harbor had unloaded holds of baled trade goods and supplies which filled the stores. It was a time of plenty. Now, heading upriver, with Iroquois boatmen hauling them over rapids and gorges by ropes, the women wondered what would be awaiting them.

At the onset of the journey from Cincinnati, one mission station was the plan. At some point during the way West plans changed. Now they would each create their own mission station. They had found it difficult to get along; the men had been in at least three fierce arguments along the way. The decision to separate into two and perhaps three mission stations instead of one, would have many repercussions. At the onset, it seemed a logical way to handle the increasing competition between the missionaries. McLoughlin warned the Americans against settling with the Cayuses; the Nez Perces told them the same. But Marcus Whitman was undeterred; now that the mission dream had become reality, he chafed at the prospect of serving as physician at Reverend Henry Spalding's mission. Good land, water, proximity to the river trade, and being on the trade highway for the Hudson's Bay Company was enough for him. He would do it his way.

It didn't suit Eliza at all, ". . . thus it seems we are about to go to our respective fields, where heathen darkness reigns, single handed and alone—." She knew they would be stronger and more capable of survival if they were together, rather than strung out across the region.[16]

Marcus and William Gray were busy building a station at Waiilatpu, "place of the rye grass," in the Cayuse people's homeland. Eliza and Henry were to go further north, to a spot along the KoosKooskie River (Clearwater River), and settle in the midst of the Nez Perce people. Gray thought he might try going up in the Bitterroot Mountains, once the first two stations were finished.

Narcissa stayed at Fort Walla Walla for several weeks as a guest of the Pambruns while the house was being built. She was happy to teach Mrs. Pambrun and her daughter how to speak and read English, and was looking forward to being "situated near one family so interesting, and a native female that promises to be so much society for me. She is learning to speak the English language quite fast."[17] If Narcissa deemed the polished Mrs. Pambrun a typical native female, she must have thought that the Cayuse women would be much like her.

She had "no plan separate from my husband's," and discovered that "nothing" was "more difficult" than her attempts "to convey religious truth in their language," to the Indians.[18]

The Spaldings went upriver to build their station while Marcus worked at Waiilatpu. Narcissa felt guilty at remaining a guest of the Pambruns, "This dear sister [Eliza] goes very cheerfully to her location, expecting to live in a skin lodge until her house is built; and this, too, in the dead of winter; But she prefers it to remaining here, and so should I."[19] Well, she should have, probably, but she didn't.

She noted that already one had died from their party. The "colored man," John Hinds, who had joined up with them at rendezvous as a laborer, had died from "dropsy" while helping Marcus build the house at Waiilatpu.

It took two months for Marcus, William Gray, two hired Kanakas from the HBC, and Hinds (before he died) to build the dwelling. It was a house, though; with a lean-to, a chimney and fireplace, and a floor. No windows or door—just blankets. But there was a fire in the hearth, and it was Narcissa's own home. "It occurred to me that my dear parents had made a similar beginning, and perhaps a more difficult one than ours." She dreamed that this was only the beginning; that someday she'd have the comfortable house and garden her own mother had enjoyed. After all, didn't all newlyweds start out with very little? Hers was not such an unusual beginning. Only that she was twenty-five miles from the nearest female she could talk with, (even in faltering English) or summon in three months when she went into labor.

Today we might think that pregnant Narcissa felt secure and in good hands with a physician husband. In that era however, medical men seldom delivered babies. Midwives were the custom, and doctors didn't bother with deliveries. It was a time when medical practitioners were seen far differently than today. Most physicians had only rudimentary education and training. There was no knowledge of disease, few surgeries, and ignorance of the causes of infection. The participation of a doctor with unwashed hands and instruments often insured a patient's demise.

On the trip so far, Marcus had used the lancet plenty, but so had Henry and anyone else who carried one. Bleeding was so common a practice that a doctor wasn't necessary. Giving dosages of calomel, too, didn't call for much knowledge. Opiates, morphines, and other strong medicines of the day didn't require a prescription—anyone could purchase them, and most people dosed themselves. When Hinds, who came explicitly with Marcus in order to receive medical attention for his dropsy, died, Narcissa must have worried about his medical abilities.

What Narcissa needed was a skilled woman who'd already been through childbirth. She could relax, knowing Mrs. Pambrun was only twenty-five miles away. Less than a day's hard ride. She could be summoned when the time came.

Eliza, though, would be farther north and east, about 120 miles upriver from Waiilatpu. Lapwai, the "place of the butterflies," would be her home. When she and Henry left Narcissa at Fort Walla Walla they were surrounded with a welcoming committee: 125 Nez Perces came to take them home.

They weren't pathetic creatures waiting for salvation. They were strong, hardy horsemen and horsewomen, who were taking the missionaries into their heartland. The Spaldings were impressed. Henry and Eliza wrote to friends back East that the Nez Perces were "certainly the most handsome Indians . . the most friendly, and most like civilized men, and live better than any other tribes on this side of the mountains."[20]

Hadn't they seen dreadful practices—an infant buried alive with its dead mother? (Henry had seen the Walla Wallas perform such a tradition) Corpses left to rot on open platforms (rather than given a Christian burial)? The filthy, naked creatures living along the lower Columbia River seemed alien to these people. That was the key to their success with the Indians: Eliza and Henry saw the Nez Perces as *people*, first; Indians to be civilized, second.

The Nez Perces treated them royally, packing all the goods, setting up camp, doing all the labor—anything the Spaldings desired, they did. Arriving at Lapwai—"this desirable spot"— they provided the Spaldings with a fifteen-foot buffalo skin lodge. The "long and tedious journey" had finally come to a close.[21]

This was Eliza's home for nearly a month, while Henry and William Gray directed the Nez Perces to carry stones and timbers two miles to build a cabin. They moved into it the latter part of December. It was a record cold winter, and temperatures got to twenty-degrees below zero (Henry recorded temperatures three times daily). Snow piled up a foot and a half outside, but they huddled in the cabin. It was 42' x 18'; eighteen-feet at one end was their living quarters (a room with buttery, closet and recess); the other end was the schoolroom.

The Nez Perces provided them food—mostly salmon and venison. They were very happy. Both wrote letters telling how relieved they were to have a roof over their heads (even if it was grass and dirt over timbers) after so many months of sleeping under the stars.

The "natives appear really . . . eager to receive instruction," so in a month's time, Eliza had a school open. The people were clamoring for it, they wanted to learn the English language and other "white ways" so Eliza couldn't see any reason to put it off until the building was completed. She had trouble learning their language, but she persisted. The Nez Perces had an oral tradition, but Eliza's written words intrigued them; they threw themselves into academics with gusto.

She'd brought some teaching materials, of course. There were a few primers (perhaps McGuffey's readers fresh from the printer in Cincinnati) and several copies of the Bible. She had to go back to the very basics, such as rote memorization, but she was an educational innovator, as well.

Pestalozzianism was a revolutionary educational philosophy of the day. Based on the principles of intellectual education promoted by Swiss reformer, Johann Pestalozzi, schools in America were slowly beginning to change. Leaving behind the old ways (rote memorization based on drill), educators were beginning to focus on hands-on learning: drawing, music, writing, and crafts. Learning was to be concrete before abstract. Students were grouped by abilities and taught at their development level. Commonplace ideas today, they were an extremely controversial departure from the accepted techniques of the time.

Eliza taught a few students verses, and they proceeded to teach others; the entire group recited in unison at times. At first Eliza copied letters to make little books for them every night; soon she had some of them copying as well.

She taught them songs, Protestant church hymns mostly, which they sang enthusiastically. A few years later she translated the hymns into the Nez Perce language and printed up a hymnal in their native tongue. Those hymns, translated roughly by Eliza over 150 years ago, are still sung by some Nez Perce people.[22]

Eliza used visual methods, just as she had been trained. She'd learned to draw and paint, part of her teacher's education preparation, another Pestalozzi practice. She painted pictures to illustrate various Bible stories, which she read to the students while natives translated the stories. It wasn't long before everyone knew the lesson. She would have needed to use every skill she knew, as eventually there were between one hundred and two hundred students (of all ages) in her classroom at one time (once the larger building was built).

She worked tirelessly by day and far into the night, copying pages, painting pictures, hand stitching little books together with needle and thread. She was "faithful" at instructing them because she knew education would be "the salvation of their precious souls."[23]

From the beginning there were differences between the two stations: Waiilatpu was situated along a major river and at the center of many Indian trails. The Oregon Trail wound right past it (in only a few years, thousands would trek past Narcissa's home). When the missionaries arrived there were between 300-400 people in the Cayuse tribe.

The Spalding's Clear Water Mission at Lapwai was more than 120 miles away in an isolated location. Off the path of the fur traders, no one passed by except Nez Perces traveling from one end of their vast land to the other. It was in the center of the Nez Perce homeland; the tribe numbered between 3,000-4,000 people.[24]

The Cayuse people were in transition: the language was changing, as the young people began to adopt the Nez Perce language. Narcissa wrote that the young Cayuses were much easier to get along with than the older chiefs. She felt it would be only a matter of time, when the young ones took over, then salvation would be easier. The Nez Perce chief Tackensuatis (nicknamed Rotten Belly) led the welcoming party to take the Spaldings up to Lapwai. When he found out the Whitmans had chosen to settle at Waiilatpu, he warned them that they had made a mistake. He told Marcus that the Nez Perces had never had difficulties with the white man as the Cayuse had. He cautioned that they would see the difference.[25]

March 14, on Narcissa's birthday, she gave birth to a daughter: Alice Clarissa Whitman, "a treasure invaluable, indeed."[26]

She wrote to her parents that, "During the winter my health was very good, so as to be able to do my work. About a week before her birth, I was afflicted with an inflammatory rash, which confined me mostly to my room. After repeated bleeding, it abated very considerably."[27]

Mrs. Pambrun had arrived two weeks before the event; summoned to act as midwife. She wasn't much help, though, because she was sick and couldn't do any cooking or housework, either. And, she'd brought two of her children along.

Narcissa was thankful the baby was a "very quiet child, and slept all night—only "nursing once, sometimes not at all."[28] Marcus ended up doing the cooking and washing, as Narcissa described the crowded household: the entire camp of Cayuses arrived, William Gray came to stay a while, Mr. Pambrun and another HBC trader, Mr. Ermatinger, stayed one night, and of course Mrs. Pambrun and the children.

Narcissa demonstrated how to dress and diaper the infant for Mrs. Pambrun and Marcus. Mrs. Pambrun wrapped her own infants "native-style," on a cradleboard stuffed with dry moss that was thrown away; cloth diapering was quite new to her.

"The little stranger is visited daily by the chiefs and principal men in camp, and the women throng the house continually, waiting an opportunity to see her," the new mother exulted. "Her whole appearance is so new to them. Her complexion, her size and dress, etc., all excite a great deal of wonder; for they never raise a child here except they are lashed tight to a board, and the girls' heads undergo the flattening process."[29]

Alice was larger than the Cayuse newborns: ten pounds, at that. The Indians called her a Cayuse *temi*, which meant "Cayuse girl," because she was born on Cayuse *waitis*—Cayuse land. "The whole tribe are highly pleased because we allow her to be called a Cayuse girl," Narcissa wrote.[30] If the Cayuses were simply overjoyed at the excitement of having a white child born on their soil (which might have been quite powerful medicine—they weren't sure about that yet), or if they were gently reminding the Whitmans that they were interlopers in someone else's domain, we can't tell. The Whitmans were too overjoyed with their precious daughter to worry about it.

Narcissa delighted in being a new mother: "I believe I was up and dressed the day the babe was a week old, and in a day or two after was about the house, and the next Sabbath walked out of doors."[31] Weakened by childbirth, not to mention the week of bleeding by Marcus before the birth, she needed time to regain strength.

In the same letter detailing the new baby to her mother, she mentioned that the spring weather had been so mild she didn't need a fire in her room very often. "Fine, healthy atmosphere— no danger of nervous affections here. I have not been troubled in the least as I used to be."[32] Whether she was referring to bouts of depression, or another type of problem, it's hard to know exactly. Now that she was a mother, with a baby to shower affection and attention upon, and a little house of her own to tidy and care for, her life was becoming much as it would have been back in New York. Things weren't so foreign; nor the heathens so prominent, now. She had her infant daughter and a house to run.

Mrs. Pambrun left after a while and her twelve-year-old daughter stayed with Narcissa to help with the housework. The Whitmans sent to Fort Vancouver for domestic workers and McLoughlin sent an orphan girl to them. She wasn't quite what Narcissa expected, ". . . said to be sixteen, but she is not larger than a girl of twelve years." The girls had no clue about housework; the orphan couldn't even speak English. "It is impossible for me to obtain permanent help here . . ." Narcissa lamented in a letter to her own mother.[33]

She wrote asking them to send ready-made clothing for her and her family as it would, ". . . save so much of my time for teaching and writing, the latter of which I have a great deal to do, and besides, my eyes suffer very much from weakness— more than formerly."[34]

Marcus had two men working for him, "Owyhees" (Kanakas) hired from the Sandwich Islands. They spoke a different language, too. Narcissa's opinion of them was quite different from her feelings about the girls (who were mixed-bloods). "They are the best for labor of any people this side of the mountains. The Indians do not love to work well enough for us to place any dependence on them. I find a peculiar tender feeling in my heart for these Islanders . . . They make excellent cooks and house servants. Our men do their own cooking, and sometimes cook for me."[35]

That spring, with tiny Alice Clarissa in Narcissa's arms, the Whitmans attended Sabbath meeting in one of the Indian lodges. Narcissa was surprised to find it, "a very comfortable place . . . remarkably neat and clean."[36]

As soon as the soil could be worked, Marcus began to set in motion his plan to eventually cultivate three hundred acres of farm ground around their home.

At Clear Water, Eliza was in her element, "We feel happy and satisfied with our situation and employment . . ." But it hadn't been without sacrifice, ". . . though it removes us far from almost all we hold dear on earth." The Nez Perce children were her focus, "for they are our hope of the nation."[37]

That December she finally got a child of her own, "Through the astonishing mercy of God . . . I was made the joyful mother of a daughter." They named her Eliza, after her mother, and the pleased Nez Perces gifted the tiny infant with a pony.

In March, Narcissa wrote to Eliza asking, "Would it not be well for us mothers to devote a special season [time] and unitedly present our infant charges before the mercy seat?" "Mercy seat" was a special spot in the front of a church where sinners sat and prayed for redemption. It was a common term pertaining to spiritual rebirth in evangelical circles. Eliza responded asking Narcissa to set the time—they would pray together for their daughters' early conversions. Eliza agreed with Narcissa that it was good to pray together because, "united prayer is prevailing prayer."[38]

There were only two of them, and they were so far apart that Eliza thought forming a formal association (a Maternal Association) for "strengthening each other's hands in the cause of infant instruction," impossible to do. They couldn't travel for meetings—but they could pray together, which she thought necessary due to their "peculiar situation."[39]

The women agreed to pray at nine every morning; they would read selected Scriptures—seeking God's help in "discharging the responsible duties of mothers & for the early conversion of our children."[40] It was a sort of spiritual telepathy between two isolated women who refused to give up their own culture against impossible odds.

Notes on Chapter Eight

[1] Ibid, p. 44.
[2] Ibid, p. 34.
[3] Ibid, p. 36.
[4] Ibid.
[5] Ibid.
[6] Ibid, p. 36.
[7] *Warren, Memoirs*, p. 67.
[8] *Whitman, Letters*, p. 37.
[9] Ibid.
[10] *Warren, Memoirs*, p. 67.
[11] *Whitman, Letters,* p. 38.
[12] Ibid, p. 39.
[13] Ibid, p. 38.
[14] Ibid, p. 40.
[15] Ibid, p. 39.
[16] *Warren, Memoirs*, p. 67.
[17] *Whitman, Letters*, p. 45.
[18] Ibid, p. 41.
[19] Ibid, p. 44.
[20] Dawson, *Laboring in My Savior's Vineyard*, p. 67.
[21] *Warren, Memoirs*, p. 68.
[22] Dawson, *Laboring in My Savior's Vineyard*, p. 71.
[23] *Warren, Memoirs*, p. 68.
[24] Drury, *Marcus and Narcissa Whitman*, p. 224.
[25] Ibid, p. 226.
[26] Whitman, Letters, p. 47.
[27] Ibid.
[28] Ibid.
[29] Ibid.
[30] Ibid.
[31] Ibid, p. 48.
[32] Ibid.
[33] Ibid, p. 48.
[34] Ibid, p. 58.
[35] Ibid, p. 48.
[36] Ibid, p. 49.
[37] *Warren, Memoirs*, p. 69.
[38] Ibid, p. 70.
[39] Ibid, p. 71.
[40] Ibid.

Chapter Nine

Mary's Choice

*As life is uncertain I write this page that should I be
taken away sudenly this book may not be seen except by
a sister or some very near and intimate friend, and I
hope that that friend will have the compassion to burn
it immediatley.*
*"Should it by chance fall into the hand of an other prey
be so good as not to read it.*[1]

Mary Richardson (Walker's) diary

On December 21, 1836, while Eliza and Narcissa settled
into their isolated homes, in Maine, twenty-five year old
Mary Richardson sat down with pen in hand to write a
letter that would change the course of her life. She'd worked
hard to educate herself, had a little school of her own to run,
was still unmarried (but only because she'd been able to rein in
her passion for a wealthy, intelligent man who was not a
Christian) and wanted to do something with herself.

She wrote to the American Board for Foreign Missions in
Boston: "I cordially acquiesce in your proposal to employ me as
a teacher of the Missionaries' children. I thought of offering
myself expressly for this employment. Perhaps I can attend to
this and at the same time be acquiring the language and quali-
fying myself ultimately for other labors." The "other labors" she
had in mind was being appointed an official missionary, one
step above teacher. "I simply suggest the idea. Of course I have
not the means of knowing whether such a thing would be prac-
ticable or not." She knew no single female missionary had been

appointed in the past. Her high aspirations had a purpose, "—I think I should take a great interest in trying to elevate the condition of Females." And she didn't want to do it in Maine, or even the slums of Boston. She envisioned herself in a far-off locale, "Perhaps there is no station I would sooner select . . . than Bangkok."[2]

For a woman of the 1830s (or any other time), she had set goals for herself that were not to be taken lightly. The eldest of nine children born to parents who were local schoolteachers, Mary was a quick study, eager to learn, and curious about everything life had to offer; she had once wanted to be a doctor, but that was impossible.

After finishing elementary classes, Mary attended classes at Kent's Hill, the Maine Wesleyan Seminary, but couldn't take examinations or gain credits for her work. Eager for recognition of her efforts, she asked a professor how she had done, "How do my papers compare with those the young men hand in? I just want to know . . ." His answer was, "They are better, much better. Aren't you ashamed of yourself, Mary?"[3]

Her father pursued farming, but failed. The depression of the 1830s was a difficult time for the nation. The Richardsons were broke, and so was everyone else in town. "Almost all the banks in the county are down. Provisions are not so high as formerly but there is nothing to buy them with," a neighbor observed.[4]

The Richardson family was resourceful. They planted mulberries and tried silk growing. Every year they gathered for pigeon season, when thousands of passenger pigeons were netted, killed, cleaned and shipped to the cities. It was a hardscrabble existence; Mary sought better for herself through books and education. After one year's preparation at Kent's Hill, at nineteen, she began teaching.

She had "beaus," sometimes too many, she would joke with her sister. "If ever I have a husband may God give me a Christian . . ." She was choosy, and not at all ready to settle down. A neighboring farmer proposed but she swore she'd cleaned enough tripe for a lifetime—she didn't want to be a farmer's wife. "Ought I to bid adieu to all my cherished hopes and unite by destiny with that of a mear farmer with little education and no refinement. In a word shall I to escape the horrors of perpetual celibecy settle down with the vulgar. I cannot do it."[5]

However, she knew she was getting too set in her ways. "I see very few men that are perfect enough to please me. If I do not get married soon I fear I shall not be able to find anyone who will suit me . . ."[6] She considered that maybe she thought too highly of herself, and chastized herself to remember that "Birds that fly high light low may be true of me yet. But I hope not."[7]

There was one suitor, a man who was cultured, wealthy and very attractive to her. He was intelligent, educated, and challenged her mind. There was one problem: he was an infidel. She was tempted to reject Christianity, so there'd be no hindrance to marrying him, but she couldn't do it. Even five years later, she wrote in her diary that she still wondered how it would turn out. She must have hoped he would attend a revival and change his mind, but that didn't happen.

She taught school, attended social and church events, and waited for something more, something that was missing from her life. Her diary entry for New Year's, "I have closed the year and begun the new, but was so busy cleaning tripe and one thing or another that I almost forgot to mind anything about it. I am a year older, a year nearer death. But I fear I am no better for having lived another year. How little good I do in the world. I wonder if I do all I might."[8]

Feelings of insecurity as well as frustration surfaced at the beginning of another school year: "I want to do a thousand things yet can not do any thing. What is the use to try to make any body think I am anything when I know I am not."[9]

Once she'd decided to go on a mission, things fell into place, except for her problems with suitors. She couldn't accept the farmer's proposal—he'd never go into the mission field. Her only hope was to be assigned as a teacher, then perhaps do a good enough job to be appointed a female missionary, sans husband.

"My mind very much excited don't know what to do have always harbored the design of going on a mission If I listen to the proposals of G. [the farmer] then fare well to the design. I have found the decision is an important one Oh may I decide aright—"[10] She was highly excited about the possibility of going on a foreign mission, yet wasn't completely sure it was the right choice to make. ". . . And now Oh! God direct my decission. lead me in the path of duty. O may I be able to scrutinise my fortunes."

Discussing her plans with family and friends, she saw how easy it was to be the center of attention; going out into the foreign missions was the most exciting thing a woman (or man) in the little Maine community could think of doing. "I wish I knew whether it is fame that is urging me off on a mission if so woe is me. God forbid that I should be influenced by unhallowed motives I do not see how it can be wrong for me to go or right to stay."[11]

She wasn't sure she would be acceptable to the Board, and left it to its decision to decide her fate. "Feel a decided determination to offer myself. If they accept me I go, if not I stay . . . By night and by day I scarcely think of any thing but becoming a missionary. I think I feel more engaged in religion than I have ever befor. May God grant that I may not mistake the path of duty."[12]

Her teacher wrote a glowing recommendation, mentioning her "vigorous intellect," and her knowledge of history, philosophy, chemistry, natural history, botany, mental philosophy, mathematics, French and Spanish. Her pastor was not so enthusiastic. Mary's father was one of the church deacons, which may explain her pastor's grudging recommendation. He pointed out that she had been skeptical of religion, but had now laid that skepticism aside. He noted that there was opposition to him from her father and family, which she was a part of.

Mary wasn't one to miss an opportunity, so she sent a letter of her own. She mentioned her good health, her joy at doing domestic chores, her aspiring mind and willingness to work. She closed with, "But I have endeavored and I hope with some success to cultivate a spirit of humility: to be willing to do something and be nothing if duty required."[13]

The Board found her application satisfactory, but as she was an unmarried female, she could only fill a teaching position in a foreign mission. She applied for two openings,

Constantinople, Turkey and Bangkok, Siam; but both were filled.

She did not give up. She merely prayed for a husband.

Elkanah Walker was born in the seaport town of North Yarmouth, Maine, a farm boy in a family of eleven. At nineteen he was a wild teenager in a Puritan community, where he spent his time taking after "dancing and frivolity" until he read a book that changed his life. He read a widely popular novel, *The Scottish Chiefs*, which was about William Wallace. First published in 1809, the book was a favorite of men nearly everywhere; mountain men read it aloud around the campfire. Fur trapper Joe Meek named his daughter Helen Mar Meek, after the book's heroine. (Later, Helen Mar Meek would be left for Narcissa to raise.) The novel stimulated Elkanah to seek adventure and make a change in his life; with a passion for more than milking cows and plowing fields, he decided to get an education.

After learning the basics he went to Plainfield, New Hampshire, to a school that offered free tuition to poor but worthy students who were planning a career in the ministry. He made friends quickly. A fellow student wrote to him about a speaker who'd described conditions in the West (the Western Reserve, at that time). The greatest obstacle to Christianity was from emigrants who had been former Christians, who now turned away. They were far from Church discipline so they threw off restraints and turned infidel, becoming bitter foes of Christianity.[14] The frontier was awash with lawless men who were a threat to the very democracy of the country. It was something a patriotic Christian needed to worry about.

But the West didn't spark his interest; he decided to be a foreign missionary and applied to be sent to South Africa. He was accepted and appointed to the Mission of the Maratime Zoolaks (Zulus). He was thirty one, an educated minister, and expecting to be sent to Africa in the fall of 1837.[15]

There was something lacking; Elkanah was another applicant whose matrimonial status was a problem for the Board. The secretary of the Board wrote to him, mentioning Mary Richardson, another Maine applicant for foreign mission service. "From her testimony I should think her a good girl. If you have no body in view, you might inquire about her."[16] Elkanah was never one to ignore good advice.

Letters flew back and forth, Elkanah traveled to Mary's home to meet her and the family. Everyone was eager for the marriage, but of course Mary had doubts. So did Elkanah. Elkanah was over six feet tall, with long gangly limbs and big feet. Mary's family jokingly referred to him as a "pelican," and teased her about his ungainly walk. She was undaunted. This was the man for her. He wanted something beyond the fields of Maine. No matter that he had no money, and absolutely no sophistication. He had an education, and bigger dreams than hers. That suited her just fine. It was the idea of marriage that chilled the blood in her veins.

Mary was quilting with friends when Elkanah arrived for a second visit after proposing marriage. "He appears much more interesting than before and I have no doubt as to being able to love him. Think there is mutual satisfaction."[17]

The farmer-suitor rushed over when he heard the news that Mary was engaged. He pleaded his case and tried to talk her out of it, telling her, "people did not think (she) was cutting a great cheese . . ." by marrying Walker.

Mary and Elkanah wrote letters back and forth, trying to get to know each other. They received word that Mary's application to the Board had been accepted; she'd been appointed "an assistant missionary on condition she be married to Elkanah Walker."[18] Whether Mary thought it unfair or not, that she wasn't allowed to go on her own merits, she said nothing.

Elkanah saw his future linked to marrying Mary Richardson; he hadn't received an appointment yet, and he needed to get her to marry him before he could enter the mission field. If the Board *suggested* marriage, he'd comply, of course. But he had fallen in love with Mary, and the Board was no longer an issue with him. It wasn't the first, though, as he'd already had several fruitless love affairs. He didn't have much luck getting women to commit their future to his. He tried even harder with Mary, signing one letter with the romantic language of flowers, "Rose Cinnamon."

Mary answered that letter quickly, "As you seem to like the language of flowers, I have selected a few symbols.

"Ivy: I have found one true heart.

"Rose Bud: Thou hast stolen my affections.

"White Poppy: Doomed to heal or doomed to kill.

"Fraught with good or fraught with ill.

"If I do not paint a group of flowers composed of these and the cinnamon rose, it will be for want of leisure . . .There is a question under discussion here as to whether long engagements are favorable to intellectual progress. What is your opinion?"[19]

What she meant by the white

Whitman College Collection

Elkanah Walker

poppy can be read either way, maybe that's how she wanted it. Obviously she hadn't given her heart to Walker completely. Not even slightly, it would appear. Then again, it wasn't Walker, the man, she hesitated about, but the act of marriage itself.

Elkanah had even bigger problems though. The Board had not come through the financial depression that swept the nation in 1836 very well. It was "embarrassed by a want of funds" and couldn't even support the missionaries already in the field. The Rocky Mountain Mission had cost plenty already. There would be no missionaries sent out in the fall.

When he broke the news to Mary, she didn't give up. She wrote him, "I have now acquired the habit of sitting up an hour or two after the family retires (something she continued to do in Oregon, too. Mary was a night-owl.) I think of you almost constantly . . . Can you endure it, to have a simple creature like me always annoying you with her little griefs and woes or inviting you to participate in her trifling joys. If you cannot, then go where the *centrifugal forces will carry you.* If I am to have a companion for life, I want one who will be willing to share all my sympathies. In a word, I want a *better-self* and I am confident that in you my desire will be satisfied.

"If I could stay young I'd like to stay single a while longer, but old maids are so abhorred, I think one does well to escape that doom if they can. Said Brother J.C. the other day, "I don't blame a girl for having anything she can get. It is such an awful thing to be an old maid." . . . There are plenty of cinnamon roses in bloom which never fail to remind me of you when I look out of my attic window."[20]

Mary may have given up on the mission idea, but she had discovered she needed and wanted a "better-self" and was trying to reach out no matter how independent her spirit was. On the one hand, she feared getting old alone; on the other she didn't want to give up her independence. Everyone around her must have reminded her she wasn't getting younger, either.

But she had another problem, too. Mary was in love with someone else. She had been for years. The man, likely a physician from a nearby town, was what she feared; he was older, wealthy, sophisticated, and everything a Christian farm girl had been warned away from—he was an "infidel." Now, Mary was torn between him and Elkanah. She felt guilty and wanted Elkanah to know she didn't have to marry him—she had better chances. ". . . he is a very literary man," she explained to Elkanah. "He is an old bachelor and has been ever since I can remember and beside that, is somewhat rich."[21] She was putting high-and-mighty Elkanah in his place.

And the mystery suitor knew how to woo Mary—through vanity and the intellect. ". . . said he would like to have me write a whole book and he would have it published if I had no objection." It must have been very difficult for Mary to give the man up—after all, her mind was her most (if not only) precious possession.

She reassured Elkanah, though. ". . . I might as well sell my soul as marry an infidel. Yet this man has always exerted an unaccountably strong influence on me . . ."[22] She wrestled with the temptation, but reassured Elkanah that she'd decided, "I am determined and fully determined that this Mary shall be Walker's and no one's else . . . be sure that I am yours and yours only." Perhaps she knew he would hear about the suitor from someone eventually, and thought she'd confess everything up front. She gave Elkanah the opportunity to write back and tell her how much she meant to him, too. But he ignored the letter.

Mary struggled on with her battle against temptation in her diary. She listed pro's and con's about the two men. Walker is "poor and of mediocre talents;" while the other man, G., is "rich and brilliant;" but G. is an infidel and Walker is to be a missionary. It would be "sinful" to love G.—but her Christian duty to love W. no matter how "little inclined" she is to do so. "I have gone so far that I cannot go back without forfeiting my Christian character," she wrote in her diary.[23]

The Board wrote to Elkanah, advising him that since the mission was postponed, he should wait to get married. But he didn't want to wait, and he urged Mary to marry him that fall anyway. He reassured her his graduation sermon was judged to be one of the best given, "This does not make me vain but does increase my confidence in my self and encourages me to feel that I have a chance to rise in the world so my Mary will not be ashamed."[24] He'd obviously been hurt by her description of the other gentleman vying for her hand. Now, without a mission post, he had nothing to offer her but himself.

But Mary, usually willing to rebel at any command from authority figures, responded to the Board's directive willingly. "Feel greatly relieved . . . Tho' I feel for you the tenderest regard and when I must be disposed of wish to fall into your hands, yet after all there is something a little dreadful to me in the thought of being married. One's destiny is so inalterably fixed." She was a modern woman, "I like to tread a devious path and the thought of following a passion so antique is rather humiliating."[25]

The mission is out, the marriage on hold. While the courtship was entwined with mission service, once the African mission opportunity dissolved, they continued to write to each other, frustrated and unsure of the future and themselves. Elkanah became depressed about his financial situation (after all, hadn't Mary written about the other man being rich?). Absolutely penniless—now out of school, unemployed, and preaching from town to town for free, he was going nowhere fast.

Mary told him, "I sometimes feel it would be better for you to ally your self with some rich heiress. I dare say there are plenty of them to be found and you could get along so much easier. But I have seen enough of the world to satisfy me that wealth has little to do with happiness."[26] She told Elkanah she loved him and that she would be miserable without him.

Again, Elkanah failed to respond with words to quell her fears about entering marriage. Instead, he saw an opportunity to put her in her proper place (her sphere) by telling her what to do. She'd written she was studying now; his response was, "I would rather recommend to you to read some good book in Female Education and some more refined authors. You need more of refinement than you do of solid sciences. You have the foundation well laid. All you need is a little more finishing to make you an honor to your sex and a worthy prize to your intended."[27] Mary may have been a modern woman, but Elkanah was a very old-fashioned man.

One wishes to see Mary's face when reading those words. Fiercely independent, she answered with a polite restraint, ". . . I hope that you will remember that I shall always retain my personal identity, though I will always try to improve myself— For your sake, my dear Elkanah. I could wish myself beautiful as Houris and as graceful as Venus. But I never did, I never will reproach my Maker. When I intended to be an old maid one consolation I had was that it was nobody's business whether I was lovely or not."[28]

Feisty, and willful, and not about to yield to Elkanah's inept guidance, Mary presented a challenge.

But plans suddenly changed in December, 1837; Elkanah received word from the Board that they needed missionary reinforcements to go out to the Rocky Mountains. William Gray had returned from the Oregon Country and was putting together a party to depart in April. Would Walker take Oregon instead of South Africa?

The offer changed the tone of their courtship immediately. Elkanah rushed to Mary's hometown and broached the question to her. He was a missionary once again; confidence restored, he preached a sermon in the local church which impressed Mary very much.

The Rocky Mountains appealed to her. As for Elkanah, "My only fear in respect to him is that I shall be vain of being his wife." Suddenly, he was no longer an overbearing clod, but a real missionary.

They agreed on a small wedding later in the spring as they weren't going out until April. Mary busied herself preparing to be a missionary, rather than a bride. Already fluent in French and Spanish, and able to paint moderately well, she began music lessons. Singing was absolutely required in the mission field—hymns were one way to take religion to illiterate heathen, so off she went to Gorham to take singing lessons. She was so involved in missionary preparations she didn't even attend Elkanah's ordination in Brewer.

She was busy, but she wasn't so cold she didn't write and let him know how she felt, "The anticipation of being connected with a sound and intelligent mind and a pious heart is more pleasing to me than the prospect of wealth or any similar consideration."[29] She'd found someone more interesting and the prospect of being a missionary's wife more seductive than seeing her own book in print.

But nothing about the mission field ever seemed stable. Suddenly Elkanah rushed to Mary with the news that Gray's party had changed plans, they would leave earlier than April. They had to hurry if they were to catch up with the others—it was a month's travel from Maine to the frontier, and there was no time to waste.

Suddenly, the prospect was real. Mary would get to see the Rocky Mountains! The Richardson family home was bedlam as they all packed Mary's things. She prepared for a six-month trip, but didn't know if she'd ever be back to Maine again. Elkanah and Mary had a small wedding ceremony the next morning at eleven, left at two-thirty, and headed for Boston to get the Board's final send-off.

Mary's mother wrote a letter to her, probably because everything had been such hurry and confusion, and she hadn't had time to tell her daughter how much she loved and would miss her. She mentions the Indians, telling Mary to, "Give my love to the Chief, his wife and all the people. Tell him it is very hard for us to part with our children, for we love them very much, yet we are willing they should go and tell them of the Savior. I hope they will be good to our children and hear all they have to tell them about the way to heaven."[30]

It was the only mention of the Indians that Mary and Elkanah were going so far away to serve. Neither of the Walkers did much in preparation for actually working with natives, besides Mary's singing lessons. How they thought they would help them never comes up. Elkanah was an inexperienced preacher, who had never seen an Indian. Mary did have years of classroom teaching experience, and with both their upbringings on hardscrabble Maine farms, they could survive. Mary's mind was taken up with worry about entering the contract of marriage, rather than Indians. To her, giving up her independence, belonging to a man, was the hardest decision to make.

They hurried off to Boston and met the Board. Elkanah received a passport for himself and "family;" permission came from the War Department to travel through the Indian country.

Mary wasn't too enamored of her honeymoon situation. She toured the city and visited relatives, rather than "stay shut up here in the abode of 'Bliss'," which she called the four-story boardinghouse. She found the other women staying there "haughty and reserved." Elkanah was sick most of the time, and spent his time in the room.

Boston was "magnificent," but she thought the western desert would be more like home to her. She felt she looked dowdy and not at all smart when she went shopping.

They went by ship from Boston to New York City, which was Mary's first time on the water. In New York they met their fellow travelers: Cushing and Myra Eells.

The Eells were newlyweds too, and just as eager to embark on missionary careers in the mysterious far-off Rocky Mountains. "Hope we shall like each other but it seems to me I could not like to exchange husbands," was Mary's opinion after the first meeting. Relieved, she judged that, "I think Mr. W. would not like to exchange wives."

Notes on Chapter Nine

[1] McKee, *Mary Richardson Walker*, p. 52.

[2] Letter, Cheney Cowles Museum, Spokane, Wash., Drury Files, #352.

[3] McKee, *Mary Richardson Walker*, p. 33.

[4] Ibid, p. 38.

[5] Ibid, p. 68.

[6] Ibid, p. 56.

[7] Ibid, p. 68.

[8] Ibid, p. 61.

[9] Ibid, p. 61.

[10] Ibid, p. 69.

[11] Ibid, p. 68.

[12] Ibid, p. 69.

[13] Ibid, p. 71.

[14] Ibid, p. 86.

[15] Ibid, p. 92.

[16] Ibid, p. 95.

[17] Ibid, p. 106.

[18] Ibid.

[19] Ibid, p. 108.

[20] Ibid, p. 111.

[21] Ibid.

[22] Ibid, p. 112.

[23] Ibid, p. 113.

[24] Ibid, p. 117.

[25] Ibid, p. 117.

[26] Ibid, p. 125.

[27] Ibid.

[28] Ibid, p. 126.

[29] Ibid, p. 128.

[30] Ibid, p. 131.

Chapter Ten

Second Wave

Myra Fairbanks, born May 26, 1805 in Holden, Massachusetts, was the oldest child of the church deacon. With seven younger siblings, she quickly learned how to be a responsible female. She was adept at handcrafts and sewing, and took great interest in fashion and style. Raised in town, she had more wealth and culture at home than the other missionary women. Nevertheless, she too, after being educated at a female seminary (at Weathersfield, Connecticut) taught school for several years.

Myra was described as round-shouldered, "from braiding straw for bonnets when she was a girl."[1] She wasn't a hardy, outdoorsy girl; she got a cough at eighteen that plagued her till she died.

At eighteen, she joined her Congregational Church's Gentlemen's and Ladies' Missionary Society, and listened to a returned missionary from India. Her interest was kindled. She, too, needed a missionary husband, though. It was several years later, while she was teaching school in Connecticut, that she met a young ordained Congregational minister, Cushing Eells. He was five years younger than Myra, but when he proposed marriage, she readily consented.

Of course, his proposal was countenanced with the warning that she would be marrying a potential missionary (as he had planned his life). Her reply was, "I doubt that you could have asked anyone who would be more willing." Willing to serve as a missionary, or willing to be his wife—both were one and the same.

They did not, however, marry right away. They pursued their individual careers, and Myra enrolled in the female seminary from which she'd already graduated to pursue further study in order to make herself useful in the mission field. She was thirty years old at the time, and was obviously not in a hurry to marry without a secure mission post. In 1837, Cushing was assigned to go to southern Africa, to the same Zulu mission as Elkanah Walker. (They probably didn't know each other, yet.) He and Myra were told to postpone their wedding until just before leaving for the mission in the fall. They agreed, but when the mission was cancelled because of tribal warfare in Africa, they did not go ahead with a wedding. In December, they received word that William Gray had returned from the Rocky Mountains, and needed missionaries to go back with him. Would they do it?

They agreed, and began preparing for the trip. Myra was told she would have to put all her personal belongings in a trunk twenty-six inches long, fifteen inches high and fourteen inches wide. She had one made of heavy leather and wood, with an engraved brass plate which said: M.F. Eells, Cola. [Columbia] River, Oregon Tery [Territory]."[2] Other supplies, books, and belongings were crated and shipped by sea. They wouldn't arrive at the Oregon mission until eighteen months later.

Myra and Cushing rushed the wedding, just like the Walkers and Whitmans had done. When they received word that Gray and the mission party would leave earlier than planned, they had a hurried wedding at Myra's family home in Massachusetts on March 5, the same day the Walkers were being married in Maine. It took them a week to go by stage to New Haven, Connecticut, where more farewells were said, then off by steamboat to New York City.

Myra only had time to pick up two pairs of spectacles, one a pair with silver bows, (she was plagued with nearsightedness—probably from sewing and reading so much) and dash a note in her diary: "Left home . . . with the expectation of never seeing them again in this world . . ."[3]

Myra's diary began the day she married, and she wrote it to be copied and mailed to her family. While she doesn't reveal the personal opinions that Mary Walker did, hers is one that carries

*Cheney Cowles Museum / Eastern
Washington State Historical Society*

Myra Eells at seventy

Whitman College Collection

Cushing Eells

more facts about daily events. She wrote it with the intent it would be read, but not with an eye to having it published.

In New York, they were feted with a going-off reception and address by the Mission Board's secretary. Two years before there hadn't been time to honor the Spaldings and Whitmans, but now, knowing those women had made it safely over the continent, it was the perfect opportunity for some public relations. The event was publicized in newspapers, and this time the mission women were in an upbeat, excited mood. No matter that the going-off speech reminded them they'd be crossing mountains "25,000 feet high"—such was the ignorance of what lay in the West—the missionaries seemed oblivious to any dangers. After all, Brother Gray would guide them, and he'd seen Sister Spalding and Sister Whitman cross the continent as easily as lacing a boot. Women like themselves had already done it, what was there to worry about?

The last couple to arrive, Asa and Sarah Smith, came too late for the speeches and reception. The women quickly took in some shopping and saw the sights, which Myra noted were "quite uncommon" to such small town residents as themselves.

They were nearly giddy with excitement, and had to remind themselves to maintain pious self-control.

The couples wasted no time hurrying to a steamboat and on to Cincinnati. There they had a reception and send-off from the local church members, including a meeting with the famous preacher, Dr. Lyman Beecher and his daughter Catherine Beecher, whom the Spaldings knew well. He gave them practical advice, reminding the virtuous missionaries that travel on Sabbath could be endured. If he went on an ocean voyage he wouldn't get out of the boat on Sunday, he told them.

The mission party headed up the Mississippi River by steamboat. The Walkers were having trouble adjusting to each other, and to marriage. "Wish I knew whether W. is satisfied with me or not," Mary jotted in her diary. "Sometimes I think I will try and get along one day without displeasing, but the first thing I know, I do something more than ever. Still I am determined not to give up trying."[4]

Marriage wasn't enough to absorb Mary, even on her honeymoon. she decided she'd like to have a botany, geology, and mineralogy collection, and what better time to start one? She was alert, excited about all the interesting things around them, and quick to notice everything. But she wasn't a minister's polished and proper wife; she realized she didn't "look smart" and wasn't interested in her appearance much.

Elkanah, awkward bridegroom and freshly-ordained minister, felt self-conscious and inadequate. He criticized Mary, probably out of his own lack of confidence, as well as his inclination to be the patriarchal husband (a new role for him).

The trip wasn't pleasant. Conditions were crowded, they were traveling with strangers, and trying to get to know each other. On the journey from St. Louis to Independence, the boat caught fire; then the captain raced against another steam boat until they crashed into each other. They had to change to a different boat with worse conditions.

Myra encountered something she'd never experienced before—slavery. The maid who attended them was a slave owned by the boat's captain. Myra was indignant when she saw slavery in action and noted it in her diary, referring to "the wretchedness of slavery." She was the only missionary woman

*Cheney Cowles Museum / Eastern
Washington State Historical Society*

Mary Gray

Whitman College Collection

William Gray

to mention slavery, although Mary had written about attending a lecture about abolitionism back when she was teaching.

Steamship travel was wild and wretched in those days. Myra's sensitive nature was shocked by what she saw and heard around her, the "profanity" and "wickedness" as well as the uncomfortable physical surroundings. She decided it could be endured though, ". . . but I am happy in the choice I have made in relation to spending the remainder of my days among the heathen. I love to feel that I am making a little sacrifice, if such it may be called, for the cause of Christ. If I am but the means of bringing one soul into the Kingdom of Christ I shall be abundantly paid for all my privations."[5]

They finally made it to Independence where "Dr. Gray met them with horses." He had four horses, three fitted with side saddles; the women mounted and for the first time on the trip, rode horseback. Myra admitted to not being much of a horse-woman, ". . . I confess I was a bit frightened, it being dark and not at all accustomed to riding, and besides, no lady had ever been on my animal's back before." The husbands led the women's horses through deep mud and over a steep hill to reach Independence.

There they met William Gray's new wife, Mary, and readied for the next leg of the journey. There were four missionary couples, now. The Walkers, Eells, Smiths, and Grays.

They made their final preparations for the overland journey. The women hand-stitched canvas into tents and sacks for the trip: two tents, eight feet by twelve feet with a curtain between. Two couples would sleep in each tent, one on each side of the curtain; the curtain could be pulled aside during meals. It was decided that the Walkers and Smiths would share one, the Eells and Grays the other.

The men bought supplies and animals for the trip, using letters of credit from the Board. They took twenty-five horses and mules, twelve cattle (some were milk cows), and a light one-horse wagon. They took only enough food to reach the buffalo range, there they planned to eat buffalo meat and pemmican.

While the men kept busy, the women practiced riding. "Ride a little way to try our horses," Myra worried. "Do not know how I shall succeed in riding." It was certainly a time to be concerned, as they now faced at least three to four months in the sidesaddle.

They planned to join up with the American Fur Company caravan at Westport and follow along with it to rendezvous in the Rocky Mountains. William Gray had no better luck than he'd had when traveling with the Whitmans and Spaldings two years earlier. The fur company didn't want missionaries along but finally relented once they promised to pay as well as take night watch.

The women rode horseback ahead with the guides to avoid the dust, the men followed at the end of the caravan, driving their herd of animals, which turned out to be more difficult than they had anticipated, the "horses, mules & cattle being unaccustomed to traveling make us much trouble . . ."[6] It must have been awkward if not ridiculous, Elkanah being the only one with a farm background who might have had the remotest idea about driving stock.

Once in motion, the party traveled hard and fast, just as the Spaldings and Whitmans had done. The line was strung out so far at times that the women traveled an hour apart from their husbands, and only saw each other during camp or at midday nooning. After the first twelve-hour ride Myra was exhausted. "Suppose this is but the beginning of hardship," she commented. The women didn't complain about the situation as much as their husbands did. Dragging along in the cow column, choking on dust all day while the women rode ahead didn't improve their attitude, when night was spent on the hard ground in a crowded tent. The men even fought over sleeping habits, Mary noting that Mr. Gray did not like Mr. Smith's "movements" and several arguments over snoring and whispering developed that would plague them the entire trip. The fact that four of the five couples had only been married a few weeks, added to the tension.

Elkanah Walker and Asa Smith both wrote complaints to the Board because they had to labor during the trip. They thought they should be treated the same way that missionaries sent by ship to stations were—as paying guests—rather than laboring their way like common members of the Fur Company.

Elkanah's brooding and depressed state of mind began to bother Mary. She confided in her diary, "I should feel so much better if Mr. W. would only treat me with some cordiality. It is so hard to please him I almost despair of ever being able to. If I stir, it is forwardness; if I am still, it is inactivity . . . . I am almost certain that more is expected of me than can be had of one woman."[7]

Mary snapped. She broke down and "had a long bawl," which brought Elkanah around. The next day she was able to write, "Today he has been very kind."

Cheered up, Mary baked biscuits over a buffalo chip fire, her first cooking since the wedding; Elkanah told her she had done "very well." He was relieved to see her acting more feminine: crying, baking, seeking his approval. This sort of wife he could understand.

The trip became more difficult every day. Myra noted a first, "Saw four wild Indians, nearly naked." Whether she was shocked, dismayed, or merely interested, it's hard to tell. Just three days later, she found travel nearly too much for her. "I am too tired to get or eat supper." It was hot, and the prairie spread out in all directions, which was eerie to Myra, used to Massachusetts village life, ". . . see no living being."[8]

Wolves howled near the tents all night, keeping them awake; horses strayed, rivers and creeks were swollen with spring rains making crossings difficult and dangerous. They were meeting Indians now, enduring cold rainstorms, "rode 21 miles today without stopping. The wind blowing so hard we can scarcely sit on our horses."[9] It was no Boston.

They were lagging behind the fur caravan, and susceptible to the Indians. Unaware of potential problems, the exhausted missionaries posted no night guard and let the livestock graze during the night. The howling of wolves, which "we imagined Indians," chilled them during the night. In the morning, three horses were gone, and the men had to go search for them. Asa Smith protested, saying he didn't want to go away from his wife. The men were frightened, and not wanting to exert themselves any more than necessary; they were already exhausted with the pace of travel and outdoor living. Someone had to go after the horses, but there was no one else to send.

Gray, as leader, took charge of the women and moved ahead trying to catch up with the fur company, probably in order to gain safety for the women. Gray had been in an altercation with Indians while on his way east from Waiilatpu the previous autumn. He'd been with a group of travelers attacked by Blackfeet, and knew what might happen if the mission party stayed alone on the vast prairie. None of the others wanted to venture onto the prairie to look for the missing horses.

When Gray and the women caught up with the caravan, Captain Drips and Sir William Drummond Stewart (the same adventuring Scottish nobleman who'd traveled with the fur company in 1836) came to the missionary camp for tea. The ladies eagerly served them biscuits and cheese, but it was not a social call. The Captain gave them unpleasant news; he wanted them to travel separately from his caravan. He reasoned that the caravan intended to put out night watches for the stock, and obviously the missionaries weren't planning to do the same. William Gray argued that they would take their share of night watch duty. Drips resisted, but Gray "did not mean to take the hint," and persisted, "as he knew it would not be safe for us to travel alone," Mary wrote.[10]

Government permission to travel through Indian Country.

Indians were all around their camp. To Myra, their painted faces, skin clothing and curiosity was frightening. The Eells had brought along a dog, King, who even attacked one of the "nearly naked" Indians outside their tent. Cushing had to pull the dog off, whip and tie him. The horses were still missing, and word came that one of the traders had seen them being ridden by Indians.

Myra was scared, "feel that I have been preserved through dangers seen and unseen." Her initiation to the frontier and to Indian life was one of fear and trepidation. She saw the overall situation more clearly than Mary Walker, who was busy bickering with her husband, or complaining about Mr. Smith's horrible table manners.

It was the Sabbath, and they were faced with life on the Plains, rather than back in New England. There would be no rest. Cushing Eells was exhausted from night watch, then the men each had to do their own labor getting their belongings across the Kansas River. The women rode a flatboat across, watched by scores of Indians lining the banks "on purpose to see us and take what they could pilfer," Myra feared.[11]

Their journey with the caravan was a lot like the missionary party's experience in 1836: grueling days of travel, exhausted nights spent in crowded tents with people they'd never met before. Meals consisted of buffalo and tea, and little else. The women had problems with hygiene and privacy; the men bickered and jockeyed for power between themselves. Gray was supposedly the leader this year, which meant they had someone to blame when things went wrong. Marcus and Henry had continually fought over who would direct the mission. One fault with the Board was that no one was officially put in charge which led to poor communication, lack of direction and wasted time reaching consensus over simple things, such as whether or not to butcher a calf when they were without food.

The women had their share of labor, too. They tried to keep things neat and tidy, and did what cooking they could over the campfires. They gathered buffalo chips, "prairie coal,"[12] when the wood ran out, and picked berries when they found them to supplement the all-meat diet.

Travel was paced at a fast walk, and no one lagged in the rear, because "they are always exposed to be robbed of their horses," or worse, "killed by wild Indians."[13] Myra's fears were real—they'd already been robbed of all their spare horses and mules. Afraid of losing their riding stock or being left behind by the caravan, the missionaries kept moving quickly rather than lag behind or stay along the way to keep the Sabbath.

The women rode sidesaddle, with heavy clothing, hats, gloves, goggles, and parasols to protect their skin and eyes from the sun and wind. Their sidesaddles had custom pockets to tuck parasols in when not in use. Each man wore a thick belt around the waist, with a knife attached; powder flask and bullet pouch over the shoulder, and a brace of pistols in holsters. Captain Drips ordered each to carry a gun laid across his horse's neck in front of him, ready for use. Asa Smith and Cushing Eells found guns abhorrent; Cushing carried one, as ordered, but unknown to Drips, always kept it unloaded.

To pass the time, the ladies listened to the wild tales of another independent traveler going along with the fur company,

Captain John Sutter, who was on his way to California. "Fell in company with a gentleman from New Orleans," wrote Mary Walker, " who has traveled in Europe, Africa, etc. who has entertained us with an account of Switzerland, Italy, etc. Gave an account of Swiss dogs digging men out of the snow."[14]

They saw herds of a thousand buffalo, and vast empty plains that Mary thought was like an ocean of grass. Prairie fires burned all around them and the weather got so cold at night that Myra complained they couldn't stay warm "with all our winter clothes on." Mary described the quarrelling going on within the group, "Our company do nothing but jaw all the time. I never saw such a cross company before."[15]

Mary and Elkanah continued to have marital difficulties. She and Mary Gray baked pot pie and bread, but couldn't keep from causing difficulties arguing with the men. In her diary, she fretted that her husband, "seems to think more of Mrs. Smith than of me. Spends a great deal more time in her society than in mine." She swore to improve her own behavior.

The weather turned cold and windy and it was the last straw; some of the missionaries began to regret having come on the journey. Mary was the only one to write about it, and figured it's cause, "I suspect more from aversion to the toil . . ."[15]

Elkanah got sick, and Mary dosed him with calomel (mercurous chloride). The caravan hurried away early one morning, before the mission party was ready, and they had to endure seven hours in the saddle without water or eating. People were beginning to wear down, "some evidence of improper feeling toward each other," Mary noted. Tempers were as "short as pie crust."

But they began to yield to the spectacular scenery. Myra tried to be optimistic even after a long day (twenty-one miles without stopping) in the saddle. She appreciated the prairie, "the scenery is so grand . . . with a pleasant sun . . . for a moment we almost forgot the land of our birth."[16]

They traveled along the Little Blue River, and soon met Pawnees along the Platte River. Myra called the Pawnees "better clad than any we had seen," and noted that they sang three kinds of songs: "the war song, the thief song, and the gambling song." That night, she noted that they were singing the thief song, which surely must have given her sleepless hours.

They passed the spot where they were told Dr. Satterley had been murdered the year before. He'd been with the Whitman-Spalding party in 1836; his young wife had died early in the journey to their mission station with the Pawnees. Now they rode past the spot where his "bones and clothes were found not long after the murder." No one knew who had killed him, speculation was that it was a white man. With dangers all around, grueling days in the saddle, drenching rains, and tests of faith, the women must have had second thoughts.

In the absolute silence of the wide prairies, they passed a circle of buffalo skulls, about twenty feet in diameter, on the ground facing the East. "It is said they kill the first buffalo they kill as a sacrifice, and pray the Great spirit buffalo may be plenty." After leaving the eerie scene, they did see several live buffalo; one of the hunters killed one for food.

Now they were in buffalo country, and would eat that meat continually as long as it lasted. It wasn't but two days, and Myra had to take Epsom salts, and Mary Gray was sick, too. Mary Walker and Myra rode in the wagon a while. Obviously, the women were experiencing dysentery from the unaccustomed red meat diet, just as Eliza had the year before. Cushing was so sick, he couldn't "eat, drink, or sit up," but they had to saddle up and continue "as though we were well." Myra was losing her optimism, "think it is trying," she noted.[17]

The next day Cushing was so sick he couldn't go on, so Myra gave him a piece of gingerbread she'd been saving—for three months. It was worth it, he recovered quickly and was able to continue.

Mary noted the geology as they passed, no matter how hard the travel. She was a scientist; her observations and descriptions read more like Meriwether Lewis' notebooks than a diminutive missionary. She noted whenever they passed basalt, described it and its relative age, and noted gypsum, and other rock formations. "Saw some minerals I very much wished to pick up." But she couldn't get on and off the sidesaddle alone.

When they reached Fort William (later called Fort Laramie), they were able to go inside a building once again.

Myra wryly described the rustic structure as looking "a lot like the Connecticut State Prison."

Indian women from the fort, wives of fur traders, came to visit the missionary camp; they were "neatly dressed and ornamented with beads." Captain Drips' Indian wife and the two wives of his assistants brought their children to meet the Americans. The children are "quite white and can read a little," Myra observed.[18]

There was time for washing laundry, doing mending, and for Mary, it was necessary to "rip and dye" her pongee dress so it could be "made over". Later it would be made over again, back to its original shape, for regular wear. By now, all the mission party must have been aware of Mary Walker's peculiar "health" problem. She was expecting a baby.

Before they left Fort William they gave away their wagon and packed everything on horses and mules for the next leg of the trip. No one was interested in trying to take a wagon through compared with Whitman's obsession with it two years earlier.

After only four days on the trail again, Mary began feeling sick. She was "bled" towards night, which only made her weaker. She nearly passed out, then vomited. Bleeding was common practice to let the blood inside the body reach a proper "balance"—-as a treatment for a woman in the early stages of pregnancy, it would be devastating. She was not better the next day, so took a spoonful of wine and went without dinner.

The ministrations worked, or she survived them, and on horseback once again she began to feel well enough to wish she could pick up some minerals she had spotted along the trail. "If I could only mount and dismount with out help how glad I would be . . ."[19]

They reached the rain-swollen Platte River, but had to wait to cross. Exhausted, Mary was dosed with calomel and "was bled toward night," but the next day was very tired, afraid and depressed. (All symptoms directly related to the calomel and bleeding.) "It would be bad to be sick in such circumstances," she feared. Her health was "feeble" and she couldn't "keep up a usual amount of cheerfulness." She felt like crying "half of the time without knowing why." Her pregnancy, her awkward relationship with Elkanah, and the exhausting trip, were coming to bear on her. "My circumstances are rather trying. so much danger attends me on either hand; a long journey yet before me, going I know not whither; without mother or sister to attend me can I survive it all?"[20]

Notes on Chapter Ten

[1] Ida Myra Eells, Mother Eells, *A Story of the Life of Myra Fairbanks Eells.* (Mimeograph, Wenatchee, Wash., 1947), p. 2.

[2] Drury, *First White Women,* p. 49.

[3] McKee, *Mary Richardson Walker,* p. 139.

[4] Drury, *First White Women,* p. 56.

[5] Ibid, p. 59.

[6] McKee, *Mary Richardson Walker,* p. 142.

[7] Drury, *First White Women,* p. 72.

[8] McKee, *Mary Richardson Walker,* p. 143.

[9] Drury, *First White Women,* p. 73.

[10] Ibid, p. 74.

[11] Ibid, p. 75.

[12] McKee, *Mary Richardson Walker,* p. 144.

[13] Drury, *First White Women,* p. 77.

[14] Ibid.

[15] Ibid, p. 78.

[16] Ibid, p. 83.

[17] Ibid, p. 88.

[18] McKee, *Mary Richardson Walker,* p. 147.

[19] Ibid, p. 145.

[20] Ibid, p. 146

Chapter Eleven

Full House

When they finally reached the rendezvous camp everyone's spirits perked up. The tents were set beside a glistening river with mountains far off in the distance; there was plenty of grass for the animals and they could once again wash laundry and cook proper meals. "Mrs. Gray baked mince pies and yesterday she fried cakes. We had baked pudding; and greens for dinner." Finally, a break from the diet of buffalo meat and tea, morning, noon, and night.[1]

Mary was glad that her, "Husband looks more happy than I have seen him in a long time." Maybe Elkanah cheered up because he had a chance to shine at last. He'd been plodding along in the cow column too long, now he could don his patched wedding coat and top hat once again. He preached beneath the trees on Sabbath, Cushing Eells preached in the afternoon, the women dressed up in their "Sunday dresses."

Rendezvous in 1838 was held where the Wind and Popo Agie Rivers meet to form the Big Horn River, in present-day Wyoming. It wasn't along the Green River, where the 1836 meeting had been held. By 1838 the fur trade was nearly over, and this rendezvous was much smaller than the past. There were few Indians in attendance except the wives of trappers and traders. Some Shawnee and Delaware were along, who worked for the fur company. There were a few lodges of Snake Indians up in the mountains, but they refused to come to the trade fair.

The mountain men showed up and bartered away their year's work in boisterous drinking, gambling, horse racing, quarrelling, and fighting. Some spent $1,000 a day, and when it was over, had nothing left to show for a year's hard work in the mountains. "White men dressed as Indians" were drunk and harrassed the missionary camp at night with loud raucous noise from tin horns, shouting, and drunken dancing. They fired off guns and even dangled a shriveled Blackfoot scalp to intimidate the Yankee visitors.

The mountain men painted their faces and carried on "as strangely as they could," while their Indian wives were beating a path to the American women's tents. With lengths of rare cloth trade goods tucked under their arms, the native women pleaded for the Americans to cut dresses for them. So they did.

Myra was able to put to use her dressmaker training, cutting and making up a dress for Mrs. Craig, a Nez Perce woman married to fur trapper William Craig (who later moved to Lapwai and incited problems with the Nez Perce and turmoil for the Spaldings). Indian women were adept with a needle, but their clothing styles had none of the geometric qualities of flat pattern work, in which Myra had been trained. She cut out dresses for several women, and a "gown" for Mr. Clark. Even Mary Walker, who despised sewing, busied herself making a "hunting dress."

The noise and dancing carried on all night for several nights, surrounding the tents with drunken debauchery. But how could the missionary wives be dissuaded from their grand adventure, now that they saw how desperate the women were for their talents? Dressmaking, while not prestigious in the eyes of the men, was what the women knew and it was what the Indian women seemed desperate for.

The Indian women were eagerly studying and appraising the technology the white women brought: woven cloth, ready-made threads in various colors, needles, sewing pins (still hand-crafted in two pieces then), sharpened steel sewing shears; these were the things that would save the Indian women endless labor. Indian women's lives were consumed with creating clothing for their families and for trade (just as colonial women had done before the advent of industrialism); now with the entrance of white women into their domain, the new ways were within reach.

While the women were busy pinning and cutting, a larger problem than drunkards began to emerge. The American Fur Company had completed trading, and was headed back to St. Louis with pelts, but there was no party from the Hudson's Bay Company at this rendezvous for the missionaries to continue farther west with. Captain Sutter was continuing on, but they hesitated to commit themselves to his leadership, as he knew no more than they. He didn't offer much security as they headed into Blackfoot country.

William Gray had assumed the HBC escort would materialize just like before, and lead them west, but this wasn't the same spot, and there were no HBC people anywhere around. Myra wrote in her diary that there was no one there to meet them with instructions—something Gray must have expected, just as the party he'd gone with in 1836 had expected to get advice from Reverend Parker. "Hear nothing from Mr. Spaulding or Dr. Whitman or the Indians who were to meet us here."[2] Had they endured the trip so far only to see their hopes evaporate?

Earnest prayers commenced, and after three weeks of tense waiting and worrying, as if in answer to those fervent pleas fourteen men from the HBC rode into camp. They'd gone to the Green River site, suspecting the trading would be going on there, but found only a scrawled note: "Come to Popeasia, plenty of whiskey and white women." Who left it, or why, has remained a mystery.

The Hudson's Bay contingent, having arrived too late to get in on the trading was willing to let the mission party go back westward with them. However, they warned the travelers that the going would not be easy. "The gentlemen tell us we have not begun to see danger and hardship in travelling," Myra wrote. There were mountains and deserts to cross yet. She'd become friends with the trappers' wives, now proud owners of new calico shirtwaists and skirts. She "bid farewell to" the "new-formed acquaintances," before starting on the trail for the next leg of the cross-continent trip.

With the Hudson's Bay men, it was hard traveling; one afternoon saw thirty-five miles in a stretch. When Mary Walker was lifted off her horse, she fainted on the ground. "In the morning spent an hour, rubbing, washing & dressing, & feel pretty well." The hardships were nearly unbearable, but there was no turning back, and no wagon to crawl into.

The line of travellers was long, the cattle lagging at the rear, the husbands walking or riding about an hour behind the women. The going became steep and treacherous, as they neared the base of snow-capped mountains. "I have suffered more from fear than anything else," Mary Walker admitted. At the foot of one rugged hill, she fainted after making the slippery descent. "I have felt that God only could make us go safely . . . Perhaps were my eyes opened I might see angels standing by the way to guard my feet from falling."[3]

It was the HBC Captain Frances Ermatinger, who alerted Myra to their passage over the "back bone of America."[4] She described the "Scenery" as "romantic," but worried about Cushing, who was "fatigued and almost discouraged."[5] Once again, making the monumental passage over the Continental Divide went nearly unnoticed by the women travellers.

"Will God give us strength and grace equal to our day? Will He sustain and comfort him in every trying scene and carry him and me to our destined field of labour?" Cushing was flagging, but Myra was determined to be strong, to complete what they had set out to do. "May we be faithful and successful missionaries among the Indians."

She could do little else to help Cushing, the trip was too physically demanding for a sedentary teacher-minister who wasn't used to the labor and exertion required of him. The customary sexual division of labor among the Americans meant that the men did the bulk of the work setting up camp, saddling, packing and unpacking the animals, tethering and watching the herd and whatever else needed to be done. The women had far less to do, but in their physical condition (not having ridden horseback much before the trip), it was about all they could do to keep up.

Riding past the snow-capped Wind River Mountains, as they crossed South Pass and entered the western side of the Rockies, they passed a huge herd of buffalo, so close they could "hear them pant."

National Park Service, Whitman Mission National Park

Waiilatpu Mission

Mary Walker noticed a far more personal event, she felt the first kicks of her unborn child, and noted the "leaping" in her diary.[6]

One day they made eleven stream crossings, another they went forty-five miles without stopping over dry, sage-covered desert. One weak calf and the dog, King, had to be abandoned along the way as they could no longer keep up the pace. The trail wound through thick forest, over steep ravines and precipices where a stumble could mean death 150 feet below.

When they finally made camp, Mary was relieved to see Elkanah was still alive, but to her dismay he'd lost his wedding coat and broken his watch in the rough going. She lost the frill from her bonnet and all the women lost part of their veils.

Mary Walker's horse stumbled, fell, and "tumbled me over his head but it did not hurt me."[7] Nor the unborn child.

When they reached Soda Springs the women made biscuits with the water, which were, "as good and light" as if they had "used the nicest yeast and let the dough rise just enough. Used nothing but the water & a little salt & baked them as soon as mixed."[7] They also fried fritters. Exhausted and starving, they were comforted by food they'd known in what seemed to be another world.

Even as Mary undertook a typically feminine job of baking, she noted the "great abundance of Basaltic rock"[8] near the springs. She described the rocks in detail, their appearance and structure and estimated their ages. For Mary, though, her health hindered her again. She was suffering an intense toothache, which kept her awake all night, even when she faced riding hard the next day; physically she was nearly at her limit. To make matters worse, while riding painfully along, her companions moved on ahead, leaving her behind, and her pony ran off into the sage, nearly getting her lost. Too weak to turn or control the horse, she had to be helped by one of the hunters who spotted her and rode along with her until they reach Fort Hall, four hours later.

At Fort Hall, a fur trade outpost in Blackfoot territory, she was able to eat breakfast, rest, and finally, have the tooth extracted. After that she felt "better."[9]

The party stayed at Fort Hall long enough for the women to wash clothes. They did their laundry in a room at the Fort which Mary judged, "in form & size & cleanliness resembles your hog sty."[10]

They saw potential around them though. "The fort is full of men with squaws & half breed children with bright black eyes, enough of them to make a fine school," according to Mary. She may have wished to end the journey right there, after all Fort Hall needed a school and missionaries—but it would not be that easy. Two men were hired on to work for the mission, James Conner, who had a Nez Perce wife, and Richard Williams. Both were ex-mountain men, looking for work in the decline of the fur trade.[11]

On their way to the next stop, Fort Boise, an HBC trading post, Mary continued to be critical of Asa Smith—she disliked the man intensely, and thought the others felt the same way. When he preached a sermon to them one Sabbath, she noted he "preached in his old patched pantaloons. Sermon rather flat."[10] Dress and demeanor was quite important among the little group of travelers who were still trying to impress one another with their professional knowledge, skill, and expertise. After all, it was a highly educated and cultivated group: three ordained ministers, all with educated wives.

At Fort Boise they were delighted to eat butter and milk, along with "salmon, boiled pudding & turnip sauce for dinner." The next day they made pumpkin pie, and ate sturgeon and turnips. There were yellow fields of sunflowers around the Fort. But it wasn't an idyllic visit; during the night the dogs barked, wolves howled and the horses spooked and broke loose. Some of the men at the fort had a "spree," and the wind blew the missionaries' tent over. Myra was fearful the "Indians about are watching for an opportunity to take whatever they could get— all cause our sleep to be filled with anxiety and dreams."[12]

Word had reached Clear Water that the missionaries were coming and the Spaldings had sent fresh horses and flour with Nez Perce couriers, so when they set out they were somewhat revived.

Days later on the trail, Connor's Indian wife went into labor so they stopped, but she did not give birth. While they held camp over, three good horses were stolen by a camp of Indians who disappeared during the night.

For some reason, the Grays chose to ride ahead on their own, leaving the rest of the party behind. They sent back word with an Indian courier that they'd reached Waiilatpu, and urged the others to hurry on.

Once again, Mrs. Conner went into labor. This time they continued on, only James Conner and the Smiths remaining with her. At noon the pregnant Indian woman "collected fuel & prepared dinner" and at sunset finally gave birth to a daughter. They were about thirty miles behind the main column but when she rode into camp with the infant in her arms, Mary described her as looking, "smart as could be." It's unusual the other women didn't all stay with her, but perhaps they were too inexperienced as midwives; Gray, the "doctor" of the party was already at Waiilatpu.

Cornelius Rogers was thrown from his horse during the next march, and was unable to ride; Asa Smith, Mary Smith and Myra turned back to bleed him while the rest of the camp waited for him to catch up. Too weak to remount, they decided to move on, leaving Rogers along the trail; the Smiths and the Conners remained with him until he was able to sit his horse again.

They passed through dense forest where Mary Walker spotted a "tiny kind of huckleberry" and "trees six feet in diameter."[13] A rider met them with fresh horses sent by the Whitmans and the party switched to them and rode at a gallop to reach Waiilatpu at two o'clock that afternoon. The six-month, 3,000-mile honeymoon was over.

At Waiilatpu the exhausted travelers were met by throngs of natives who'd heard that more Bostons were coming. The reinforcements met the Whitmans and Spaldings for the first time, and thought they "all appear friendly and treat us with great hospitality." The Whitman home was not what they had expected: Myra could "not describe its appearance as I can not compare it with anything I ever saw." The house, an improvement over the hurried cabin of 1836, sat along the banks of the Walla Walla River, and was built of adobe—sun-dried blocks of mud. "There are doors and windows, but they are of the roughest kind; the boards being sawed by hand and put together by no carpenter, but by one who knew nothing about such work, as is evident from its appearance." Inside, the furniture was "very primitive." The bedsteads were "boards nailed to the side of the house, sink fashion," with blankets and husks making the bed. In spite of its appearance, though, it was "good compared with traveling accommodations."[14]

The house was surrounded by a "number of wheat, corn and potato fields" and there was a "garden of melons and all kinds of vegetables." The Whitmans feasted the new arrivals on melons, pumpkin pies, and milk, but just as they sat down to eat the house was "thronged with Indians" and they had to stop and shake hands with at least fifty Cayuses who came to look them over. That night they dined on a "fine dinner of vegetables, salt salmon, bread, butter, cream, &c" and the "long toilsome journey at length came to a close."

Mary Walker was exceptionally relieved to "find so comfortable a house prepared for me & find it very gratifying to meet mothers who know how to sympathize with me." Eliza and Narcissa now each proudly sported infant daughters born in the mission field. If they could do it, so could Mary.

The next day each missionary man spoke to an assembled crowd of Indians, with Henry Spalding interpreting their English words. The Indians gave speeches, too, which Mary thought "rather sensible." A young Cayuse man said he agreed with the missionaries' talks but he was "always concerned about trade," and he criticized the Hudson's Bay Company trader at Fort Walla Walla (Pambrun), calling him a "bad man." An old chief "seemed inclined to smooth over what the younger one had said," by saying that the incident with Pambrun had just been unruly young people who had tied and beaten the trader. Hadn't they just seen Pambrun recently? Wasn't he fine now?

It had been four years earlier that the Indians, angry at fur prices, had kidnapped and held Pambrun until the HBC raised prices. The missionaries would probably not have understood what they were talking about.

Several of the older chiefs, "complained that the young people were getting very unruley, and would not obey the chiefs . . ."15

The new arrivals were able to be more critical of the Indians than their predecessors had been. Mary Walker noticed that the Cayuses at Waiilatpu weren't grasping the essence of Christianity, and how easily they misunderstood the behaviors expected of them. She saw them line up to go into the house's schoolroom for worship, and realized they considered lining up to be worship. They were eagerly getting into lines all the time, all over the place.

There was friction against the new practices the missionaries had introduced, too. An old chief had been in the practice of ringing a bell and summoning the people to his lodge to worship. But since he hadn't learned the Bostons' prayers and songs as quickly as the others in the tribe, they now worshipped in their own lodges, leaving him without the importance he felt due him. The missionaries, so thankful at ending their torturous journey, seemed to give little attention to the Cayuses— after all they were the Whitmans' "people."

The new reinforcements were ready to settle down and get to work, but where would they begin the great work they had come so far to do? Establishing new mission stations seemed to be logical—after all, this group hadn't gotten along together any better than the Whitmans and Spaldings, a lot of "hardness" existed among them. Again, separate stations were considered instead of everyone working at one central location; a decision that would only lead to more discontent, competition and finally disaster.

It was voted that the Smiths would stay with the Whitmans at Waiilatpu; the Grays would go to work with the Spaldings at

Lapwai; and the Walkers and Eells would set up a new station with the elusive Flathead Indians they thought lived farther north in the mountains. Exactly where, they couldn't know for sure yet. Exploration would tell. Also, advice from the Factor at the HBC Fort Colville, farther north along the Columbia River, would be considered. Going into the Bitterroot Mountains was out of the question—Blackfeet there were too dangerous and unpredictable. Settling farther down the Columbia was out of the question, too. Methodist missionaries were moving into that area, carving up the Willamette River Valley into settlements, and many of the river tribes had already disappeared from disease.

The hired men, Connor and Williams, brought along to work during the trip overland had to be paid. It was the first argument among the missionaries. The men wanted cash, that's what they'd been promised when hired on. Dr. Whitman refused, saying they should be paid in goods. The newly-arrived missionaries were embarrassed and dug into their own pockets to pay them in "specie," in order to prevent "trouble."[16]

Coins were hard to come by in the Oregon country. The lack of available money plagued Oregon's settlers for decades. At the time, Spanish silver coins were commonly exchanged; gold hadn't been discovered in the West, yet, so it wasn't a common form of exchange. Paper money and bank drafts were ridiculous, in a country where the mails took over two years to be answered, and where no banks existed. Everything was traded under the auspices of the HBC, either in beaver, or in like goods.

On Sabbath, the new arrivals joined the First Presbyterian Church of Oregon, which had been founded the previous August and included the Whitmans, Spaldings, a Hawaiian couple named Maki, and Charles Compo, a French Canadian—their first convert—previously a Catholic. Being together, worshipping and singing hymns, strengthened them all. Even the hard times between them all seemed to disappear as they looked forward to doing the glorious work they'd come for. Mary wrote in her diary that night that "We feel we [have] great cause for gratitude & much encouragement to go forward in the work."[17]

While the brethren conducted their business meeting (at which the women could not participate) the six women organized the Columbia Maternal Association, the first women's club on the Pacific coast. There were already hundreds of Maternal Associations on the East coast, part of a women's movement that was quickly spreading across the country.

Although only two of the women were mothers at the time, Mary Walker (and by now Mary Gray, as well) were expecting, and they all hoped to achieve maternal status eventually. The women would be separated by distance, but they resolved to observe the same time each day in meditation and prayer, at nine each morning, just as Eliza and Narcissa had been doing. This invisible and spiritual tie bound them together in "discharging the responsible duties of mothers."[18]

The members agreed to observe two Wednesdays a month in reading scripture and prayer; those living near each other would meet together at that time when possible. They held their "Maternal meetings" regularly for years, but this first meeting was the only one at which all members were present. Eventually five wives of "independent" missionaries and two wives of HBC factors (at Fort Colville and Fort Walla Walla) were invited to join.

Members wrote papers on selected subjects and passed them on, in round-robin fashion. Getting together to hear the papers read was simply too difficult.

The Mother's Magazine, the official publication of the mothers' club movement was read avidly, and members sent letters to the editor for publication. Narcissa Whitman at one time sent eighteen dollars to pay for subscriptions for the Oregon women.

In the far West, as elsewhere, women's clubs provided a framework for expressing women's pent-up ambitions and aspirations. These clubs were the seeds of a growing move towards women's rights, particularly suffrage. Participating in formal organizations allowed women to use their skills and expand their abilities within an extensive supportive framework.

The Columbia members took up the task of corresponding regularly with other Maternal associations in Prattsburg, New York; Constantinople; Cape Palmas, Africa; Singapore; and the Methodist missions in the Willamette Valley.

Then as now, one of the first topics to be addressed by the Columbia Maternal Association was the, "Importance of the aid

& cooperation of our husbands in training our children in the way they should go."

By the end of the business sessions, William Gray had become "Mister" Gray to the new arrivals, rather than the "Doctor" they'd been introduced to, and considered him to be. Whitman had been surprised and furious when he heard the new reinforcements referring to William Gray as *Doctor* Gray, and grilled him about the new title. Gray had spent several weeks at a medical school while organizing his party of new missionary recruits; he'd been trained in some basics, and felt the title was earned. Whitman sent an angry letter to the Board, accusing Gray of being a fraud, and the others never referred to him as Dr. Gray again.

Elkanah and Cushing left to explore their new station, looking for a location and making contact with the factor at Fort Colville, Archibald McDonald. The new arrivals at Waiilatpu tried to settle in; the trip had been long and difficult, but living in the crowded house with the Whitmans was nearly as bad. Not only were the missionaries shocked by the primitive living conditions, the Indian people weren't quite what they had expected, either. Mary was annoyed because the Indians kept looking in the windows. She'd pull the curtain, but that made it too dark, so she'd eventually open it and they'd be back at the window. ". . . I cannot drive them away because I know not what to say . . . They annoy me very much and I will teach them better manners as soon as I can acquire language enough." She questioned the Indians' motives for wanting religion, feeling they were influenced by vanity and curiosity, but she admitted she was out of her league, ". . . I suspect I know just about as much about them as they do about religion."[19]

While the Whitman's house was crowded with visitors, Marcus decided to escape on a trip to Fort Vancouver for supplies. He hurried and bustled about so much that Narcissa snapped and started crying. After that, Mary observed, he went more calmly.

Mary was pregnant and waiting, if not patiently, at least politely. Elkanah sent her a letter from Ft. Colville advising her to learn the Nez Perce language, to be careful and not injure herself, and as if to remind her to keep her quick temper and sharp tongue under control, he added, "Remember that you are not mistress of the house and you have nothing you can call your own, and that you are entirely dependent on others."[20] Perhaps his words were a veiled threat to her concerning her need to become a more submissive Yankee wife.

Mary seems to have understood what he meant, because she answered with a letter reassurring him that she remained on good terms with Mrs. Whitman and that Narcissa (of course they never referred to each other by first names) seemed to be pleased with Mary so far, "If she were not I would be likely to know it as she is not sparing of hints to others when they do not suit her."[21] Narcissa had words with quiet Myra, angrily accusing her husband (Cushing) of caring for nobody but his wife.

Narcissa had worries on her mind over little Alice's health. She wrote her parents about the baby, ". . . our dear babe, she has been sick ever since he left and continues to be more so." Marcus had left for two weeks on a trip to Fort Vancouver to order supplies for the reinforcements. ". . . we have neither of us had a quiet night's rest for some time . . . Her body is covered with a rash much resembling the one I had just before she was born; has considerable fever and coughs a good deal." The rash worried her, but it wasn't mentioned by any of the other women in their letters or diaries. Narcissa must have kept it to herself, caring for the infant in her bedroom without letting the others know about the illness. William Gray, with his recent bit of medical training probably would have helped out if asked. She chose not to.

Mary was in a different predicament: "Find it very unpleasant being with Indians . . ." She thought they smelled offensive, and she couldn't bear to be around them. She busied herself writing a Nez Perce/English dictionary, and promised to work with the Indians and learn about them when her "senses become less acute."[22]

Notes on Chapter Eleven

[1] Ibid, p. 148.

[2] Drury, *First White Women*, p. 97.

[3] McKee, *Mary Richardson Walker*, p. 151.

[4] Ibid, p. 103.

[5] Ibid, p. 103.

[6] McKee, *Mary Richardson Walker*, p. 152.

[7] Ibid, p. 153.

[8] Ibid, p. 155.

[9] Drury, *First White Women*, p. 110.

[10] Ibid, p. 111.

[11] Ibid, p. 114.

[12] McKee, *Mary Richardson Walker*, p. 157.

[13] Drury, *First White Women*, p. 116.

[14] McKee, p. 159.

[15] Drury, *First White Women*, p. 117.

[16] Ibid, p. 118.

[17] Warren, *Memoirs of the West*, p. 67.

[18] McKee,*Mary Richardson Walker*, p. 160.

[19] Ibid, p. 174.

[20] Ibid, p. 175.

[21] McKee, p. 176.

[22] Ibid, p. 176.

Chapter Twelve

Personal Problems

We begin to have horse flesh served on the table. But I cannot overcome prejudice enough to taste it, though it looks as tempting as any meat.[1]

Mary Walker

Mary and the other new arrivals would become well-accustomed to horseflesh. During the first year at Waiilatpu the Whitmans butchered a large number of horses for eating. They would continue to trade for eating horses from the Cayuses for five years, until their own beef herd was well developed.

The Indians were the source of the horsemeat and labor, too. Mary noted that, "We have Indians to do our drudgery. They need a great deal of over sight. They save our strength, but wear out almost our patience . . ."[2] These were women hired from the Walla Walla tribe, a small, weak group the Cayuses looked down upon. The Cayuses never would work for Narcissa; which she resented, calling them "too proud."

Mary prepared the lean-to she was given as a room; because she was about to be "confined," she was the only one besides Narcissa who had a private area. "Had the floor washed and built a fire to dry it. Put up my curtains in the evening. After nine o'clock made 2 table cloths. Went to bed about 12 o'clock."[3] She must have annoyed the others with her practice of staying up so late in such crowded quarters. Elkanah was away with Cushing, searching for a mission location, and she was in a crowded cabin of strangers, about to go into labor. It was "very trying" to have her husband gone. She wished she could be "where no one else scarcely could see me."[4]

For Myra, the transition from traveler to missionary was disconcerting, too. The mission wasn't what she expected. Not only was the house too small and crowded, she discovered that William Gray had not given them correct information. He'd promised them that they would be able to purchase all the items they needed once they got to Oregon. For that reason, they had traveled light, and shipped some items by sea to Fort Vancouver.

Meanwhile, they had no shelter, no food, nothing at all. ". . . we are dependent on the mission family at present," Myra wrote, which was difficult because the Whitmans had little to share with them, and a baby to care for as well. Myra was older and had enjoyed a career and her own life for many years, marrying Cushing at age thirty-four. She wasn't a young girl, but rather a mature woman who had been led to expect something a bit more settled. She now discovered that there was nothing available, except items brought from a "foreign Post."

She lamented not being properly prepared for her situation; if she'd known the circumstances, she would have brought what she needed. "Had I known that there was not a spinning wheel in this whole country, I should have been exceedingly anxious to have one sent with my things." Clearly, the brethren of the mission hadn't put much thought into the women's roles or how they would keep house in the wilderness. The women, with no idea what to expect on the frontier, had not been given any information or direction before heading West. The reinforcements probably questioned William Gray, but he typically reassured them everything was taken care of, and could be easily obtained in Oregon. He didn't want to hinder his chances of returning as the head of his own contingent by having any of his recruits get cold feet about heading into the unknown.

Myra tried to figure out how to be of service to the mission. A skilled seamstress, she realized she could be of great value with her needle, but that would be only for the Americans, who had cloth available. ". . . at present I cannot teach the Indians to sew or knit because they have no cloth to sew nor yarn to knit

. . ."[5] She realized that perhaps they didn't actually need her skills, since they relied on skins for clothing, "Of course they have no need of cotton cloth . . ."[6]

Assessing the situation, she was superfluous, unnecessary, without value. The shock and dismay must have been palpable for her. Instead of showing her temper, or her disappointment, she hid it well. Only in a letter written while at rendezvous, waiting for the HBC escort, did she express her sadness. "It costs me tears every time I write home," she revealed. She never uttered cross words, or wrote about the shortcomings she saw in the people around her. She was a lady, a wife, and a missionary. She endeavored to prepare future female travelers for the passage by writing a lengthy letter to her sister telling of the trip overland and giving advice on what women should bring along. She recommended "good strong colored clothes" for the horseback journey. A lady's dress should be green merino or pongee, with a loose calico dress to wear when she doesn't need a cloak. Men's and ladies' underclothes should be "colored"—white must have been impossible to keep clean in the dirt and dust. She advised three sets of underclothes for the trip; four sets for travel while still in the States and for use on arrival in Oregon. A Florence bonnet or variegated straw bonnet would be best, and if a woman expected to have any sort of headgear in Oregon, she must bring her silks, ribbons, lining and trimming. Two or three verage veils were necessary to protect the face from sun and wind while riding. Myra recommended a bonnet cover and cape made from India rubber, as protection while riding in the rain. Myra had succeeded in getting to Oregon with her umbrella, but she advised others that it was too windy and they were easily broken. The other missionary women had all lost or broken theirs on the way. Footwear should be gentlemen's calf (leather) shoes—"a good supply"—and plenty of stockings, as well.

Travelers needed to supply their own bedding. Myra suggested each lady bring a small dark-colored bed quilt, a pair of sheets, four pairs of calico pillow cases and two pillows. Last, no woman should leave the States without plenty of sewing pins, needles, scissors, pen knives, and silk and thread of all kinds and colors—with plenty of brown. Lastly, a lady needed to bring along a stock of raisins or figs, "for her own comfort."

The women at Waiilatpu that winter: Myra, Mary Walker, Sarah Smith, and Narcissa, had a trying time. (The Grays had gone to stay with the Spalding family at Clear Water.) Narcissa and Asa Smith fought about the lack of food in the pantry—one day he was upset that there was only milk and melons, and Narcissa accused him of eating more than his share. Laundry never got underway until evening, something Mary resolved to get done early in the morning once she had a home of her own. Moody Narcissa spent her time in her room, writing letters. The other women shared the other bedroom and the chores. When Mary Smith asked Myra to help sew a new dress for Narcissa, Myra refused, saying she didn't like the style of the proposed dress. After some chiding, she admitted that since Narcissa wrote all the time, and that her (Myra's) time was just as valuable, she did not feel under the least obligation to make a dress for her.

Mary Walker was shocked at Myra, but there were so many other spats going on in the crowded house it was nearly impossible to say who was right. When Sabbath came, she searched her heart for sinfulness, because she could "Detect so much in others that I fear I do not see it quick in myself & husband, as I do elsewhere."[7]

It was a trying time for all, Mary reflected in a letter to Elkanah that, she thought she was "much more cheerful, happy & contented than Mrs. Eells. She is rather unreconciled to the idea of spending the winter here. She does not seem to like Mrs. Whitman very well."

By mid-November, the women at Waiilatpu were stretched to their Christian limits as far as getting along with one another. Narcissa, put in the role of hostess to people she had never met before, was not at her best. She seemed to be overwhelmed by the household duties expected of her, but was also reeling from the loss of her domestic servant, an orphan girl sent up by the HBC, who had died weeks before the reinforcements arrived. She had hired Indian women to help her, but nothing was going right. Maria Maki, the Hawaiian woman hired with her husband to work for the Whitmans, was on her sickbed, her husband weeping at her bedside. Narcissa's biggest concern was always obtaining domestic help, something she frequently wrote to her own mother about.

The new arrivals were willing to do what they could, but it was nearly impossible without Narcissa's direction or cooperation. The women were not used to doing much of their own work, except for Mary Walker, who in spite of late stages of pregnancy, threw herself into doing what was necesssary. She washed clothes, hung out laundry, scrubbed floors, baked—did whatever she could to get Narcissa to act cheerful; to "melt over her tallow."

In spite of Mary's efforts, Narcissa treated the newcomers rudely. She spent days in her room with Alice Clarissa, writing letters to family or other missionaries. It was the only room with a stove; the fireplace kept it so cold inside the rest of the poorly-built house that frozen door latches stuck to the fingers.

They watched Narcissa withdraw alone, disregarding the house and the others. Mary couldn't figure her out, which made it difficult to please her. "Think her a strange housekeeper," she decided. There was no soap, they were running out of candles, (a disaster when the women were up all night reading books or writing letters), and they had gone a week without any bread. The Whitman's weren't starving, the garden and field (seventeen acres that year) had provided enough to eat.

Mary saw much to be done, but no one interested in doing the work. Mary blamed the others' for their lack of assistance around the house. She felt Narcissa had "less help from the other ladies than she ought." Maria Maki, the servant, wasn't recovering, and Mary noted that "Mr. W. has not bathed for some weeks." To make it even worse, the only food they had was boiled wheat, potatoes, and horse meat and salmon traded from the Indians.[8]

The stress, bickering and overcrowded house began to wear on the women. Mary observed that Narcissa was in a "sad mood," and she herself "went out doors, down by the river to cry."[9] It would be a long and dreary winter.

On December 7, at nine o'clock in the morning, Mary Walker "became sick enough," and went into labor. "Began to feel discouraged, felt as if I almost wished I'd never been mar-

ried. But there was no retreating." Definitely not, when in the
final stages of labor. "Meet it I must," she resolved. After two
hours, her son was born and she forgot the pains over, "the joy
of possessing a proper child." Elkanah returned that night, "full
of kisses for me and my babe."[10]

But Mary's relief was short-lived, when she discovered she
was unable to feed the newborn child. The baby's sucking produced paroxysms of pain which she could hardly endure. Mary's
breastfeeding ordeal was painful: she was very nervous, the
milk caked in her breasts and she feared she would have two
"broken breasts," which would mean disaster for the baby—and
any future child she might bear. Myra took care of Mary, applying compresses to alternately steam and draw the breasts, then
covering them with sticking plaster. Eight days later, she was
still trying to make a go of nursing Cyrus. She was getting
somewhat better, but the baby was not getting enough to eat.
The breasts continued to be painful, and she was taking mor-
phine and calomel.

Narcissa was nursing little Alice Clarissa, now nearly two
years old, and nursed tiny Cyrus at first. The baby found it easier to nurse from Narcissa than Mary and began refusing
Mary's breasts. Narcissa's solution was to wean Alice Clarissa,
letting her milk dry up, so Cyrus would be forced to nurse from
Mary. Narcissa went even further, refusing to give Mary a bottle so she could feed the child cow's milk, but Mary "made out to
find one & so fed him."[11]

Mary confided in her diary that she was "sometimes discouraged & fear I shall never do anything to benefit the heathen & might have stayed at home." She was still trying to
recover from three "relapses" after the birth, as well as disas-
trous breast inflammations. She was frustrated that she wasn't
getting her health and strength back faster.

Mary refused to give up easily. Her own milk supply nonexistent, she tried "to invent artificial nipples," but to no avail. The
women had a "maires tit" cut from a horse that was suckling a
foal, which they hoped would succeed. If that worked, Mary
would "rejoice."[12]

A horse's teat seems outlandish today, but they were only
doing what they had heard could be done. The original sucking

bottle was made from a cow's horn in the late eighteenth century, and highly recommended by doctors at the time. This was followed by the glass bottle, with a nipple made successively of parchment and leather, sponge, heifer's teats kept in spirit, wood and India-rubber.[13] The mission women had no access to a milk cow, except the one they were dependent upon for milk, so they couldn't butcher her in order to use her teat. A horse was the logical choice. But it simply wouldn't work.

Behind all their efforts was the knowledge that the baby might die. Infants who were "dry-nursed" rather than breast-fed had very high mortality rates. In the early nineteenth century, seven in ten dry-nursed children died their first year. They were desperate. Fortunately, Mrs. Compo, an Indian woman married to the mission's hired man, had a three-week old infant. She had enough milk to nurse Cyrus, so that with supplemental feedings from Mary, and from cow's milk, he survived. Even though Mary was ". . . glad my babe can be supplied with milk" there was a problem: ". . . it comes from a black breast." Something Narcissa was not going to let her forget.

Narcissa wrote to another female missionary about the baby's birth, and the problems Mary had with nursing. She described how Mary had "suffered much from sore breasts and nipples, & what to me would be the greatest affliction, no nipples at all." Her vanity over her own prowess at motherhood showed, along with her disdain for how Mary had to handle things: "Her poor babe had to depend upon a foreign native nurse or milk from the cows."[14] No doubt Narcissa made much of Mary's failure at the first demands of motherhood.

Tensions and tempers continued to build in the crowded house. Narcissa grew more anxious, until Marcus decided to take her and Alice Clarissa away for a visit with the Indians. Eager to be out of the confines of the house, Narcissa busied herself getting ready for the trip. Mary noted wryly in her diary that Mrs. Whitman had got up early in the morning and done her wash, "Query. Did she every do such a thing before?" According to Mary, "Mrs. W. has dealt so largely in powder & balls of late that perhaps her absence will not detract much from our happiness."[15]

The Whitmans went to the Tucannon River to camp with a small band of Nez Perces, where Marcus did some preaching, and Narcissa sat in the tent and wrote letters. She was so relieved to get away from the strangers who had taken over her house, that she confided in a letter to her sister Jane that, ". . . we have been disappointed in our helpers last come, particularly the two Revs. who have gone to the Flatheads." She meant Elkanah Walker and Cushing Eells. "They think it not so good to have too many meetings, too many prayers, and that it is wrong and unseemly for a woman to pray where there are men."

That was true. Walker and Eells were Congregationalists; the Whitmans and Spaldings were Presbyterians. The American Board for Foreign Missions was a cooperative venture. The groups differed in how women were to be allowed independence and authority in the church. Congregational practice at the time did not allow women to pray aloud or sing hymns in a mixed group. To Narcissa, the excitement of religion was embodied in a boisterous revival meeting—which was certainly not the demeanor the two new preachers approved of.

"And how do you think I have lived with such folks right in my kitchen for the whole winter?" It must have been very difficult, surrounded by a vast empty land filled with Indians who spoke a foreign language. The missionaries had indeed huddled together for months of intense stress. Narcissa admitted she hadn't been able to handle the change in the mission, "This, with so much care and perplexity, nearly cost me a fit of sickness; and I do not know but it would have taken my life had it not been for the journey . . ."[16] The journey into the mountains to stay with the Nez Perces had been her salvation.

Spending time with the Nez Perces made the Whitmans see the Cayuses in a different light. Narcissa thought the Nez Perces were not so, "hardened in sin; or rather, they were not so proud a people as our people, the Wieletpoos, are."[17]

Most of the Cayuses had abandoned the grounds at Waiilatpu for the winter, choosing to camp farther down-river where they could trade for salmon from river tribes along the warmer banks of the Columbia River. The Indians only visited the mission seasonally, giving very little chance for the Whitmans to do actual mission work.

The Whitmans had very few opportunities to learn the absent Indians' language, either. Narcissa wrote to Mrs. Perkins, who was the wife of a Methodist missionary newly-stationed at Wascopam, near The Dalles. When Mrs. Perkins wrote with questions about what progress Narcissa was making in working with the Indians, Narcissa's answer was defensive, "I do not see how you get along and learn so many languages. What is the particular benefit? We hear so many spoken but we intend to learn only one, and make that the general one for the country."[18] What language the "one" was, she doesn't say. At the time she wrote the letter she'd been living "with" the Cayuses for two and a half years. She told Mrs. Perkins that they had decided to travel out to meet the Indians a little, as they were continually "roving" and the Whitmans spent the "greater part of our time alone" at the mission station.[19]

While the Whitmans were away from Waiilatpu, the other missionaries got along fine; no conflicts ensued, the Smiths built and moved into a small house of their own near the Whitmans' and all were making plans for their move out into their stations come spring. Mary, Myra and Sarah Smith went riding, and walking outdoors—noticing that it was a "beautiful country." They dipped twenty-four dozen candles, did laundry, and everything seemed to "move on pleasantly."[20]

Mary even wrote poetry, she was feeling so light-hearted, and she worked on her clothes, remaking her pongee and her delaine dresses back to their original design for everyday wear now that the baby had been born and her figure was back to normal, which necessitated considerable hand stitching. For years, these dresses would undergo transformation every time Mary gave birth to another baby.

The quiet activity gave them a chance to rethink their priorities. Mary wrote an interesting comment in her diary, "I have been thinking to day that if I did not know I should sooner suppose myself in the house of a Southern plantation than a Christian missionary. I witness much that seems wrong to me."[21] At that time, the mission employed several people: Margaret McKay was a live-in domestic, the Compos and the Makis were four more workers, and there were no doubt others. Mary had no experience with slavery, so she might not have been referring to the number of people working on the grounds. Maybe she was disturbed by the lack of work the missionaries seemed to do. After all, there were no Indians about, there was a "big" house, and now the Smiths' smaller house, and the grounds were constantly growing.

The peaceful, contemplative mood changed quickly, though. When Narcissa and Marcus returned, tempers flared again. It was "Adieu to peace & order," as Narcissa seemed at first to be in good humor, and to have evinced a change of heart, but "at supper table & even before she began to show out."[22]

Narcissa spent the next four days in her bedroom, giving the others no explanation of what was wrong. She came out once, "in the greatest agitation" and begged the others to pray for her and forgive her, but they weren't satisfied that she meant it.[23] She went back to her room, not even coming out for meals the rest of the week. When Marcus decided to take her to visit the Spaldings at Clear Water, she came out, and dined with the rest.

Her behavior made the others very uncomfortable. They had no idea what they had done, or what Narcissa wanted from them. "She says we do not know her heart," Mary wrote. "I fear she does not know it herself." Something was wrong. "I would like to know how so much unpleasant temper can consort with such high pretentions to piety," Mary wrote, letting her anger show. "If she is a good woman, I hope grace will so abound in her as to render her a little more pleasant."[24]

She was still reeling from the difficulties between them over nursing Cyrus. Narcissa had accused Mary of not loving the baby, and refusing to nurse the baby only because her "heart had not been big enough." She called Narcissa's taunts "cruel & without reason." In her defense, Narcissa said the others "thought her out of humor when it was anxiety for the salvation of sinners that caused her to appear as she did." This caught the others off-guard, and they thought she was trying to "make a cloak of Religon." They "felt worse than before."

In spite of the bickering with Narcissa, Myra and Mary were eager to get to the Spokanes, ready to embark on their effort at working with the Indians, and willing to do whatever it might take. "I like Mr. & Mrs. Eells better than I used to do, think we shall live quite happily," Mary noted. "When I get there I think I shall not be a slothful servant."[25]

When Sabbath arrived, Narcissa spent the entire day in prayer. Suitably impressed, Mary thought maybe they'd been too harsh on her. "I fear we are too severe in judging her & that we are not after all as pious as she. Perhaps our beseting sins are as heinous in the sight of God as hers." To make amends the next day Mary baked plenty of gingerbread for Narcissa and also got supper.

Marcus decided to visit the Spaldings, so Narcissa and Alice Clarissa again left the mission house and their visitors. The reinforcements weren't really visitors, as they felt that they were as much a part of the mission as anyone. Because the men were preachers, they were the actual missionaries. Every foreign mission had a medical doctor, sent to care for the mission families—not the natives. That was Whitman's status, anyway. He was to be there to serve the real missionaries, the preachers of the Gospel. It irritated them that he took it upon himself to administer to the financial and secular affairs of the mission, but since no one was supposed to own anything—they had all accepted personal poverty as part of the mission life—there was no need to feel that the Whitman's even "owned" their house. Everything was to be considered mission property, and all were equal in access to it.

While the Whitmans were at Clear Water, Cushing and Elkanah returned to retrieve their families. They had met with the Hudson's Bay Company factor at Fort Colville, Archibald McDonald, and had settled on a spot to build their mission station. The women must have been eager to see the spot once they heard the romantic name: Tshimikain, "Place of the Springs."

After seeing the Indian situation at Waiilatpu for months, Elkanah and Mary wanted to settle the Spokane Indians in one location, so the children could be taught in school. Like the Spaldings, they felt that white settlement would only ruin the Indians. "To settle the Indians will be the surest way to prevent the country from being overrun by a lawless . . . mass that will be very likely to pour into the country from the four quarters of the earth."[26] If lawless people came to Oregon (such as the mountain men who were scattered about) and those who had been "outlawed from civilized society," then the "hope of the Indian and all hope of doing them good will end."[27] There was little time to waste, as they knew more Americans would surely be coming.

Notes on Chapter Twelve

[1] McKee, *Mary Richardson Walker*, p. 180.

[2] Ibid, p. 181.

[3] Ibid.

[4] Drury, *First White Women*, p. 118.

[5] Eells, Ida Myra, *Mother Eells*, Wenatchee Mimeograph, 1947.

[6] Ibid.

[7] Drury, *First White Women*, p. 130.

[8] Ibid, p. 135.

[9] Ibid.

[10] McKee, *Mary Richardson Walker*, p. 181.

[11] Drury, *First White Women*, p. 138.

[12] Ibid, p. 139.

[13] Fielding H. Garrison, *The History of Medicine* (Philadelphia: W.B. Saunders Company, 1929), p. 402.

[14] *Whitman, Letters*, p. 76.

[15] Drury, *First White Women*, p. 142.

[16] *Whitman, Letters,* p. 78.

[17] Ibid, p. 77.

[18] Ibid, p. 75.

[19] Ibid, p. 74.

[20] Drury, *First White Women*, p. 143.

[21] Ibid.

[22] Ibid.

[23] Ibid, p. 144.

[24] Ibid, p. 145.

[25] Ibid.

[26] McKee, *Mary Richardson Walker*, p. 177.

[27] Ibid.

Chapter Thirteen

First Born

A t Waiilatpu, the Cayuse Indians were "more noisy & mischievous" than the women had "ever knew them." They were in "considerable excitement"—telling the Americans that, "the Doctor says they will go to hell any way & they are not going to restrain their children to be good or try to be good any more." Mary was "sorry" to see them so "ill disposed," but she figured they were "anxious to devise some way of getting into heaven without repenting & renouncing their sins."[1]

When Elkanah and Cushing returned to take their wives to the new mission station near the Spokane Indians the excitement dissipated any worries about the Cayuses. Ignoring the turmoil brewing around her, Mary wrote in her diary, "Farewell to Waiilatpu . . ." It was nearly spring, a time of new beginnings, and she was on her way to start her new home. The climate at Waiilatpu was very mild, and she noted in her diary, "Frogs are singing;" they were embarking on a new beginning.

It was mid-February and as they went north from the mild climate along the Walla Walla River bottom, snow began to swirl around them. They slept in tents, and one night so much snow piled up outside, they couldn't move camp. They had to cross the high water of the swollen Snake River, then traverse the treeless windswept plains.

Travel on horseback, with a two-month old infant, was not easy. Baby Cyrus rode in front of Elkanah, on a large pillow fastened to a specially-constructed pad which he used instead of a saddle—the entire affair was a make-shift attempt to transport an infant. A blanket was spread over his lap on which another pillow was laid, then the baby. The sides of the blanket were wrapped up over Cyrus and a "girdle passed around Mr. W. and the child so that he hardly requires holding."[2] Mary, on sidesaddle, would have found it difficult if not impossible to balance the infant with her.

A milk cow was taken along for the baby's nourishment and Cushing rode ahead and built a fire to warm the infant's milk for periodic feedings. Mary noted several times that the baby was difficult—indeed he cried nearly the whole time. His mouth was raw and sore, possibly an infection from the variety of unsterile items the women had tried using to feed him, and his little feet were nearly frostbit; "swollen like a puff," Mary noted. She tried to wrap him warmly, but it was "Not very comfortable taking care of babe."[3]

When they finally reached their chosen spot, the women must have been shocked and dismayed. At Tshimikain, the "Place of the Springs," in a picturesque little valley, the "houses" that Elkanah and Cushing had ready for them were what Myra called, "log pens." Neither man had any skill at building, nor any experience. Without tools, lumber, or trained workmen, their finished efforts must have been sadly inadequate. To complicate things, they had run out of food. Their Indian guide, Solomon, went seventy miles north to Fort Colville to see what he could obtain for them there. While he was gone, the rest of the Indian escort worked with the men to cover the log houses with grass, pine boughs, and mud chinking.

When Solomon returned nearly a week later he brought a welcome invitation from Archibald McDonald, the Hudson's Bay factor at Fort Colville, for the women to come stay at the fort until their houses were complete. Elkanah rode north with the women and baby, while Cushing stayed behind to guard the supplies and see what he could do about finishing the two cabins.

They took the precious milk cow along, but stopped within a day's ride of Fort Colville, saved up a supply of milk and sent the cow back to Tshimikain with an Indian escort. There were already dairy cattle at Fort Colville and the cow was too precious to lose for any reason. Perhaps they thought it best not to flaunt the cow's existence; cattle were well-guarded by the HBC, and the company had a strict policy of *never* selling or trading a cow to anyone, even ex-employees of the company.

Keeping cattle out of the hands of would-be settlers meant fewer people would try to set up housekeeping in the fur company's domain. Lack of a milk cow was the one thing that would make an American woman resist going into the wilderness; without a family cow, they would be taking very great risks that babies would starve to death. If a mother couldn't nurse the baby for any reason, or if she died or sickened—an infant would perish.

Mary and Myra were relieved to find themselves welcome and comfortably treated at Fort Colville. They were happy to meet Mrs. McDonald—the former Jane Klyne, half-Cree daughter of an HBC postmaster—now a woman of refinement. She was twenty-nine years old (Mary was twenty-eight, Myra thirty-four), and had young children of her own. She spoke excellent English, and eagerly befriended the women.

A visiting trader described the McDonald household as quite pleasant. When eating dinner with the family, he'd felt like he was back home in "some domestic circle."[4] McDonald was a devoted father and family man, a contrast to some of his cohorts in the fur trade. Jane had quickly learned to read and write under the tutelage of her husband. He was intensely proud of her accomplishments and boasted of her to everyone. She was skillful at managing a complex household: all work was done by servants but she never sat still. He bragged about her "Butter, Cheese, Ham & Bacon" besides taking pride in her ability to master literacy. She was a devout Christian (Archibald McDonald was a Scotch Presbyterian) and welcomed the missionary wives.

Jane was gracious and intelligent; she was intent on protecting her own interests as well as those of her children by adopting white ways as quickly and completely as possible. In the past few years she and other mixed-blood wives of fur trade executives had been shocked by the Governor of Rupert's Land, who had "turned off" his fur-trade mixed-blood wife for an imported European woman. So had other top fur trade men. It was the beginning of a new era for mixed-blood women who feared their husbands (many married for years, but only in the "custom of the country"—not by the church or state) might abandon them for white women.

If Jane feared Archibald would abandon her and their children, she was doing everything she could to prevent it by adopting his culture. The arrival of white ladies in Canada threatened to undermine the status of the mixed-blood women of the fur trade upper echelon. Perhaps they knew their men well, or perhaps the women were able to quickly seal their place in their husbands' hearts—only half a dozen "country marriages" were abandoned by men seeking European imports and the higher social status that conveyed in developing Canadian society.

Archibald had noticed the change in his wife; he wrote that she was well aware of the potential that he might abandon her if she failed to bring herself up to his standards. "I already feel the beneficial effects of the Govr & McTavish's marriages," he wrote. Certainly, Jane was coddling and pleasing him to no end. She had "picked up sense enough to infer from their having changed partners, that the old ones were difficient in learning & that her own case may be the same when tis my turn to visit my Scottish cousins."[5] HBC gentlemen were given periodic vacations to Scotland, where they visited, relaxed, and often recruited new employees for the company—and mingled with white women.

Jane's welcoming and socializing with the American women certainly impressed Archibald, and cemented her status with him. It's doubtful he would have ever dropped her, he was quite a character and may have enjoyed milking the situation for his own domestic advantage.

After all, fur trade wives (of upper level employees) were notoriously independent, frequently took lovers, and seemed to give their husbands endless worry. Even Governor Simpson, on an early tour of the forts, had criticized the men for spending so much time worrying about whether their wives were being faithful or not.

Fort Colville was well-furnished with windows, tables, chairs, and so many conveniences that Mary feared she wouldn't want to leave. The HBC farming operation yielded 1,500

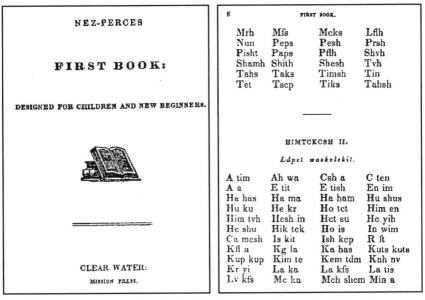

Two pages from Spalding's Nez Perce dictionary, the first book
published in Oregon Country.

bushels of wheat and 7,000 bushels of potatoes. There were
fenced fields, a sawmill and large herds of cattle and pigs.

The McDonald children were well-educated; Mary
described them as, "well I think as any I ever saw in N.E. (New
England)."[6] Jane taught the children herself, something that
impressed the Americans as being quite the proper motherly
role. Being in a large happy family was a joy for the women who
had so recently endured the stressful atmosphere of Waiilatpu.
Mary was delighted that Archibald McDonald showed so much
interest in the geology book she had toted across the continent.
She lent it to him, and he spent quite a bit of time reading it
during her visit.

On Wednesday, the women embarked on their usual
Maternal Meeting, this time they were thrilled to enlarge their
membership by adding Jane McDonald as a member. Mary
called it "quite an interesting meeting." Certainly, they must
have felt they were doing what they had come to do—civilizing
the heathen. They considered Jane McDonald to be "nearly
white," but she was still part Indian. The fact that they welcomed and added her to their group was significant. For Jane, it

may have been quite an accomplishment; as a member of the Columbia Maternal Association, she was certainly cementing her position as a proper matron.

Mary was pleased that "Mrs. M'D. is fond of making improvements," so they embarked on cooking lessons, among other things. They taught her to prepare a "variety of Yankee dishes" which included toast, custards, puddings, gingerbread and other foods she hadn't tried before.[7] Since every HBC post had a cooking kitchen run by male cooks and servants, Jane had no need to do much of her own cooking, but it gave the women an opportunity to share and spend time together.

Mary was given the services of a mixed-blood servant girl, Lizette, who cared for the baby during the day. She stayed in Mary's room watching little Cyrus and knitting, a skill Mary was happy to teach her as well.

Mary, Myra and the McDonalds went to the Indian village outside the Fort where they toured the Indians' "lodge for worship." The building was typical of the region, a pole frame structure covered with grass mats. The roof had a high peak with a grass-covered floor that was swept clean down the center to create an aisle. A cloth was spread on the ground at one end for a pulpit and the worshippers sat on the grass as if in pews. The chief led the services.

While waiting at Colville, Mary spent some free hours reading from books she'd brought, mostly the memoirs of women who'd married missionary husbands. Reflecting on why she had come West and what she was really doing made her despondent. She asked herself, "I have desired to become a missionary & why?" She felt guilty about all the months that had passed since she left Maine, and thought maybe the only reason she'd become a missionary was to "avoid duties at home." After all, what had she done, except busy herself with her own and her family's needs?

"If I felt a sincere interest in the salvation of the heathen," she reasoned, "should I not be more engaged in acquiring the language that I might be able to instruct them?" She admitted to herself that she'd avoided doing that, and had looked for opportunities to keep herself busy doing anything but learn the language.

Mary's competitive nature surfaced, ". . . as I do not like others to excell so I feel a wicked satisfaction in seeing them as little interested as myself." She was talking about the other
women, particularly Myra, Narcissa, and Mary Smith, her associates the past winter. She had no idea what tasks Eliza
Spalding and Mary Gray were taking on, but she must have
noticed the other wives' lack of interest in working with the
Indians.

When Elkanah returned to escort them to their new homes
at Tshimikain, Mary knew they wouldn't have many conveniences, but at least they would be together. It was very pleasant at Colville, and she reminded herself that it was not difficult for a female to abandon a palace for a cottage, if it meant
being with the one she loved.

Elkanah and Cushing had been busy at Tshimikain,
besides finishing up the rough "cottages," they'd been bargaining with the Indians over slaughtering their dogs. Elkanah worried that he'd gotten himself in hot water with the Indians over
it, but there was no way they could live there, with so many
aggressive, nearly-wild and half-starved dogs. He and Cushing
had told the Indians that unless they slaughtered their dogs,
the missionaries would not move there. They'd eventually com-
plied and gotten rid of the dogs. Henry Spalding had faced the
same problem at Clear Water, and while the Indians didn't
retaliate, it was an awkward hurdle to the initial relationship.

Indians seldom fed their dogs, figuring they had to earn
their own survival. Things were hung beyond the dogs' reach in
an Indian camp, and guards were stationed to defend the home
when others went root digging or hunting. Innocent travelers
often discovered that their moccasins had disappeared during
the night, as starving dogs took whatever they could devour.
Father Pierre Jean DeSmet, the intrepid Jesuit missionary,
wrote about the same problems with famished Indian dogs.

When the women reached Tshimikain again, they found the
men had finished two cabins, each sixteen-feet square. There
were no windows or doors. Openings were covered with deer
skins or woven grass mats the Indians had made. Each had a
chimney made of mud and grass adobe blocks and a fireplace.
Neither woman ever had a cooking stove in the nine years they

stayed at Tshimikain. They always cooked in the fireplace, with the help of a tin oven for baking. The floor was stamped earth covered with pine branches. Beds were "sink-style" as Myra called them—wooden platforms nailed to the wall, with legs made of slender log poles. Mattress ticks were filled with straw.

The men had made tables by pushing four stakes in the ground and fastening three precious boards from Waiilatpu over the top. Stools were cut from logs. They ate with the dishes they'd used on the trip and a few they'd obtained at Fort Colville.

Mary wrote succinctly in her diary, "Reached home about noon, very much fatigued. Commence house keeping."[8] For Mary and Myra, housekeeping meant washing laundry in Tshimikain Creek and packing the heavy load of wet clothes back to hang out on a clothes line. There were candles to dip, water to haul, a garden to plant. Ominously, Mary noticed red dots on little Cyrus, and realized he'd come down with chicken pox, "suppose he took it of the Indians at Colvile."[9] That meant even more work, caring for the sick baby.

A packet of letters arrived from Wailatpu, with the surprising good news that the Hawaiian natives' Christian church had adopted the Indian mission as a foreign mission to their own, and had sent them $400. The Hawaiian missions had been established a few years earlier, and had been very successful. With more assets and personnel, and the assistance of the Hawaiian monarchy, the church there had fluorished. Now, they were established enough to reach out to help their closest mission friends, those in Oregon. It's surprising to learn that the Christian natives of Hawaii were eagerly donating to save the souls of American Indians in the Pacific Northwest.

Mary had hired an Indian girl to help care for baby Cyrus while she did other tasks. Mary still dressed and fed Cyrus (mostly milk porridge now), but he was sitting up and wanted playthings, and the babysitter was absolutely necessary to keep the five month-old infant safe and busy. Rough log floors, open fireplaces and burning candles must have made caring for young children challenging on the frontier, unless a domestic could be taken in.

It was salmon time, and there were nearly a thousand Indians gathered at the river. From four to eight hundred salmon were taken daily, caught in barriers (weirs) the Indians built out into the river. The fish weighed from ten to forty pounds apiece. The missionaries traded for both fresh and dried fish and often made meals of salmon. There's no mention that they ever tried fishing themselves, but they often traded with the Indians for salmon. The missionaries refrained from any activity that could be considered "heathen," after all, they had not come to learn to live like the Indians, but to teach them the Yankee lifestyle.

By summer, the families were settled enough that the Walkers traveled south to the Spaldings' home near Lapwai for the annual Mission Meeting. Myra was sick, which explained the reason the Eells remained at Tshimikain. (She suffered menstrual problems and several miscarriages and was bedridden for hemorraging, several times being near death.)

At Clear Water, Mary was able to visit with Eliza Spalding, Mary Gray, and a new arrival at the mission, Mrs. Hall, who had just arrived with her husband, E.O. Hall, from the Hawaiian mission in the Sandwich Islands. Mr. Hall was the printer for the Sandwich Island Mission of the American Board and had brought a printing press donated to the Oregon mission by the Hawaiian mission. While it was a great ordeal to bring the heavy press upriver and overland, by canoe and horseback, it was extremely difficult to bring Mrs. Hall the distance, too. She was an invalid, and couldn't ride horseback, so was brought by canoe.

The women had an opportunity to chat and bring each other up to date on events as they did laundry and ironing together. Narcissa was certainly a topic of their conversation, and Mary wrote sarcastically in her diary that Eliza Spalding "likes Mrs. Whitman as well as any of us."[10]

The brethren busied themselves with meetings, and Mary tried to sew Elkanah a proper spencer (jacket) so he might appear more presentable. Since he'd lost his wedding jacket on the overland trip, he'd probably not replaced it with a good jacket to use during preaching. Since his arrival in Oregon he hadn't had many opportunities to preach formally. In the Indian lodges, his apparel didn't matter, but at Lapwai, at the annual mission meeting, each man needed to appear at his best in front of the other three ordained ministers. There was also a much larger audience of Nez Perces to impress. There must have been a pressing reason, because Mary hated to sew, and she spent two of her days at Clear Water making the coat. Myra Eells wasn't there to do the sewing for her, so it must have been a project that couldn't wait.

They spent ten days with the Spaldings at Clear Water, then rode north to Tshimikain again. The Whitmans hadn't made the trip to Clear Water to meet with the other mission members because Marcus was too ill to make the trip.[11] Several of the other mission members were bedridden or too sick to do much during the ten days, too. The temperature was ninety-six degrees, and the heat affected them all.

Mary swung up on her sidesaddle for the trip home to Tshimikain. Elkanah carried their little boy in front of him on his saddle. They had gone forty miles when an Indian messenger caught up with them. He brought news from Clear Water that a courier had come from Waiilatpu with the sad information that the Whitmans' little daughter, Alice Clarissa, had drowned.

Alice Clarissa Whitman was two years old that September day when she fell into the Walla Walla River where it flowed within feet of the Whitman's home. It was Sabbath, and Narcissa was engrossed in reading, Marcus absorbed in a book, too. Margaret McKay, a young girl hired from the HBC as a domestic servant, had set the table for the Sabbath meal. Little Alice had fussed with the dishes on the table, and had taken two of the English china cups down from the table. Later Narcissa would remember the child saying, "Mama, supper is almost ready; let Alice get some water."

No one noticed the girl missing, until Narcissa told Margaret to go find her. Margaret didn't see the girl, but passed the garden and remembered she needed to pick some vegetables for dinner. No one paid any more attention to the toddler's absence, until Mungo, a Hawaiian boy hired from the HBC as a laborer for Marcus, came to the house to tell the Whitmans that two of their china cups were in the river. Marcus told him to leave them alone, after all it was Sabbath, and tomorrow would be soon enough to retrieve them from the water.

Narcissa put down her book, though, asking how they had gotten there. Who had taken her cups? Why were they put in the river? Marcus responded that probably Alice had done it. Finally the two of them put down their reading matter and went outdoors. They looked in the garden, but Margaret was alone there. She hadn't seen the child. Narcissa remembered the little girl's comments about water, and raced to the river. She, Marcus, and others went up and down the bank, looking for the girl but saw nothing.

Narcissa saw "an old Indian" go into the water, swim beneath the water's surface and emerge with the body and the words, "She is found."[12] The old man was Chief Umtippe. Marcus tried to revive the child, but she was dead.

Grief, loneliness, guilt—Narcissa felt them all. The only thing she cherished in the world, little Alice Clarissa, had been taken from her.

An Indian messenger was sent north to the other mission parties, but the only ones to come for the funeral were the Spaldings and Mr. Hall, the Hawaiian mission printer. Pierre Pambrun, from Fort Walla Walla, the nearby HBC post came too. Henry Spalding performed the service, and the little girl was buried near where she had been born. The first white child to be born, and to die, in Oregon Country.

Henry Spalding wrote poignantly in his diary, expressing the fear that was in all of their hearts: ". . . the first of our little no.[number] who found a grave in these dark regions. Who is to be second. Oh my soul who is to be second."[13]

Notes on Chapter Thirteen

[1] Drury, *First White Women*, p. 146.

[2] McKee, *Mary Richardson Walker*, p. 187.

[3] Drury, *First White Women*, p. 148.

[4] Sylvia Van Kirk, *Many Tender Ties: Women in Fur-Trade Society, 1670-1870* (Norman: University of Oklahoma Press, 1980), p. 126.

[5] Ibid, p. 209.

[6] McKee, *Mary Richardson Walker,* p. 191.

[7] Ibid, 193.

[8] Drury, *First White Women*, p. 154.

[9] Ibid, p. 156.

[10] Ibid, p. 159.

[11] Ibid, p. 159.

[12] Drury, *Marcus and Narcissa Whitman*, p. 353.

[13] Clifford Merrill Drury, *Diaries and Letters of Henry H. Spalding and Asa Bowen Smith Relating to the Nez Perce Mission, 1836-1842* (Glendale, CA: Arthur H. Clark Company, 1963), p. 266.

Chapter Fourteen

Dissension

Narcissa didn't let the child go easily. She sat with little Alice Clarissa's body for days, holding the corpse until it began to "change" and physical deterioration began. Only then could she finally accept putting the toddler's body into the shroud she'd made from one of her own dresses.

After a simple burial ceremony, the Whitmans went to Lapwai with the Spaldings for a few weeks. The Grays were living at Lapwai, too, and the three couples tried to make amends, to get over the differences that had grown to divide them. The Whitmans believed their daughter had been taken from them by the Lord because of their own sins, and they apologized to the other missionaries. Grief and fear for their own families enveloped the others; it was a time of forgiveness and compassion.

Alice Clarissa's death tormented Narcissa for years. She eventually accepted the loss, holding to her belief that the girl had died for the mission cause. She believed the Lord had taken her child from her because she'd been so overwhelmed with responsibilities teaching the Indians; something Narcissa had been unable to do without Alice Clarissa being "exposed to the contaminating influence of heathenism and very much neglected."[1] Unwilling to accept responsibility for the toddler's drowning, she angrily blamed the Indians. Now she had another reason to hate them; she distanced herself more and more from the Cayuses.

The death of Alice Clarissa was a turning point for the Indians, too. They had hoped the white missionaries brought eternal life and supernatural powers. So why did their cherished daughter die so easily—just like a Cayuse child? Were they really that powerful? Just when the Indians were seeing proof that the missionaries were simply ordinary people, another newcomer to the region fanned the sparks of their discontent.

Just days after the girl's burial, word came to Waiilatpu that the Hudson's Bay express had arrived at Fort Walla Walla. Twice a year the express passed through the country, carrying supplies and mail from Fort Vancouver upriver into New Caledonia, for the trek to Montreal. Marcus Whitman and Henry Spalding hurried to the fort, eager to see what mail and freight might be waiting for them. They were surprised to meet two of the Company's top executives accompanied by a Catholic priest—Father Demere—who was on his way to Fort Colville where he intended to set to work.

Asa Smith wrote about it to the Board, "At this very moment the Catholic priest is at Walla Walla instructing the people & the Indians are gathering together there to listen to the false doctrines which he inculcates. Already has the priest denounced us because we have wives & the people told that they are going to hell because they are unbaptised."[2]

In the mid-nineteenth century, Americans feared European threats and worried about infiltration and subversion. Leaders warned of a worldwide conspiracy against American liberties that intended to alter the population (and the voting patterns) of the U.S. The Jesuits, a "mysterious" foreign Catholic order of missionaries were thought to be zealously infiltrating the continent bent on bringing hordes of pauper immigrants who were responsible for violence, filling the prisons and workhouses and quadrupling the taxation. Worst of all, these Catholic hordes would go to the polls (the males at least) "to lay their inexperienced hand upon the helm of our power," exercising their right to vote.[3] Catholic voters were thought to favor "authoritarianism" in government and might in fact one day allow the "potentates of Europe" to gain control of the U.S.

Fighting the spread of Catholicism in the Indian country was imperative, lest the wild Indians be seduced by "demonic foreign powers" who would enlist them to "devastate the country." It was a seductive fear, spread through a population that had recently elected Andrew Jackson, and his feisty brand of "common man" philosophy.

Not just Protestant missionaries felt that way; the Secretary of War, John Calhoun, and fur trade leaders like Jedediah Smith and William Sublette echoed the sentiments, as well as a growing public who hid behind the Know Nothing party's shield.

Weapons of choice in the "war on Popery" were free public schools, the Bible (and the literacy to read it), religious tracts, colleges and universities, and a free press for the discussion of all issues.

That's why the arrival of Catholic priests alarmed the Protestant missionaries and prompted them to set to work learning the Indian languages as quickly as they could. "Had we now a translation of some portion of the bible to put into the hands of the people we might hope to check the progress of error. But without this our efforts will be feeble," Asa Smith worried.[4]

Asa and his wife, Sarah, had gone to live with a band of Nez Perces farther up the Clearwater River from Lapwai. Near what is now Kamiah, Idaho, they settled close to the spot where Lewis and Clark's starving expedition was rescued by Nez Perces about thirty-five years earlier.

Asa was a linguist and scholar, and consequently had never developed skills that were essential to survival in the wilderness. He referred to Marcus Whitman and Henry Spalding as acting like "western men," a derogatory referral to the way they threw themselves into hard labor, rather than being intellectuals. He had nearly as much medical training in college as Marcus Whitman, but didn't practice it. Asa was bright, he was an educated, ordained minister; but he was an obnoxious bore and none of the other missionaries got along with him. He struggled from abject poverty to receive his education, accolades and respect, but he found the reality of being a missionary a far cry from the success he expected.

Sarah was the youngest of the missionary wives and the only one who didn't bear children. Attractive and appealing, when Mary Walker met Sarah she described her as, ". . . a little dear."5 Sarah had plannned to locate as a missionary wife in Siam, to be near her sister, who was already married to a missionary stationed there by the ABCFM. When the western mission opportunity presented itself, she and Asa considered it, and under extreme pressure to decide immediately, accepted William Gray's invitation to go back to the Oregon country with him as reinforcements. It was a decision they regretted almost immediately. By the time they reached rendezvous during the overland trip, Sarah was so despondent she, "seemed to cry half the time."6 There wasn't anything she could do about her fate—there was no going back.

At Waiilatpu, Sarah and Asa had difficulty getting along with the Whitmans. After the arrival of the reinforcement of 1838, the Grays and Spaldings were stationed at Lapwai, the Walkers and Eells waited to go to Tshimikain, and the Smiths were assigned to work with the Whitmans at Waiilatpu.

But before the Walkers and Eells left for their station, Asa determined he couldn't work with Whitman. He told the others if he was forced to work with Whitman, he'd leave the mission completely. Negotiating went on, several different sites were discussed, the brethren even voted to locate Whitman at a different location, one more central to all of their extended locations. His position was mission doctor and in order to fulfill his responsibilities to treat the mission families he needed to be centrally located. That didn't go over well with Marcus or Narcissa. They had located first, had situated themselves on prime land for farming and couldn't be forced to move. Asa had hired the Nez Perce chief, Lawyer, to teach him the Nez Perce language, and was making progress in writing a lexicon of the language. Lawyer evidently realized there was dissension among the missionaries and urged Smith to locate farther north among his Nez Perce relatives, in the heart of the Nez Perce territory.

Asa and Sarah moved up the Clearwater River to the base of the Bitterroot Mountains. They lived in an extremely rough cabin, intending to camp there only for the summer. Sarah wrote to Mary Walker that the cabin was situated in a pleasant little pine grove, and she described it as having "three rooms: kitchen, buttery and bedroom" and added that it had only taken a week to build.[7]

When Henry Spalding saw the cabin he thought it entirely too primitive. It had no floors or windows, and was without any comforts. Sarah had been raised in a deacon's household in Massachusetts—she knew nothing about surviving in the wilds. Asa, the scholar, was out of his sphere, too. They took a milk cow with them, and survived on "pudding & milk," which even Henry Spalding thought was "quite too simple."[8]

In November, they decided to stay through the winter at Kamiah, and some of the brethren came up to help build a better cabin. Sarah proudly drew a floor plan of the larger, more civilized building—her "new" house—and sent it to Mary Walker. It was about fourteen by twenty-eight feet; and had two small windows; one in the kitchen, and one in the bedroom. It was a decided improvement over the "mere shed," they'd been in for nearly seven months.

While at Kamiah, Sarah became very ill; at least that's how Asa described it in letters to the Board. In separate letters he referred to her "affection of the liver," a "spinal affection," and her inability to endure it any longer. "The hardships and exposures she has passed through have been too great for her constitution to bear up under."[9] It was not a pleasant time for Sarah. The Nez Perces called her "The Weeping One." She had been treated for some time with "mercurial remedies."[10] Asa also "put a blister" on Sarah's spine from time to time.

Sarah wrote to Mary Walker and Myra Eells telling them, "O I want to see you more than words can express."[11] Mary sent her pieces of ribbon in letters, which Sarah was grateful for, but felt obligated to send some tiny gift in return, although she had absolutely nothing to give. "I think you are getting me quite in debt. But I am waiting for my ship to come in when I shall remember it." What else could she do?

Even though she was living in such dire straits, she noted that there was another woman who desperately needed their help. Two couples had arrived from the States, planning to work as "independent" missionaries. Reverend and Desire Griffin, and Mr. and Mrs. Munger (he to be a mechanic, or skilled laborer). They'd been denied assistance from the ABCFM, and had no connections or support. Why they came, unless it was purely missionary zeal, was not known.

This put the missionaries in a quandary. They were delighted to have more hands to help with the work, but how were they to proceed without irritating the American Board? They hesitated to accept the new arrivals as their own, yet they couldn't send them elsewhere or ignore them. There was nothing to do but put them to work.

Henry Spalding hired Griffin to work at Lapwai, and the couple settled there. But Sarah Smith saw the dilemma that Desire Griffin faced: the woman had no lodging, no supplies, and was thousands of miles from home with no going back. Sarah must have sympathized with her situation, feeling she was in a similar fix.

In a letter she addressed to both Myra and Mary, she asked "What is best for us to do about giving to Mrs. Griffin?" The new arrival had nothing. Sarah wanted to give whatever they could to the newcomers. Her husband felt differently. "They have come in opposition to the Board & ought not to be assisted," was Asa's opinion. But poor Desire had come "without a sheet or pillowcase" and where else would they get anything if the other missionaries didn't give it?

Eliza Spalding had given them three broken plates and enough wide striped cotton to make a pair of sheets, Sarah informed the others. Sarah confided that if Asa agreed to it she would give Desire whatever she could. She pointed out that the woman had arrived with "plenty of clothing probably more dresses than I shall have after mine get here." The Smiths had shipped belongings by sea, and were still waiting for them to arrive.

Oddly, the newcomer, Desire Griffin, had brought a large and elaborate wardrobe, but absolutely no household equip-

Desire C. Griffin

Reverend J.S. Griffin

ment or supplies. "She has two pretty silk dresses, several muslin & fine calico, & two or three pieces unmade. She has more neck dresses [a sort of collar] than she will ever need & all *very pretty.*" It seemed like the two independent missionary couples were not independent at all. They had come with no clear idea of what they would do or where they would go. They immediately became dependent on the Oregon ABCFM missionaries for survival.

Sarah Smith was trying to do the best she could, putting a curtain up around her rough bedstead and trying to sew a rag carpet for the "little parlor." Asa grew furious at the idea of her doing such a menial task, threatening that he would burn the carpet—that it "was selling his wife too cheap to exchange her for a carpet."[12]

So Sarah turned to making new clothes for herself. Not that it mattered what she wore at the isolated camp. She described to Mary the "good black bombazine dress" she had made to wear that winter, and a cape lined with flannel to go with it, "so I shall be warm."[13] She was like many frontierswomen who equated style and fashion with civilization and fought to maintain standards of style in dress, no matter what.

Sarah's sweet personality and earnest pursuit of feminine friendship was displayed on the outside of the letter. Letters were folded several times, then sealed with sealing wax, envelopes were not commonly used at that time. She knew Tshimikain was getting a shipment of letters and supplies from the States at the same time, so she marked on the letter, "Not to be read for a month," and the date. Inside the letter she'd told Mary she'd done that so it wouldn't be opened until "you have seen & read everything else & begin to want something more. Then perhaps you can bestow a thought on your sister here in the wilderness all alone."[14]

Sarah had more to worry about than loneliness; the winter after they moved into the little cedar house, the milk cow ate a poisonous weed and died. The loss to them was "beyond calculation."[15] The Lord had given; the Lord had taken away. But nothing they faced would be as difficult as what Christ had endured, so they stuck it out.

To make things more difficult, the Nez Perces were beginning to make them uncomfortable. Asa described them as "increasingly selfish and depraved;" they only wanted missionaries to live with them in hopes of gaining some "temporal benefit."[16]

It was disturbing and unnerving for the Smiths, particularly Asa, as they discovered the Indians weren't so easily turned into Christians. They'd both read about the Rocky Mountain mission effort in publications before they decided to join it. The articles had been optimistic and stressed the importance of the mission and what success it was about to have.

Now, on the ground, they saw their expectations had been "raised to the very highest pitch," only to be disapppointed. Asa's dreams had fallen far short. He felt it was because of the highly optimistic stories, which he blamed on Henry Spalding (who had written them) and the American Board (who didn't dissuade such "vivid imagination").

Asa wrote to the Board that the Nez Perces were "self-righteous," and "consider themselves already good." They had "left off their old practices of lying, stealing, &c, & are now worshipping God & giving heed to his word"—but that wasn't enough. They weren't reborn, yet, and refused to go farther. Asa was stymied.[17]

As if to bolster his point that the mission effort was becoming useless, he pointed out that he'd counted the Indians, and there were far fewer than they had first believed. After an extensive and laborious job of taking a census with headmen using sticks to represent each person, Asa determined there were no more than 3,000 Nez Perces and Cayuses, combined. He made the point that the mission might better serve the hordes of Asia (perhaps Siam?) more efficiently. There were so few Indians, so scattered, and besides they were already a "dying race"—were they wasting their efforts on them?

He maintained that the Nez Perce numbers were dwindling due to disease (small pox in 1770 and again 1806) and war with the Blackfoot and Snake nations. He noticed that very few men were left; the villages were largely female. Using the figures Smith provided, men made up an average of less than twenty-percent of the tribe.[18] A man of narrow vision, Asa didn't realize that many of the women were slaves, and blatantly ignored the fact that female souls should be saved as well as males. To Asa, saving females was just not as important.

He described the "horrible degradation of the females." Adultery, polygamy and a high incidence of abortion made their lives miserable, he noted. There were few small children; he estimated that at least half the infants died. Deaths had outnumbered births since he'd come to Kamiah. Did the Board intend to leave him there, stranded, with a people who were to be extinct almost immediately?

Asa was miserable and doubting the value of his efforts, but he realized something important about their socio-political system: "this people have no form of government, & no law among them. . . . There are indeed those among them who are called chiefs. But these have no power. Their law is mere advice. The people regard them or not as they please. To be chief amounts merely to nothing."[19]

Asa was thorough, reminding the Board that they'd spent $17,000 on the mission up to that point (winter of 1840). Were they wasting money? He admitted, ". . . it is the work of years. People at home who have no experience cannot realize it."

Asa's letter was brutally clear, poignantly begging to be released and stationed elsewhere. Because of the difficult overland and ocean mails, the Board received it a year after it was written.

Settling at Kamiah, in the heart of the Nez Perce nation, Asa and Sarah Smith had put themselves in the most isolated and tenuous situation of all the American Board missionaries. They had gone to such a remote location that no travelers ever passed by. The Kanaka hired man deserted them after a few months because he was so lonely. Even the Nez Perces were absent for periods of up to six months at a time, off to hunt buffalo on the Plateau or in the Bitterroot Mountains gathering berries and roots.

The Smiths had no chance to do any missionary work, and were barely able to subsist; the Nez Perces forbid tilling the soil. They planted a small garden for their own subsistence, but it failed. Sarah's health grew worse. Her "spinal affliction" may have been something she had earlier, in New England, which had made her family quite concerned about whether she could make the overland trip. Even if she had been in perfect health, the overland ride by horseback would have been injurious to her spine, and the destitute living circumstances along with overwhelming depression, nearly killed her.

Sarah became so bedridden that Asa had to take over all the household tasks. He wrote to the Board that he had little time to do any missionary work, as he was doing the laundry and cooking. He grumbled that they had gone all summer without "ironing their clothing." A serious step down, the pair were living like animals in depressing isolation from the rest of the Mission. Asa took out his anger in long letters of complaint to the Board. Sarah stayed in bed and cried. The Nez Perces became more and more impatient with the pair. They wanted the missionaries to replace the declining fur trade. They expected, "to make the stations their trading posts," and the Smiths had no intention of establishing trade, nor an adequate supply of any sort of goods.[20]

Besides, Asa had grown so angry about their situation that he began to resent the Indians. He wrote the Board that the Indians shouldn't be provided with a grain mill, as "I think they had better pound all the grain they have as they pound their roots, untill they shall learn to *appreciate* the favors that are bestowed on them."[21]

Asa's anger towards the Indians focused on the Spaldings and their work with the Nez Perces at Clear Water. He accused them of allowing Indians to join the church when they weren't sufficiently prepared. He told the Board that the Spaldings had a "great desire" to get natives into the church, and if he and the reinforcement hadn't arrived in 1838, "probably there would before this have been a large number [of Indians] counted as members of the church of Christ."[22]

Dissension built between the brethren of the mission; Asa Smith's letters to the Board described in minute detail the bickering and petty arguments and posturing between the missionaries. Disagreement was largely over how to best work with the Indians. Several felt that the Spaldings were moving too far, too fast, in settling the Nez Perces. Seeing little progress around them, several of the brethren proposed selling out the mission to the Methodists, who were settling the Willamette, and had a mission station at The Dalles. The Methodists had more people (hundreds were arriving by ship) and more money (over a hundred thousand dollars from the president's "secret service fund"), and were proceeding to colonize the country for the United States.

Notes on Chapter Fourteen

[1]Jeffrey, *Converting the West*, p. 145.

[2] Drury, *Spalding and Smith on the Nez Perce Mission* (Glendale, CA: Arthur H. Clark Company, 1958), p. 110.

[3] Miller, *Prophetic Worlds*, p. 69.

[4] Drury, *Spalding and Smith*, p. 110.

[5] Drury, *First White Women*, p. 274.

[6] Ibid, p. 275.

[7] Ibid, p. 276.

[8] Ibid.

[9] Ibid, p. 277.

[10] Drury, *Spalding and Smith*, p. 112.

[11] Ibid, p. 117.

[12] Ibid, p. 118.

[13] Ibid.

[14] Ibid.

[15] Drury, *Spalding and Smith*, p. 125.

[16] Ibid.

[17] Ibid, p. 134.

[18] Ibid, p. 137.

[19] Ibid, p. 139.

[20] Ibid, p. 151.

[21] Ibid, p. 154.

[22] Ibid, p. 158.

Chapter Fifteen

Slavery

The Nez Perces and Cayuses recognized that the mission was faltering, the financial support from Boston was now nonexistent; the only trade goods arriving were barrels of old clothes donated by penny-pinching Yankee church women.

What the natives had hoped for had not come about. They desired a trade network to replace the dwindling fur trade, and expected the Americans—the missionaries—to set up a network of trading posts.

Instead of bringing a wide assortment of goods that the Indians could barter for, the Americans only brought dissension and bickering, and the Indians were often included in it. The arrival of Catholic priests added to the mix, because both faiths taught diametrically opposite views on many religious issues; the natives were continually told by the one faith that the other was wrong. Who could they believe?

The Jesuits didn't participate in the fur trade either, but they traded guns and ammunition to the natives figuring that to arm them for the hunt or against their tribal enemies would help provide stability while they concentrated on saving their souls.

The "pathetic" Indians Narcissa and Eliza had seen as they traveled down the Columbia River to Fort Vancouver had appalled them and made them thankful they would be working with the people from the mountains—the Cayuses and Nez Perces—who were noble horseback tribes.

What the women didn't realize was that many of the people they observed were slaves. The Chinook, the populous people that had run the river trade from the mouth of the Columbia since early Spanish ships plied the inlets of the Northwest Coast, were expert traders before the white men's ships arrived. They'd dealt with trading tribes from the vast regions to the north, south and east.

Astute Chinooks levied duties on all goods that passed through their land, everything going from points in California to Alaska. Their culture was based on barter: lesser tribes caught fish and traded it to the Chinook, who saw such work as beneath them; they traded dentalium shell "money," slaves, and later guns and European trade goods, to all the tribes who needed to pass through them to obtain access to the white traders.

The Pacific Northwest was an area heavily invested in the traffic of human chattel. For generations before the coming of the white men, the river had served as a conduit for captured slaves. In fact, the Columbia River was called the "River of Slaves" or "Slave's River" by prehistoric people in the area.[1]

The lives of slaves were tenuous because they weren't valued for their labor, only for prestige. They could be killed on a whim, or to impress another. They were forced to kill for their masters, and were made to taste all foods first (to identify poison) and to forge ahead when traveling, in case of attack. Some tribes marked slaves by putting out one eye; nearly all kept their slaves' hair shorn; and a dead slave's body was abandoned without burial. No freeman would touch a slave's dead body—it was left for the carrion.

On the Plateau, the climate and topography made slaves less important. People living inland, like the Cayuses and Nez Perces, needed to travel to obtain their seasonal food supply but travel was difficult with slaves; a village on the move had trouble capturing, controlling and maintaining a slave population. Providing subsistence and keeping control of slaves was as much a hindrance to their masters as their additional food gathering labor was a help. Inland tribes didn't lend themselves to such an aristocracy based on trade profits. The few captives they kept were humiliated and persecuted, but in time they were socially integrated with their captors, many marrying into their masters' families, their children being accepted as members of the tribe.

When white traders arrived on the coast, the price and demand for slaves shot up. With a wide array of trade goods available in exchange for furs, the Chinooks who controlled the trade with the Europeans responded by trading slaves for furs, which they could trade to the white men. As the demand for furs shot up, so did the price of captives. Inland tribes, who had relied on horses as trade chattel, now needed something that the Chinooks would trade for. The Chinooks didn't want horses—useless animals to people who based their economy on the rivers and waterways. But Chinook traders could barter slaves to the tribes in the far north, the Tlinget and Haida, who fueled their voracious desire for captives by making slave raids on adjoining villages. As the demand grew, the Cayuses began supplying more and more slaves for the coastal markets.[2]

The arrival of the horse on the Plateau in the mid-18th century accelerated the slave trade, too. On horseback, people could move swiftly, strike and ride off with captives before the foe recovered and retaliated; captives on foot couldn't escape their masters who were on horseback. Among the greatest equestrians in history, the Nez Perces and Cayuses had a special acumen for horses. Plunder and revenge was easier on horseback. Tribal boundaries changed, aggressive peoples expanded their territories, those less able to challenge them became subservient. Sedentary people like the Walla Wallas were intimidated and forced to perform menial tasks for their Cayuse captors.

The Cayuses, fierce horsemen adept at using whips, knives and guns, dominated the Plateau tribes. A few powerful Cayuse families owned huge herds of horses, slaves, and even surrounding hunting lands; none could or would challenge them.

Even Cayuse women were brutal—fur trader Alexander Ross tried to establish a trade fort near the confluence of the Columbia and Walla Walla Rivers in 1818. He wrote that the Cayuse women's torture of slave captives was "heinous." The men gave fresh captives to the village women, who, "armed with the instruments of torture, keep all the time jeering them with the most distorted grimaces, cutting them with knives, piercing them with awls, pulling them by the hair and thumping them with fist, stick or stone, in every possible way that can torment without killing them." He watched in horror, as the "loss of an ear, a tooth, the joint of a finger or part of the scalp torn off during these frantic fits are nightly occurrances."[3] Fort Nez Perce, his facility, never did work out, the natives there thought fur trapping and preparation was work for slaves, and refused to do it.

The Northwest slave trade was centered on one spot: The Dalles. Situated on the Columbia River where the water's natural flow was interrupted by a rugged section of boulders and falls, anyone traveling the river was forced to stop and portage past the dangerous terrain. At that spot, trade goods could be "taxed" by the Indians who hired themselves to do the portaging.

Numerous travelers' accounts describe the prostitution and gambling that went on at The Dalles. Slave women were routinely put out to prostitution to earn profits for their owners. Male slaves were hired to portage fur company boats and belongings up and down the rugged cliffs. Similar to castles on the rivers of Europe, camps were established to profit from the flow of goods and peoples on the Columbia River.

The Nez Perces and Cayuses, imperial horsemen, had augmented their income by raiding tribes farther downriver, and bringing captives up to The Dalles for sale. They'd gone as far as the Willamette Valley with their slave raids. That explains the Nez Perces' fear of going farther south than The Dalles with Lewis and Clark. Traveling with the Expedition, they were not in a war party and were highly susceptible to rataliatory raids by those villages they'd plundered for captives in the past.[4]

The trading season at The Dalles lasted from August through October, coinciding with the salmon runs. As emigrants began to pass through from the United States into the Willamette Valley, the Indians began to trade directly with the whites for clothing and goods. As the travelers passing through increasingly became families rather than single fur trappers, they were not interested in bartering for prostitutes, so the Indians traded horses, canoes, and salmon, and acted as guides for the travelers.

The Indians wanted cloth garments for their own use, and as a medium of exchange in trade as well. A good man's or woman's cloth outfit could purchase a slave, which could be taken elsewhere and bartered for up to five horses.[5] The common fee for river laborers was a shirt, and the Indians became incensed when tight-fisted emigrants tried to pawn off worn-out garments.

How many natives were enslaved? Estimates run as high as a quarter of the population, during contact times. Pre-contact numbers are impossible to estimate. Why didn't they escape? Usually the stigma attached to slavery was so heavy that a returned villager who had served as a slave would be treated as such even after he'd escaped. "Once a slave, always a slave," was the common belief.

And, if a slave did attempt to escape, she (most slaves were women) was faced with nearly insurmountable hurdles in language and terrain in order to return to her people. Since slaves were taken far from their homes and traded off to even further distant people, a Shastan slave from northern California could easily be stuck in a southern Alaska village. With no knowledge of geography, and a variety of unknown languages surrounding them, there was little hope of ever going home again.

The coming of the fur trade companies did not end the slave trade, rather it accelerated it. Employees of the Hudson's Bay Company were allowed to buy slaves and employ them for their own family's use. They cut wood, hunted and fished for the families of the men who spent their time working for the Company. Men hired to go on trapping parties took their slaves along— each man taking two or three of his own—to do the hunting and caring for horses and camp. The use of slave labor cut the Company's expenses for labor by about half.

The Company didn't acknowledge the use of slave labor for its own purposes, but did try to end the Indians' practice of buying and selling slaves because of the effect it had on fur trade practices. When the HBC traders tried to raise fur prices, the Indians quit trading furs with the Company, instead taking their fur harvest to the slavers and bargaining for additional slaves rather than trade goods.[6] That affected the Company's year-end profits.

Slavery had been abolished in Great Britain in 1833; but not the U.S., where it had been in practice for two hundred years. Did the Oregon missionaries even consider Indian slavery an issue—moral, religious, or spiritual? Reverend Samuel Parker noticed the Walla Wallas, who he was told were freed slaves of the Nez Perces. Elkanah Walker mentioned in 1841 that the Spokanes held only one "genuine" slave in their midst.[7] In 1836, the year the Spaldings and Whitmans arrived in the Oregon country, a female slave was priced at between eight and fifteen trade blankets.

While the missionaries seemed to ignore or not even realize the slave-based economy that swirled around them, their actions affected the slave-vs-master relationship immensely. The practice of gathering all the people together for mass teaching and preaching was highly abrasive to the aristocracy of the Cayuses and Nez Perces. Because the Spaldings practiced a type of teaching where head chiefs were taught a Bible story or prayer, and were then sent to small groups to teach, they were able to maintain a social order that was important to the Nez Perce ruling class.

The Whitmans and the Smiths, however, persisted in trying to teach everyone at a mass session. This was shocking and irritating to the slave owners, who might be taught the same lesson, side by side, with their human chattel. No doubt some slaves learned hymns or passages as quickly or quicker than their masters. Not teaching the chiefs or aristocracy first, was highly upsetting to the social order by which the Cayuses measured themselves.

As time progressed, the Indians grew more and more angry. What deference was paid to an upper caste aristocrat who owned a thousand horses and dozens of slaves, if he was expected to stand and sing a hymn along with slaves, who were considered to be less than dogs? The upper class would have tried to keep the slaves from attending worship sessions with the missionaries, and would have used them to do the physical labor the missionaries were expecting to teach to the Indian men. When a field was broken and plowed, or a log building erected, slaves were directed to do it. The missionaries didn't mention the difference, only that the men of the village seemed haughty and could never be made to do honest work.

The missionaries adopted abandoned slave children, taking them into their houses as their own. Narcissa took in a little boy who had been badly abused, directly related to his slave position. Part "Spanish" the boy had probably been taken in a slave raid farther south, having passed into hands of northern tribes from the Santa Fe trade.

At first, the missionary women seemed to fit into the natives' world. Narcissa hired Indian women to do domestic work, employing Walla Wallas since the "Kayuse ladies are too proud to be seen usefully employed." The fact that she hired Walla Wallas confirmed more deeply to the Cayuses that anyone who cooperated or worked for the missionaries was acting as a menial servant.[8]

Why didn't anyone mention this slave economy? Was it too controversial, too sensitive an issue back in the East? Possibly the missionaries simply failed to clearly distinguish slave women from free women. Seeing the lives of all Indian women as degraded, they didn't notice the finer divisions within female Indian society. Since slaves mingled freely with freemen among the Nez Perces, it was difficult to tell who owned whom.

By winter, 1840, Asa and Sarah Smith were desperate for another location. While they waited for a response to their request for another appointment to Ceylon or Lahaina, Asa wrote to the Walkers that, "I expect that we shall remain through the winter, but fear we may see much difficulty." Sarah was getting worse, "Mrs. S. being feeble is seriously affected by these things . . ." It was a time for prayer, ". . . we are in the hand of savages & what they will do with us, we know not . . ."[9]

Surrounded by disappointed Indians who were growing angrier every season, and relegated to struggling for their own survival, the bickering missionaries were on the edge of disaster. They realized that their mission hopes would not be fulfilled.

To make the failure more distasteful, Father Pierre Jean De Smet had begun settling Jesuits from Europe in Indian missions on the west side of the Rocky Mountains. Up in the Flathead country, priests were baptizing "a great many children" and the priests were passing out "the image of the cross or other emblems of Popery." Asa's Nez Perce teacher, Lawyer, reported meeting the priests in the Flathead country, where the Jesuits had "tried to get the cross on him."[10] Would the Indians fall prey to Catholicism?

But the Smiths wouldn't spend another winter in their cabin at Kamiah. The men who "pretend to own this soil"—the Nez Perces—came to Asa and Sarah's house and demanded that they pay for the land under it. The Indians used "the most abusive language" and ordered them to "leave the place on the next day."[11]

No doubt Sarah was ready to flee in a minute, but Asa was not so easily moved. "After hearing their abuse for a time I began to think it was time to begin to think about moving . . ." and he told them he'd leave as soon as he had his belongings packed. They had a sleepless night, "Mrs. S. in great fear & is nearly sick in consequence of it." The hired man, Jack, slept in the house with them, "sharpening his knife" and ready with it at his side in case of an attack.

At about the same time, the Spaldings were having difficulty with some of the Nez Perces at Lapwai; threats and anger pervaded both Indian and white households.

The Nez Perces were embroiled in a bitter fight for tribal leadership, with different factions either attacking or embracing the Americans. Political divisiveness was natural in tribal social systems, the Americans added to or accelerated the problems. Perhaps the unsuspecting missionaries became a focus for Indian anger because they were virtually helpless and easily sharpened the division of tribal affiliations.

Asa and Sarah, terrified and alienated from both the Indians and the other missionaries (because of Asa's continual fighting with the other brethren), stayed on. They didn't leave Kamiah until April. The probable reason is that they had no funds of any kind. Without trade goods, or any supplies, they were paupers dependent upon the goodwill of the Indians. They had nothing to barter for assistance in moving their possessions downriver to Lapwai.

And, once they got to Lapwai, what then? They would be chastised by the other missionaries for "giving up", for leaving the post the Lord had called them to. If they could handle that humiliation, then what? Go to Fort Vancouver? How? And why? Until the Board contacted them with another posting, and paid their passage by ship to that next mission station, they were strangers in a strange land, with nowhere to go. So they spent the winter, huddled together in fear and anger, waiting for a letter that never came.

The difficulty of getting mail to Boston and back heightened all the mission's problems. It took seven months, quickest, to get the mail to Boston overland, up through Montreal. It took about fourteen months to go by sea. That was one-way, double the time allowed to get a reply. Asa had been in the Indian mission for two years before he ever received a letter from the American Board secretary in Boston.

So the Smiths waited, relieved when the Indian troublemakers left the area and went to The Dalles for the winter. Henry Spalding sent another newly-arrived "independent" missionary couple, Reverend Clark and his wife, up to stay with the Smiths. All was peaceful, sort of. For Sarah, that winter was hell. Asa wrote the Board that the situation was "extremely unfavorable" to her health. She was lonely, and "being feeble & able to do but little, her mind is left to prey upon itself, her spirits sink, & she often feels that our lonely situation is more than she is able to endure."[12] Her spinal problem was also getting worse. Sarah spent most all her time in bed, barely able to sit up for months.

The only solution was to head downriver to Fort Vancouver, and out of the mission completely. Asa managed to get a large canoe built so that Sarah could ride comfortably. Their possessions were packed on horses and sent to Waiilatpu. In order to portage around rough waters, Sarah was carried, "on a hammock suspended on a pole & carried on the shoulders of two men."

Once they got to Fort Vancouver they were able to obtain medical attention for Sarah from Dr. Barclay, the HBC doctor there. Undoubtedly, Asa didn't think much of Dr. Whitman's medical abilities, as he wrote the Board that Dr. Barclay at Fort Vancouver was a "Physician of thorough education" of which the Smiths had "formed a high opinion."[13]

The Smiths embarked for the Hawaiian Islands on an American ship which left Vancouver in mid-summer, but after going downriver to Astoria, the ship was sold, and they had to go ashore and wait for another opportunity to leave Oregon. They finally got to Hawaii at the end of January.

The Sandwich Islands mission was a delightful change for the Smiths. The climate was much better than along the Clearwater River, and they were welcomed with open arms. Mission workers were needed in Hawaii, and there wasn't the bickering and lack of direction Smith had bristled over within the Oregon mission. Most of all, the natives were very different from the Cayuses and Nez Perces.

Asa noticed his wife's health showed a "definite improvement" within weeks of arriving in the islands. The Smiths had found their calling; they were assigned to the station at Waialua on the island of Oahu where they worked as missionaries for the next three years.[14]

In 1843 they adopted three girls whose missionary parents had died at the Sandwich Islands mission. In 1845 the Smiths and daughters set out on a return trip to New England, which took them to the new and booming city of Hongkong, then to Capetown, and finally to Boston. Asa became a pastor in Massachusetts; Sarah, frail from her years in Oregon and the subsequent around the globe trip by ship, died from "consumption" at the age of forty-one. The following year, Asa married a second wife twelve years his junior.

Notes on Chapter Fifteen

[1] Robert H. Ruby and John A. Brown, *Indian Slavery in the Pacific Northwest* (Spokane, WA: Arthur H. Clark Company, 1993), p. 60.

[2] Ibid, p. 223.

[3] Ibid, p. 238.

[4] Ibid, p. 235.

[5] Ibid, p. 283.

[6] Ibid, p. 140.

[7] Ibid, p. 246.

[8] Ibid, p. 239.

[9] Drury, *Spalding and Smith*, p. 193.

[10] Ibid, p. 193.

[11] Ibid, p. 194.

[12] Ibid, p. 205.

[13] Ibid, p. 215.

[14] Ibid, p. 216.

Chapter Sixteen

Strange Journey

According to the Indian story of the ash fall, the people were very much frightened at the terrible uproar as they supposed the world was coming to an end. But the chief's uncle dreamed that it wasn't thunder, but the rolling of the heavens.

Mary Walker writing on the Spokane Indian legend of "Time of the Great Thundering."

The Indians believed the Great Thundering was a sign that before the world ended, a people of a different color, wearing strange clothing, speaking another language would come with books. These strangers would teach them and then the world would be destroyed.[1]

The Indians thought the fur company voyageurs were the promised people. But it was not so. Mary felt this explained the natives' extreme interest in books and papers, especially those with images on them. Post traders had given out pieces of paper which the natives worshipped, paying homage and offerings to whoever owned the paper.

"It has been said if we had come here first we should have received a great amount of presents from them," Mary noted.[2]

There were still remnants in the region of the volcanic ash fall from an eruption of Mt. St. Helens between 1770-1800. The "dry snow" and its six-inch depth, mystified the Indians, who had danced and prayed to it, asking for an explanation.

Early travelers, particularly Lewis and Clark (who kept extensive journals) and David Thompson, who came down the Columbia River from Canada (and kept voluminous written records as well), were greeted with reverence and awe. The fact that these men spent their spare time writing in journals, graphing astral observations, and drawing maps, gave natives the impression that they were perhaps the prophesied saviors. They greeted them with reverence and awe—were these the Gods who would bring the end of their uncertain world and the dawn of a new one? When the missionaries (and their books and papers) arrived, the suspicion, or hope, may have surfaced again.

Eliza Spalding was teaching in her schoolroom one morning when several "painted" and nearly-naked Indian youths began taunting her from the open doorway. She told them to leave, then hung a blanket over the doorway when they refused. They persisted, showering her and the students with insults and threats.

Henry Spalding was drawing fire from one band of the Nez Perce led by a white "mountain man," William Craig, whose wife was the daughter of a headman. (Myra had helped her make a dress at the rendezvous, years before.) Craig stirred up the natives against the mission, telling the Indians that the Spaldings should give the Nez Perces more goods, more food, and build houses for them. He stressed what an insult it was for the Spaldings to expect the Nez Perces to build their own houses. He obviously understood the social hierarchy, and the wealthier Nez Perces began to listen to him. He told the Indians that they must run the Spaldings off, and that he should take over the buildings, and then the tribe would be given whatever they wanted.

Henry and Eliza were helpless in the growing controversy. Not all the Nez Perces turned against them. But the rivalry between various bands escalated. The Spaldings turned to fasting and prayers; unable to accept the harm William Craig meant to do them. He was from the same background as themselves. "How is it possible for a man born of Christian parents (his parents were members of the Presbyterian church) to be guilty of such deeds of darkness?" they wondered.

It was an "awful state of things" and all they could do was visit Craig, and "converse on the subject of religion . . . & pray with him, leave a testament, a sermon & tract."[3] When Craig and another mountain man left the area to go to the Willamette Valley, the Spaldings breathed a sigh of relief. They hoped to see "peaceful times soon."

At Tshimikain, the Eells family (Myra and Cushing had two young sons now) lost everything when their house burned to the ground. Doubling up with the Walkers, the two families worried about what had caused the fire. One of the chief factors at a Hudson's Bay Company fort was murdered by Indians.

It was a dark time. Trouble was all around: Mr. Munger, one of the independent missionaries who had arrived a few years past, had become insane. News came from the Willamette Valley that he had "attempted to nail himself to wood-work above his fire," evidently trying to crucify himself above the fireplace. He had "fastened one hand, probably fainted, fell on one side into the fire & so burnt that he lived but 4 days."[4] The Americans in Oregon had realized Munger was going increasingly insane, but had no way to return him and his wife to the East. There were no more fur trade caravans across the Rocky Mountains; the fur trade had ended, and so had the annual mountain rendezvous. Without money for ship fare to Boston, the missionaries were stranded in Oregon.

Eliza Spalding began to hemorrhage severely following a miscarriage, and Henry sent for Dr. Whitman. But the doctor had been having his own bouts with poor health. Many times he refused to make medical visits to the mission families because of his own fragile condition. He usually sent calomel medicine, with written instructions for dosages. When Spalding sent for Whitman this time, he got a "letter not very kind" relating to "Mrs. S's state of health."[5]

Henry and the Nez Perces doctored Eliza, and after days of being bedridden with fever and loss of blood, she recovered. Within a month was able to go horseback riding with Henry, only to be "thrown most frightfully" but "little injured."[6]

The Spaldings' milk cow and calf were poisoned, and native children were caught stealing their corn. The final insult came from the Islands: two missionary couples bound for the Oregon mission had heard of the difficulties in Oregon and stayed in Hawaii rather than continue on as reinforcements for Oregon.

At Waiilatpu, the Whitmans were having "new trouble with the Indians." The Indians there had "endangered" Marcus's life and had broken down the door of the Whitman's house.[7] Fort Walla Walla was torched and burned.

While the natives had their own axes to grind, there was ample upheaval and distress rooted within the mission. The men and their wives turned against the Spaldings, blaming them for everything that had gone wrong. They complained that the Spaldings were too optimistic, too involved with the Indians, and had welcomed too many natives into the church. When Henry proposed baptism and membership in the Presbyterian Church of Oregon for several Nez Perces, and the Cayuse headman, Five Crows, Marcus Whitman promptly refused. The other men wrote letters of complaint to the Board in Boston, blaming Henry for many of the wrongs for some time.

Unable to comprehend why there was so much jealousy and bickering, the Spaldings attempted to apologize for whatever wrongs they had committed. Their only request was that the Indians be welcomed into the church. Again, they were refused. Whitman was visiting Lapwai when the difficulties erupted, and took away the Clear Water blacksmith tools and other items, promising to send replacements from Waiilatpu. They were never sent.

Of course the Indians, living and working so closely with the Americans, knew what was going on. This only caused greater divisions and squabbling within their villages, too. Add to that the presence of several more disenfranchised mountain men, all claiming the missionaries were shortchanging the Indians, and there was bound to be trouble.

Dismayed but undeterred, Henry and Eliza continued their projects, building a weaving loom and grist mill with the help of anyone who would still work with them.

Trying to push on with their purpose, the Spaldings worked harder. Eliza taught the school, even with her children underfoot. Little Eliza was now four and the baby, Henry Hart, two. Henry continued working closely with the Nez Perces, renewing his efforts to settle them. He soon had the grist mill operating and had built a water-powered sawmill. Eliza taught weaving and some fine woven cloth was being produced by native women on the loom.

William Craig, seeing the bickering and conflicts between the other missionaries and Spalding, must have sensed that the Spaldings meant to do good for the Nez Perces. He took the job as mission hired man for Henry, and they seemed to be getting along.

To add to the tense situation, Americans in Oregon country were told England had declared war on the United States. If that was true, what was their position? How would the Hudson's Bay Company react?

With autumn, 1842, came the annual mission meeting and the group faced a difficult directive from the Board. Orders had come from Boston: Henry and Eliza Spalding were to be recalled from the Mission. The others were to locate at Tshimikain, where some success with the Spokanes was felt evitable.

Even though the other men had written letters pointing out all Henry's shortcomings and blaming him for so many lost opportunities, when it came time for him to vacate the mission, the others realized their own successes paled in comparison to the Spaldings'. Reverend Asa Smith and his wife Sarah had left the Oregon mission in 1841; William Gray and his wife Mary, had left that very year. Their absence seemed to reduce the dissension. Perhaps the remaining missionaries could get along?

The Spaldings weren't given the exact reason for their censure. Defensive and misunderstood, Henry wrote to the Board that they had only received "one side of the question," and had not given him a chance to defend his actions. He apologized for trying to settle the Indians, but justified his efforts because "if the people cannot be collected & brought under regular preaching of the gospel, & into schools for several months in the year, there is but little hope for them."[8] From that point on, Henry wrote less frequently to the Board, and his letters were seldom reprinted in the *Missionary Herald.*

The remaining brethren decided to write letters to the Board petitioning to save the Clear Water Mission. Marcus Whitman proposed to take the letters East himself. The meeting ended, the men rushed home to compose their letters. But Marcus didn't wait. He hurriedly departed from Waiilatpu without even taking his comb and compass, and rushed off before Narcissa could ask him to obtain a pair of spectacles for her in the East.

It was nearly winter, and Marcus had no traveling party, only an American lawyer who had come to Oregon with a recent group of emigrants and wanted to go back. He had no supplies, no money, and left before he even received final advice from the other mission members. This hurried and frantic ride east was characterized for decades as Marcus Whitman's ride to save Oregon for the United States. Embroidering his efforts as based on patriotism in the face of a British threat, he has been eulogized as a western Paul Revere, riding to alert Congress to save the territory for the United States.

Why would someone like Whitman ride East in the manner he did? It was winter. The Rocky Mountains were impossible to cross. He headed south, through Mexican territory He nearly froze to death several times during hazardous river crossings and got lost in a blizzard. His face was so frostbitten he became disfigured.

One explanation for Whitman's rash act was his poor health. His long-time sickness in the side may have been related to syphilis. He'd been ill periodically, then had minor recoveries. Treating himself with mercury, he was able to hang on, but his behavior became more and more erratic. Like Munger in the Willamette Valley (who may have been syphilitic—insanity one symptom of the disease), Whitman attempted to do a grandiose deed that made no sense. Riding eastward, without supplies, escorts, extra horses, or even a compass, he headed into the winter like a madman.

When Whitman arrived in the East, people were shocked at his appearance—he was brutish looking, clothed in skins and furs, his face disfigured from frostbite, his manner nearly savage. When he showed up at the ABCFM office in Boston, they were furious with him and he was promptly chastized. Why had he left the mission without permission? Why did he look as he did? The Board insisted he clean up and put on decent clothing.

A larger question hangs on his personal life. Why did Marcus Whitman leave his wife alone at the isolated mission station of Waiilatpu when it was increasingly difficult to get along with the Indians? Why didn't he take her to nearby Fort Walla Walla, or down to the Methodist mission station in the Willamette Valley, or at the least, send her with an escort to stay with one of the other mission families, such as the Spaldings? It's incredibly difficult to understand that the man abandoned his wife and home and tore off on a cross-country trek with no real purpose. No mission letters, no supplies, and no cash. Did he really plan to return?

It hardly seems Whitman went to "save the mission" for he had not worked with the Indians for a long time, and had little hope of getting along with the other missionaries. Failure was clear to be seen.

That autumn one particular visitor had passed through Waiilatpu with the emigrant wagon trains (the mission station had become a way station for Americans on the route to the Willamette Valley) with news for Marcus that may have pricked his interest.

Elijah White had visited the Whitmans in the past, and had gone East and brought back a group of settlers. He revealed to Marcus that he had been paid a significant sum of money by the U.S. government. The president reportedly had a "secret service" fund, which was used to finance the Methodist missionaries and their settlement for Americans in the Willamette Valley. Marcus, always interested in financial opportunities for himself (that's no doubt why his mission station became a source of supplies for travelers, charging what travelers claimed to be exhorbitant prices) may have hoped his plans could be funded in the same manner.

While Marcus was in the East, a comet appeared in the night sky in February (1843). It created a stir in New England where prophets awaited the end of the world, expected to arrive that year. Followers had sold or given away all their property and stood on hilltops waiting for the coming of the Lord. The country was in "financial embarrassment"—several states were nearly bankrupt and the government's credit at home and abroad had been destroyed.

Narcissa, abandoned and alone for the winter, with health problems of her own, grew despondent. Her vision was nearly gone, she hoped Marcus would obtain new spectacles for her in the East. Winter pending, she settled in for a restless season. She was isolated, without the companionship of others in the mission (who found her difficult to deal with and tried to avoid her), without close ties to friends and family back in New York, and without a husband to rely on.

Narcissa was gloomy, despondent and hopeless; she'd fallen into a deep depression after the loss of little Alice Clarissa, and she couldn't pull herself out of it. She developed "inflammation of the kidneys and was brought very low."[9] Her health was growing worse, and Marcus treated her with mercury, something that would have increased her depression. As her physical strength ebbed and her vision faded, she was utterly without hope.

Without Alice, Narcissa needed to create a new purpose in life for herself. Motherhood was the role she had most enjoyed. Why she failed to conceive another child after Alice Clarissa is unknown. She never wrote about her feelings towards another pregnancy, she never hinted at the possibility the couple would have another child, or that she hoped to become pregnant again. It's possible one or both of the Whitmans had become sterile, one side effect of syphilis.

When she had the opportunity to take in two-year-old Helen Mar Meek—the daughter of a former fur trapper Joe Meek and an Indian woman—she eagerly did so. The next year she adopted another girl, six-year-old Mary Ann, daughter of Jim Bridger and an Indian wife. She felt the Lord had taken her own child away, but had also meant for them to take in the "outcasts of the country and suffering children."[10]

The children gave her more reasons to turn away from the spiritual work of the mission and concentrate on the maternal duties within her home and family. She was an enthusiastic parent and a dedicated disciplinarian. She had advised other women to avoid treating servants too well, or they would show saucy and difficult behavior; with children, it was the same.

The girls required "tight reins" constantly, and Narcissa devoted herself to providing that guidance and control. This time, she was not going to make the mistakes she thought she had made with Alice. She didn't allow the children to come in contact with the Cayuses at all. She kept them in the house nearly all the time. She didn't allow them to learn a word of the Indians' language. Pursuing the maternal ideal of her era, Narcissa was finally able to escape from missionary work.

When Marcus left on his hurried trip east, Mary and William Gray were still staying at Waiilatpu. In fact, William had built a rather large house from adobes for the couple, which the Whitman's sarcastically referred to as "the Mansion House." The Grays were unhappy though, and William's bitter letters to the Board had been partly responsible for the Board's order to dissolve Waiilatpu and Lapwai.

The Grays were planning to head to the Willamette Valley, abandoning the mission, when Marcus left. Within two or three days after Marcus' hurried departure, the Grays left and Narcissa was all alone at Waiilatpu, except for a hired man who slept outside the Whitman house.

Narcissa was in a vulnerable position, and she knew it. Why she didn't leave with the Grays is unknown. Perhaps they too, abandoned her. She stayed at Waiilatpu alone, with her adopted girls.

It was only two days before a terrifying incident frightened her away. During the night she heard noises at her bedroom door; and the sounds of someone unlatching the door. She leaped from her bed and pushed against the door, keeping the intruder from entering. In the darkness she couldn't recognize whoever was trying to break into her room, but after "the ruffian pushed and pushed" at the door Her screams finally frightened "him" away. She was "dreadfully frightened" and called for the hired man to sleep in the kitchen the rest of the night.

Historians are divided on whether Narcissa was ever really in danger. There's no proof the attempted assault ever happened. Alone and frightened, she could have imagined it, or could have been experiencing paranoia due to health problems or medications.

There is little doubt the Indians in the area, or the mountain men residing near them, might have attempted to hurt Narcissa. The Whitmans had endured various threats and attempted assaults from the Indians in the preceding years, but they ignored the building hatred. Threatened with guns, axes and slapping, Marcus had simply ignored the Indians, even when one of them "pulled his ears," in an attempt to make him listen to their admonitions that he leave the area.[11] He left his wife in a perilous situation. If the assault didn't really happen, and Narcissa fabricated it on purpose, it gave her a good excuse to leave Waiilatpu.

The next day Narcissa sent word of the incident to Fort Walla Walla and was quickly escorted to safety there. This gave her a way to exit Waiilatpu without embarrassment over being abandoned by her husband. As she left, she reasoned that the Indians didn't really want her to leave, and that they were regretting the "cause."

Shortly after Narcissa left Waiilatpu, the grain mill burned to the ground. She didn't know whether it was on purpose or from "carelessness" of the Indians, but she felt it was what they deserved. They had been ungrateful of her sacrifices and this might make them a "better" people.

Narcissa and her two adopted girls spent the rest of the time during Marcus's year-long absence as guests first at Fort Walla Walla, then of various Methodist missionary families in the Willamette Valley and with the McLoughlins at Fort Vancouver. She enjoyed her stay among the people whom she closely identified with, and thrived in the social atmosphere she had missed for so long.

But Narcissa was not well. As she was escorted away from Waiilatpu, she had to be driven in a wagon, lying on a trundle bed. She was dosing herself with quinine and calomel and was unhappy and uncomfortable. Her health was deteriorating; she was very "debilitated" and blamed her "prolapses" (of the uterus, presumably) on her problems. She was unable to "walk & even to move my limbs without groaning."[12] Her eyes were getting worse, she was by now unable to sew or read much and wrote with difficulty. Her eyes gave her "considerable pain." While at Fort Vancouver, the doctor there dosed her with iodine to shrink a tumor in her side that was thought to be an enlargement of the right ovary.

Marcus' departure was not unnoticed by the Cayuses. They were certain he'd gone to get troops to make war on them, and rumors flooded the area that he intended to return and kill all of them. It probably was best for Narcissa to abandon her home, as she couldn't supplicate or reassure the Indians by herself.

It was October when she finally got word that Marcus had returned to Oregon. He had brought his young nephew, Perrin, and a large party of emigrants. He'd also brought word from the Board that the Whitmans would be allowed to stay at Waiilatpu, and the Spaldings at Lapwai.

While Narcissa was delighted to see her husband again, she was devastated that none of her relatives had come with him. She'd pleaded with her family for years to come to Oregon, and had written endless letters begging them to make the trip. None had come though, and she was faced with returning to missionary work again.

Returning to Waiilatpu held no joy, only darkness. In her own house again, she stayed in her bedroom, an invalid once more; she had two attacks of fever and an inflammation of the bowels and bloating. She felt she would die. Marcus discovered a "beating tumor" in her abdomen that he determined to be an aneurism of the main aorta.[13] Narcissa was in the later stage of syphilis.

The parasites that cause syphilis weren't identified until 1905, but medical texts as early as the 1500s described many aspects of the disease. Much more easily contracted than today's strains, it could be passed by contact with a wound or even a drinking vessel. In the 1830s it would have been quite difficult *not* to contract it, particularly for a country doctor.

Fever and skin rash, like Narcissa suffered the week before Alice's birth, and Alice contracted when she was six months old, could be symptoms of syphilis.. After the rash phase, the disease often recedes for three to ten years before changes in blood vessels cause weakening and rupturing of the walls, leading to a ruptured aorta or brain aneurism.

The brain itself undergoes drastic changes including a phase in which the patient has ideas or schemes that are rational, but unusual or grandiose.[14] Victims usually carry on normal lives however, but are riddled with impotence, headache, painful joints, and character changes. A chronic fatigue with loss of memory and aches and pains sets in, appearing as a total exhaustion of the nervous system.

Mercury was given as treatment (usually calomel). In 1825 potassium iodide was introduced, too, but nothing really worked. Until penicillin, in the twentieth century, there was no cure for syphilis.

Emigrants who came with Marcus during the 1843 trip were staying at the station, and a school for the children was started. The Indians were ignored as a steady stream of American emigrants refreshed themselves and their supplies at Waiilatpu. Marcus considered whether they should make a land claim on the mission grounds, unwilling to see it claimed by emigrant arrivals who were streaming in to take over the country.

Several Cayuses had begun small farms around Waiilatpu and rode out to meet oncoming wagons with food and horses to barter to the emigrants. When Whitman began doing the same, he was seen as a competitor. The bustling mission was a stopping place for supplies and the Whitmans were becoming rich in the Indian eyes. The Cayuses clearly saw what was happening and forbid Marcus to break any more new ground to the plow, charging that he was making "money out of their lands by supplying Emigrants."[15]

The following year more emigrants passed through Waiilatpu; the emigration of 1844 numbered over 1,500 and was a virtual horde. The Whitmans heard how many were on the way, and eagerly prepared for them. That meant more than having ample foodstuffs to sell, it also meant readying security.

The emigrants that Marcus brought back with him in 1843 had not been without fault. They had ridden ahead of him to Waiilatpu and broken into everything, stealing and helping themselves to whatever was in storage. Even in Marcus' absence during the eastern trip the Cayuses had been careful to not loot the mission. It was his own comrades, the men he'd led across the continent, who helped themselves to his supplies. Eighteen forty-four would be different. Both Whitmans were ready this time.

For Narcissa, life at Waiilatpu had taken a welcome twist. She was no longer living in an isolated mission post, surrounded by drum-beating, wailing savages. She was now mistress of a burgeoning waystation on the Oregon Trail. Hundreds passed through her influence. Suddenly, she found herself the center of attention, as the station became a post "about which the multitudes will or must gather" as they passed through to the Willamette. Vitally important to the settlers, her expertise, advice and assistance were invaluable to the weak and ailing emigrants. Marcus and Narcissa were respected—something they had been unable to achieve as missionaries.

With the struggling travelers, numerous weak and helpless people came as well. Six children from one family—the Sagers—were orphaned when their parents both died during the journey to Oregon. The Sagers ranged in age from five months to thirteen years. The Whitmans were implored to take them, and after some discussion adopted the youngsters.

With the six orphans, Narcissa delved into motherhood in a grand style. These children, the infant girl especially, would replace Alice, and give her the joys she relished. She had ignored dozens of Cayuse orphans. But these were white children.

Such a large step, adopting so many children, was not taken lightly. Narcissa and Marcus discussed it for some time. Narcissa told the children she would take in the girls, but that the boys (ages thirteen and eleven) would be sent to the Willamette Valley, to find homes with other settlers. Marcus wanted to keep the boys, reminding his wife that the father of the children had asked that they be kept together in his dying words. He reminded Narcissa the boys could do plenty of work around the house, too. He finally convinced her, telling her if she was "going to have the girls," he must "have the boys."[16]

Narcissa was happy to have the additional children, even if some were boys. It gave her even more opportunity to retreat from whatever demands the mission still placed on her. While Mary Walker fretted at how little missionary work she was able to do because of her own children, and Eliza Spalding despaired her pregnancies because they took her from her work, Narcissa saw no problem with retreating from missionary work.

Narcissa now had more control over her own life. Her home was nearly as comfortable as it would have been in New York. The house was whitewashed with green painted trim, with a curio cabinet, bookshelves, a clothes press, and dainty blue and white painted china imported from England, purchased from the HBC. The windows were glass, with divided lights and protected with painted wooden shutters. Fences ringed the yard, and gardens of fruits, vegetables and flowers made it very appealing.

Narcissa saw her new purpose, mothering the Sager orphans, as the will of the Lord. She wrote a letter about her new situation to the *Mother's Magazine*. The letter was published and widely distributed. In her writings, she now concentrated on the Sager children, and barely mentioned the two girls she'd adopted earlier, Helen Meek and Mary Ann Bridger. The Sagers were white American children, and the other two were half Indians, children of fur trappers. The Sagers were something she could attribute to divine providence, the other two girls were merely abandoned children.

The arrival of the orphans, along with the new situation as mistress of a growing plantation on the route to Oregon, helped Narcissa's spirits. There were plenty of American women passing through to visit with, and hiring domestic help was no longer a problem, as so many destitute widows and orphan girls were coming to Oregon.

There was companionship and help with the domestic work and she began to feel good again. Narcissa was the happiest she had ever been in Oregon. Her health improved enough that she was able to ride horseback (on sidesaddle) to the annual mission meeting at Tshimikain, something she hadn't done in years. Her temper was growing softer, her insistence on having control somewhat mellowing.

Narcissa's time was spent with rearing her brood of wild children. The older Sagers arrived unable to read, something deplorable to her. A teacher was hired from the flow of westward travelers and a school started for the American children who either lived at the mission or were children of other missionaries, or Hudson's Bay Company officials. The Walker's son, Cyrus, was put in school at Waiilatpu, along with the Spalding's daughter, Eliza.

The Cayuses were forgotten, their unwillingness to change and accept the Americans' cultural behaviors was no longer worth the struggle. The efforts to keep the Indians out of the Whitman's house was finally over; now it was filled with boarders. Narcissa noted that they set the table for twenty, three times a day, and "it is a pleasing sight."[17]

Like many women who settled the West, Narcissa dreamed of building better schools: an academy or even a college, at Waiilatpu. The Whitmans planned to enlarge their mission station by building houses where mission mothers could live while their children attended the school. She even hired an emigrant teenager, Lorinda Bewley, who had some polish and style, to teach her daughters how to do fancy work. Narcissa was able to put together a life somewhat like what she had left in New England, against incredible odds.

Narcissa felt that by showing the Indians an example of Christian family life, she was doing them as great a service as missionary work. By showing a positive influence to the heathen, she was convinced she was helping them. But it was not enough.

She wrote to her mother, "The poor Indians are amazed at the overwhelming numbers of Americans coming into the country. They seem not to know what to make of it."[18]

At Tshimikain, Mary Walker tried again and again to work with the Spokanes, but her husband opposed it. She showed the chief's wife how to make bread and fry fritters, but Elkanah put an end to it. ". . . as usual when I attempt to do with or for an Indian, get a good scolding for my indiscretion."[19]

Elkanah, jealous of Mary as always, couldn't accept her successes, even if they were within the domestic sphere. After seven years, he'd had no success saving the souls of converts. While he tried to build a chapel for the Indians, "a company of strong men" sat gambling nearby. His ears were "annoyed by night at the songs of the gamblers."[20] His evangelistic efforts had barely made a dent in the Spokanes' world.

Mary could only offer small mercies to the women. She overpaid them on trades. When informed a woman who'd done housework for her had lost her baby in childbirth, she welcomed the woman who' had "walked a quarter of a mile barefoot on the frozen ground after sunset." Mary gave her "some motherly advice, some bread and meat and a pair of shoes . . ."[21]

Her despair over the mission work, or rather her inability to do any mission work, surfaced again, "How little time we spend on the Indians compared with our selves . . . Have been thinking how stagnant my thoughts are."[22]

Prevented from working with the Indians by Elkanah, Mary turned to her lifelong interest—natural science. She collected and pressed a variety of plant specimens, but one of her toddlers observed her interest in plants and ate some flowers that caused him to vomit "at short intervals, for some hours"— a peculiar problem for female naturalists, who happened to be mothers.[23]

In midwinter, Mary summoned Doctor Whitman as she was about to be "confined" once again. He replied that he couldn't make it. With Myra's help, and the aid of her Indian domestic (a girl who lived with the Walkers), Mary delivered another boy, Jeremiah.

The Indians recognized Mary's interest in the natural world and brought items that they thought might interest her, such as the "green clay" old Solomon gave her. She was pleased—more diary space describes the clay than the newborn.

While Elkanah was away from Tshimikain on mission business, Mary adopted another pursuit: taxidermy. She bought dead animals (a "mocking bird," rattlesnake skin and a couple of ducks) from the Indians to dress and stuff. When Elkanah got home he hit the ceiling, getting "out of sorts not liking my new trade of stuffing birds, etc." But she was able to win him over, "Had a talk in the morning with Mr. W.—got permission to pursue collecting objects in Natural History."[24]

She jumped right into her new interest, bartering with the Indians for "stuffed skins," but realized the odor was a problem. "Think I will wait until I can procure arsenic before I collect more . . ." But she couldn't resist; the next week, after doing her distasteful household duties, she "spent the afternoon skinning a crane. Think I will not undertake another crane soon . . ."[25]

Everything seemed to be getting along fine, until Mary heard disturbing news the spring of 1845, "Doctor Whitman entertains fears that his people intend taking his life. We think they will not do it, but it is trying to have them conduct as they do . . ."[26]

Notes on Chapter Sixteen

[1] McKee, *Mary Richardson Walker*, p. 254.

[2] Ibid.

[3] Drury, *Spalding and Smith*, p. 308.

[4] Ibid, p. 328.

[5] Ibid, p. 311.

[6] Ibid, p. 312.

[7] Ibid, p. 323.

[8] Ibid, p. 335.

[9] *Whitman, Letters*, p. 98.

[10] Jeffrey, *Converting the West*, p. 171.

[11] Ibid, p. 180.

[12] Ibid, p. 179.

[13] Ibid, p. 181.

[14] Frederick E. Cartwright, *Disease and History* (New York: Dorset Press, 1972), p. 56.

[15] Jeffrey, *Converting the West*, p. 182.

[16] Ibid, p. 187.

[17] Ibid, p. 193.

[18] Ibid, p. 203.

[19] McKee, *Mary Richardson Walker*, p. 249.

[20] Ibid, p. 265.

[21] Ibid.

[22] Ibid.

[23] Ibid, p. 266.

[24] Ibid, p. 280.

[25] Ibid, p. 280.

[26] Ibid, p. 280.

Chapter Seventeen

Death at Waiilatpu

May 15, 1846
"This country needs those who are able and willing to found and support society, religion, and schools. There are the best inducements to young men to come and locate a mile square of first-rate land in a better climate than in any of the States . . . A good title will be secured to all who located and reside on or occupy land or mile squares, according to the Oregon laws."

Marcus Whitman's letter to
Narcissa's sister and brother[1]

In 1846 the news that the British had given up the Oregon land claims to the United States spread quickly through the Pacific Northwest. Things would no longer be as they were. Since 1843, American settlers in Oregon had been claiming land in 640-acre chunks. This generous opportunity beckoned to the rest of the nation. Wagons were making the trek now without much ado, and there seemed to be no limit to the prospects for a person who arrived in Oregon.

In July of 1846, Narcissa wrote home that, "The Indians are very quiet now and never more friendly . . . So far as the Indians are concerned our prospects of permanently remaining among them were never more favourable than the present."

Missionary efforts at Waiilatpu had gone by the wayside, but she and Marcus now had other matters to be concerned with, "I feel distressed sometimes to think I am making so little personal effort for their benefit, when so much ought to be done, but perhaps I could not do more than I am through the family."[2]

Narcissa had no interest in the Cayuses at all and seemed to be reassured that there had been ". . . some deaths among them of the most important Indians, the past winter and spring," which meant they were dying off.[3] She would finally be able to focus her energies elsewhere.

Happily ensconced in her parlor, "with six girls sewing around me . . ." life was bright again. Raising her orphans gave her the opportunity to do what she was best at, "I must be with them or else they will be doing something they should not, or else not spending their time profitably. I could get along some easier if I could bring my mind to have them spend their time in play, but this I cannot." It was a committment she applied herself to with wholehearted effort and devotion; she was a Yankee mother, determined to mold the next generation.

At that time Oregon Territory was one of the most isolated parts of the continent. News from the outside world arrived so long after events occurred that it seemed to be another world entirely.

When the fad for mesmerism hit New England, Mary's inlaws tried contacting her through it. They needed to know exactly where the Walkers lived, ". . . how far from Wala Wala river or from some particular place," that could be located on a map. They had seen a man who "magnetized a girl and carried her to Oregon but did not know where to find you; he went near the Columbia river and followed the bank some way and went over mountains but could not find you . . ." The man could "visit" Mary at any time, and tell if she was "sick or well." Elkanah's sister realized it was very "strange," but reassured Mary that the man wasn't possessed by devils because people said he was "too good a man," for that. The clever man thought about writing to Mary and telling her how it was done so she could "visit" Maine. It took "strong nerves" and "fluid passing from one to another," which may have been some sort of electrical current, a popular technique at the time.[4]

In early 1847, Peter Skene Ogden (factor at Fort Vancouver—McLoughlin had retired from the position) wrote a New Year's letter to the Tshimikain mission, which included news of the outside world, "The potato disease is causing famine in Ireland and cholera is spreading in the States."[5] The Mexican War and the Oregon boundary were the main political concerns.

It was also the harshest winter yet in Oregon. Bread dough froze when set out to rise in the kitchen, and the Indians' horses died. The Indians came to the missionaries' doors all the time, to trade roots for medicine. They "talked insultingly" to Elkanah, and he blamed Mary for their unpleasantness.

Lonely and depressed, fighting the cold and a tiny house full of young children, Mary wrote about missing her young brother in her diary, having no way to know he'd been dead a year.

When spring arrived, word came to the Plateau natives that there were more Americans coming West than could be counted. The Cayuses saw this as an opportunity to make the most of the produce and grain they were growing in their own tilled fields. (Since 1845, some Cayuse landholders had been hiring white men to break their fields and till the crops they grew for trade with emigrants.) Horses could always be traded to the travelers, too. The emigration for 1847 *was* huge, there had never been anything to rival it in scope. Over four thousand travelers made their way across the continent, to look for land in Oregon. Mormons were on the move with thousands settling near the Great Salt Lake. The Indians were well aware of all movement across the West, they kept highly sensitive lines of communication open between various native trading groups, and knew exactly what was happening. Whites were flooding in.

But not every Cayuse found opportunity in trade, many saw the onslaught of Americans as impending doom. Hadn't the emigrants caused plenty of trouble? Weren't they difficult to barter with, demanding and insolent, quick to resort to the gun or threats?

As fall 1847 came, and the hundreds passed through Cayuse land for the Willamette Valley, trouble began to brew. Measles was sweeping through the region, leaving dead children and feverish anxiety in its path. At Waiilatpu, measles came with the emigrants, and the Whitman family was hit hard by it. The buildings on the mission grounds were filled with Americans moaning feverishly on sickbeds. The Sager children, Mary Ann Bridger and Helen Meek, all came down with the disease. Cayuse families were reeling from the disease, burying nearly half their population within weeks. What was going on? Who was to blame? Dr. Whitman, rushing from bed to bed dosing the ill with ineffective medications, was easily seen to be the culprit.

In 1847 there was no cure for measles; while inoculation was practiced most Americans developed an immunity to measles through contracting a mild case in childhood, and wouldn't have sickened and died as quickly as the Indians, who had no immunity developed through the generations. Whites became ill and were bedridden, but most eventually recovered. Not so in the Cayuse lodges.

Many Indians followed the practice of hiring native shamans to cure the sick. If the shamans succeeded, they were well-paid, if they failed and the ill person died in their care, they were killed in retribution. Now, watching Dr. Whitman's ineffective potions, and seeing that the whites recovered more easily from the measles, while the Indian children nearly all died, the natives argued over how to treat the white doctor.

The Whitmans had ignored the Indians' threats and demands that they leave the mission in the past. There had been repeated periods of hostility, the Cayuses blaming the Whitmans for a variety of problems. Marcus had been threatened by Cayuse men who accused him of administering poison in the guise of medicine. He'd always ignored or scoffed at their threats. Marcus hadn't bent to the demands of the missionary brethren, he certainly wouldn't listen to a handful of troublesome Cayuses.

But others, like Dr. McLoughlin and Cushing Eells, realized that the Indians were trying to force the Whitmans to leave. Tomahas, a Cayuse man, threatened Marcus with a club and demanded that he leave, but still Marcus and Narcissa stayed on, unwilling to recognize they were putting themselves in increasing danger.

In the face of the Indians' admonitions, Marcus decided to expand the mission, offering to buy Wascopum, the Methodist mission station at The Dalles which the Methodists had abandoned because of the difficulty in working with the Indians located there. He sought the site as a way to ensure access to the Columbia River as far as Fort Vancouver. He needed to reach out if he wanted to keep the emigrant trade he'd found plopped in his lap; a short-cut had been established on the Oregon Trail that bypassed Waiilatpu. The 1847 emigration would be the last to pass through Waiilatpu, as a "good southern route is now open into the head waters of the Willamette, and all will wish, probably to go that way, as it will be much nearer and better."

Marcus's visions became as grandiose and expansive as ever. As a mission station, Waiilatpu had been a resounding failure (not one Cayuse had ever been baptised in the eleven years he'd been there). Now that it was an emigrant supply station, the trail was being diverted elsewhere. A month before hatching The Dalles scheme, Marcus had written to Henry Spalding that he was ready to call it quits and file a land claim and retire.

Obtaining Wascopum allowed him to open a new shorter road from Waiilatpu to The Dalles, making it more appealing to the emigrant trains. Now that he saw his future tied to white emigration, he acted as a protector for travelers, warning Indians that if they raided the wagon trains, "The Great Father of the Bostons would send men to defend these travelers, and that shiploads of soldiers and guns would arrive to kill all the Indians who molested his people on their way to the distant valley." Marcus even kept watch on angry Indians, and threatened to have them "shot like a dog" if they did anything.[6]

Waiilatpu had become a white settlement. The winter of 1846, up to fifty Americans had lived with the Whitmans, in 1847 seventy were settling in. Angry Cayuses watched as the Whitmans appeared to give supplies out to whites, while charging the Indians for anything they wanted.

Marcus needed help to realize his ambitions. His nephew, Perrin Whitman, had come West with Marcus, and was now working alongside him. He wrote to Narcissa's sister's husband in November, urging the man (a minister) to come to Oregon. He extolled the opportunities in Oregon, and added that if he (Marcus) hadn't been alert and busy, the "Jesuit Papists would have been in quiet possession of this the only spot in the western horizon of America not before their own." He warned that the Catholics were "fast fixing themselves here," and praised the American emigrations for arriving in order to "hold on and give stability" or it would have been but "small work" for the Catholics and the "friends of English interests," to have "routed" the missionaries, and the country "might have slept in their hands forever."[7] He rationalized that his missionary work had saved the country from the Catholics by opening the land to Americans. No mention was made of the natives.

Marcus' letter revealed his noted lack of manners and brash personality. In the same letter that invited his brother-in-law to come to Oregon, he accused the man of being a "step" away from mental "derangement," reminding him that "Mental disease is not suspected by the person who is the subject of it." To soften the words, he added, "There are few who are possessed of perfectly balanced minds."[8] If he used such rude and careless statements to a man he was urging to come visit and settle near him, one shudders at what he must have said to the Cayuses whom he held little respect for.

At the Mission Meeting that fall Whitman announced his expansion plan and ordered the Walkers to move to Wascopum. Elkanah refused, but he did go with Whitman to look at the Wascopum site. On the trip down the Columbia he resolved to remain at Tshimikain, writing to Mary that, "The Doctor appears a broken down man," adding that Whitman "says he is so."[9]

During his visit at Waiilatpu, Elkanah was insulted when Whitman slept during his sermon, and wrote to Mary that he was thankful to have her and "not another," boasting that, "I think we are the happiest couple in all Oregon & love each other better than any other two." His glimpse of the Whitman's home life must have made him uncomfortable.[10]

At Lapwai, competing Nez Perce factions argued over the benefits of allowing the Spaldings to remain. Two part-Delaware ex-fur trappers, Tom Hill and Joe Lewis, were inciting

Nez Perce anger against the missionaries and stirring up tensions. Vandals tore down the fences, broke windows in the school, and destroyed the mill dam.

Paul Kane, a Canadian painter, was making a tour of the Columbia River drainage. He concentrated on painting portraits of Indian warriors, the fiercer the better. He found angry subjects among the Cayuses and painted portraits of several of the powerful head men; just sketching them made him fear for his own life.

When Kane arrived at Fort Walla Walla he found the Cayuses in an uproar. The son of a chief had been murdered when a horse trading deal went bad in California. A band of warriors had gone there to avenge his death, but over thirty of them had died of measles. Now the disease was felling every family in the village. Weren't the Americans behind this? Clamors for revenge were all around. Kane worried about the safety of the Whitmans and rushed to Waiilatpu to warn them of pending disaster. Wouldn't they come to the fort for a few days, just until the epidemic was over?

Whitman refused to take Kane's warning seriously. There's no way to know what he was thinking, but he "did not apprehend they would injure him."[11] Kane reluctantly hurried back to the safety of the fort.

Marcus was busy, he couldn't be swayed from putting his plans into action. He'd just brought two ox teams and wagons from The Dalles, loaded with threshing machine, cornsheller, ploughs and other goods for the mission; one of the largest supply trains he'd ever received.

Narcissa became nervous over the Indians' change of attitude; in spite of her letters saying everything was going well with the Indians, she had noticed the problem in the summer and fall of 1847. She told other women at Waiilatpu that she worried they might all be killed. While the Whitmans discussed the problem discreetly, the Sager children picked up the message. One of the girls began having nightmares. Was there going to be a confrontation?

An emigrant overheard Joe Lewis, one of the recalcitrant ex-fur traders, talking about pending Indian trouble; the news caused one family to pack up and leave Waiilatpu, where they

This portrait of Abigail Walker, daughter of Elkanah and Mary Walker, saved the life of John Mix Stanley. The New York painter was scheduled to go to the Whitman Mission at Waiilatpu. But he had to wait for eight-year-old Abigail to recover from the measles before he could finish the painting. He was still at Tshimikain when the Whitman massacre occurred.

Historical Photograph Collections, Washington State University Libraries

had planned to spend the winter. When a white child died from measles, Narcissa breathed a sigh of relief. Maybe the Indians would see that God was taking white children, as well as Indian. When she took one of the warriors into the sickroom to view the lifeless body, he laughed.

Warnings of unrest were all around. Marcus even admitted to one of the visiting Americans that if things didn't improve, the Whitmans would "have to leave in the spring."[12]

Opinions were divided as Cayuse factions took sides over the issue in heated discussions that filled the lodges. Many clamored to kill the doctor immediately. Hadn't his failed medicine been like poison to many of them? Weren't over two hundred already dead because of the man? Rivalries between various clans developed, even between young and old leaders. The dwindling tribe was rife with grief, fear, and conflict.

The morning of November 29, 1847, was a dark, dreary winter day. Many were still sick, but most of the children were in the mission school room, studying under the direction of a hired male teacher.

Narcissa, depressed and unable to eat breakfast, had been crying. When she went to the kitchen, she discovered it was "full of Indians." She hurried to the parlor for Marcus. He went into the kitchen, bolted the door behind him, and within minutes the rest of the family heard angry voices, shouting and the crack of a rifle shot, coming from the kitchen.

Narcissa screamed, "The Indians will murder us all!"

Marcus had been hit with a tomahawk twice in the back of the head and had been slashed repeatedly across the face. He was bleeding profusely. Narcissa and two other women who were in the house at the time dragged his body into the sitting room where they tried to save him. There was no possibility.

Outside the Indians went on a rampage, killing American men who were butchering a beef in the yard. The children tried to hide in the school room after seeing their schoolmaster murdered in front of them. Narcissa looked out the window and was shot in the chest. Laying on the floor, she began to pray, for the children, the "little ones," and for her mother, so far away. She was helped to a bed upstairs, where her blood drenched the precious bed linens and smeared on the children who snuggled close to her in fear.

John Mix Stanley, a New York painter, arrived at Tshimikain early in November and spent several days with the Walkers where he was warmly received. He set about painting a portrait of little Abigail Walker, but the eight-year-old girl broke out with measles and was bedridden with a fever. He waited until she recovered, finished the painting, and traveled southward to Waiilatpu. Accompanied by Solomon, a Spokane Indian guide, he was to alert Dr. Whitman that Mary Walker would need his professional services within days—she was nearly due with another baby.

The two Eells boys and the Walker children had recovered from the measles which spread through the Spokanes' winter camp, too. Only one Spokane death was attributed to the disease. The missionaries at Tshimikain had no medicine to give them, but "for want of other medicine & not knowing what is best, we give them Cayenne peper tea & light cathartics to bring out the eruption on the skin." For their dry, sore throats, they gave nitre. "These simple remedies may excite the smile of a regular physician," but "as long as they continue effective we shall administer them."[13]

It worked. By December, the children at Tshimikain had recovered. Mary was ready to give birth in a week or two and bustled about getting ready for the big event, and Dr. Whitman's visit. She baked a dozen mince pies and cleaned house. But the Indian messenger brought chilling news. He didn't bring the doctor, only a letter from John Mix Stanley. He told them about ". . . one of the most tragical massacres on record in Oregon."

In a "trembling" voice, Elkanah read the news that the Doctor, his wife and most of the men and youths at Waiilatpu had been "killed by the Cayuse Indians, and that the women and children had been taken prisoners." A "black cloud of horrors" settled around everyone at Tshimikain.[14]

Stanley had arrived at Waiilatpu nearly in the middle of the massacre, and had fortunately detoured before being killed, too. He'd been confronted by an angry Cayuse warrior along the trail, but his life had been saved by Solomon, who'd claimed Stanley wasn't an American. Stanley had been informed that a "party of Indians started to Mr. Spalding's to complete their horrid butchery . . ."[15] William McBean was the factor in charge of Fort Walla Walla; he sent a frantic message to Fort Vancouver for boats to evacuate "such as may escape."[16]

Were the Tshimikain mission families to be next? Mary feared so; prayer was the only answer. "May God have compassion on those who survive and stay the hand of the ruthless savages. We are safe only under the divine protection." Who else could they turn to? "May we trust only in God."[17] There were no laws, no enforcement, no U.S. Army posts, nothing to protect them. They were absolutely dependent upon the Spokane Indians for survival. Stanley's letter didn't say Indians were coming to kill them at Tshimikain, but then again he didn't say they weren't coming, either.

Mary gave birth to a nine-pound baby boy, John, named perhaps after Stanley, on the last day of December. Now the Walkers had six children, five boys and a girl, with the three youngest boys under four years of age. The Eells had two little boys. With so many young children—one a newborn—there was no possibility of making a quick escape, even if they found a way to attempt it.

Worry, fear and frustration filled their days; they didn't know the fate of the Waiilatpu residents, whether they were rescued, murdered, or "perishing with cold or hunger."[18] It wasn't until January 20 that a letter came to Tshimikain from Henry Spalding, letting them know his family was still alive. From December 9 until that date, they had no idea if the rest of the mission members were dead or alive, or what was happening among the Indian tribes. Rumors were rampant but the Spokanes remained firmly behind their

Historical Photograph Collections, Washington State University Libraries

Eliza Spalding Warren was ten years old when she witnessed the Whitman Massacre.

missionaries. They vowed to defend them if it came to that. But none of the Spokanes would venture south to take messages; they warned Walker and Eells to darken their windows at night and keep their doors locked.

At Waiilatpu, the remaining Americans were being held hostage by the Cayuse faction in control. There was only one American who knew the Nez Perce language, the same language spoken by the Cayuses. Ten-year-old Eliza Spalding, the missionaries' daughter, was staying at Waiilatpu to attend the school for white children. Knowledgeable about Indian ways, she'd been immersed in the language and lives of the Nez Perces since birth, entirely opposite to Narcissa's children. Now, knowing exactly what they were saying, and what they meant to do, the child was frozen in fear. Like the rest of the school-children, she watched the bloody tirade without making a "cry or scream."[19]

The oldest Sager boy had his throat slashed from ear to ear and lay dying on the floor. Wounded men tried to make a run for it or hide behind bushes. As wounded Narcissa was being carried out of the house on a lounge, shrieks and yells erupted among the Cayuses. She was shot a final time, then slashed on the head and face with a war club. Little Eliza put her apron up over her face; she didn't want to see the guns pointed at her.

The melee continued for days; the Cayuses forced the women and girls to cook for them, making them taste the food first to be sure there wasn't poison in it. They took most of their clothing, then put them to work sewing clothing for the Indians. The captives were "worn out and fatigued with fright and horrors."[20] Fort Walla Walla, and their only hope for safety, was thirty miles away, and the country was "full of Indians."[21] Would anyone save them? They knew that wasn't even a possibility, as no one in the outside world knew what was going on at Waiilatpu, unless someone had escaped during the bloody seige.

Unknown to the hostages, the Osborn family, a married couple and their two tiny children, had hidden under the floorboards of one of the buildings at Waiilatpu, and slipped away in the dark of night. It took them three days, hiding in the bushes without blankets or food, keeping the toddlers silenced when Indians passed nearby their hiding place. Mrs. Osborn had been ill and was barely able to continue. When they were finally outside the gates of Fort Walla Walla, they were refused entrance. McBean, the factor at the time, told them to go away, that he wouldn't give them refuge because he "was afraid the Indians would attack the fort and kill them all."[22] His scantily manned outpost held less than a dozen men at the time.

Mrs. Osborn heard the devastating news and collapsed on the ground, telling them she "could go no further and would die outside of the fort gates."[23] Finally the Factor relented and allowed them to come inside.

At Waiilatpu, fourteen bodies lay strewn about the grounds for three days before Father Brouillet, a Catholic priest who had recently settled nearby, arrived and directed the burial in a hastily-dug common grave. As he was leaving, Eliza Spalding told Brouillet's half-blood interpreter to warn her father not to

The death of Marcus Whitman.

come to Waiilatpu, that "they will kill him sure if he does."[24] She knew Henry Spalding had plans to return to Waiilatpu before heading north to Lapwai. If he was still alive.

But a Cayuse man heard her speaking and told her he intended to kill her father, brandishing the pistol he intended to do it with. He followed the priest and his escort when they left Waiilatpu. On the way, he lit a pipe with his pistol's flint, and forgot to recharge. They met Henry on the trail, and Brouillet gave him a furtive warning which allowed him to escape into the woods.

Knowing Indians would be waiting along the trail for him, Henry made his way under the cover of fog, staying near bushes along the river, finding only wild rose hips to eat. His horse wandered away and his ill-fitting boots, sent in a donation barrel from Boston, were impossible to walk in. Barefoot, he struggled over the rocks and prickly pears until he finally reached the Snake River and a Nez Perce camp.

One man who'd escaped the slaughter at Waiilatpu arrived at Lapwai to warn Eliza Spalding, but she refused to leave immediately. She was adamantly against packing up and leaving because it was the Sabbath. Clinging to her religious practices, she remained in her home until the next day. Perhaps Eliza was trying to buy time until help arrived, Henry returned, or until arrangements were made for the family to stay with William Craig's family. At least it gave her an extra day. She no doubt was as fearless as the Nez Perces claimed; nothing ever frightened her.

Henry made it to Lapwai and found Eliza and the three younger Spalding children waiting safely at William Craig's cabin, a few miles away from the Lapwai mission grounds. Speculation remains whether Eliza and the children were whisked to safety or were taken into custody, to be used in later bartering if the Cayuses attacked the Nez Perces.

Little Eliza and the other fifty-eight hostages were held at Waiilatpu for three weeks. Forty were women and children. "Young women were dragged from the house by night and beastly treated," one raped by the man who had murdered her father. Three of the captive children died from illness; the two Sager boys were murdered. The terror seemed unending. Ten year-old Eliza Spalding shrunk to a "skeleton," collapsed from exhaustion and became mute, "her mind as much injured as her health."

It went on for days until word came at last that rescue was near; they had been "bought by the Hudson Bay Company of Vancouver."[25] The HBC put together a ransom offer; boats were sent upriver from Fort Vancouver laden with goods to trade for the white prisoners. Peter Skene Ogden, HBC factor who replaced Dr. McLoughlin, skillfully bartered with the Cayuses for the release of all fifty-one captives. When released by the Cayuses, the hostages rushed to safety at Fort Walla Walla in overloaded wagons pulled by ox teams. The teams were pushed so hard during that thirty-mile trip that two oxen fell dead in their tracks. There was no time to look back.

When the Spokanes learned the Americans at Tshimikain were considering going to Fort Colville for increased security, the chief objected. Sensitive to ridicule from other neighboring tribes, they insisted the Americans were safe with them. The Spokanes didn't want anyone to think they'd been unable to protect their teachers.

The mission families considered the few options available to them; they were safe with the Spokanes, unless whites in lower Oregon began retaliating against Cayuses, who might come north looking for allies in an all-out Plateau war. Then what would happen to them?

Mary was anxious, it seemed "almost as bad as death to think of leaving" the mission.[26] She'd made Tshimikain her home for seven years; six Walker children were born there. To leave their homes meant hardship for the Eells and Walker families. Mary worried about what they would "eat and what shall we drink and wherewithall shall we be clothed." They were penniless in a country that offered very few amenities to those who had nothing to bargain with.

Myra and Mary kept terror at bay by embarking on an overwhelming amount of household tasks. They cleaned tripe, made tallow, dipped candles, boiled beef. After dipping seventeen dozen candles, Mary was exhausted, but she still worried. Where would they go? How would they live? Food, clothing—basics of existence dominated her mind.

Then an urgent warning came from Factor John Lewes, the chief trader and McDonald's successor at Fort Colville; things had gotten dangerous there, the men of the fort had armed and they feared an attack on the fort and Tshimikain.

Mary, holding herself together on faith alone, spent time showing an Indian girl how to skin a bird and woodchuck. She was trying to ignore the signs of pending trouble, hoping things would somehow be resolved. Mary's diary entry in March, 1848 sums it up, "It is a long, tedious winter."

The Tshimikain missionaries stayed in their homes until March, when word came that there was a war raging—a battle had taken place with "300 Americans, two hundred half-breeds and two or three hundred Cayuses warring." The rumor was that "one hundred Nez Perces [were]on their way to join the Americans."[27]

When the news came that Oregon militia volunteers were battling with Cayuses to the south, the difficult decision was made to seek refuge at Fort Colville. They stayed there with Factor Lewes until May, when they were given no choice but to head south with an escort of American troops that came to get them. They headed south on pack horses, sending some of their belongings by canoe.

Passing through Waiilatpu, a grim scene greeted them: fences were broken down, buildings looted and burned. The grounds were strewn with garbage and broken items ransacked from the buildings before they'd been torched. The smell of burnt wood, rotting bodies and waste permeated everything. The shallow common grave had been disturbed and "bones & hair of the Missionary & wife with others had been scattered over the plains by the wolves . . ."[28] One of the Walker children watched as his mother picked up a bit of Mrs. Whitman's golden hair and showed it to Mrs. Eells. None wanted to linger; the "shortest time was sufficient."[29]

Notes on Chapter Seventeen

[1] *Whitman, Letters*, p. 205.

[2] Ibid, p. 207.

[3] Ibid.

[4] McKee, *Mary Richardson Walker*, p. 249.

[5] Ibid, p. 273.

[6] Jeffrey, *Converting the West*, p. 212.

[7] *Whitman, Letters*, p. 216.

[8] Ibid, p. 215.

[9] McKee, *Mary Richardson Walker*, p. 277.

[10] Ibid, p. 279.

[11] Jeffrey, *Converting the West*, p. 213.

[12] Ibid, p. 216.

[13] McKee, *Mary Richardson Walker*, p. 286.

[14] Drury, *Elkanah and Mary Walker*, p. 203.

[15] Ibid, p. 203.

[16] McKee, *Mary Richardson Walker*, p. 288.

[17] Drury, *Elkanah and Mary Walker*, p. 202.

[18] McKee, *Mary Richardson Walker*, p. 289.

[19] Warren, *Memoirs*, p. 25.

[20] Ibid.

[21] Ibid, p. 26.

[22] Ibid, p. 27.

[23] Ibid.

[24] Ibid.

[25] Ibid, p. 30.

[26] McKee, *Mary Richardson Walker*, p. 293.

[27] Ibid, p. 294.

[28] Drury, *Elkanah and Mary Walker*, p. 219.

[29] Ibid, p. 220.

Historical Photograph Collections,
Washington State University Libraries

Amelia Lorene Spalding Brown
was born at the Lapwai Mission
Dec. 12, 1846.

Chapter Eighteen

End of the Dream

"Mrs. Walker is much cast down, more so than I have ever seen her before," Elkanah wrote that summer.

". . . we have not felt that interest in any undertaking here which we used to feel while laboring for the Indians. Our hearts seem constantly inclined to return to the Indians . . ."[1] Eliza Spalding wrote to an eastern friend.

In the Willamette Valley, the missionary wives found they had to beg charity, stay in houses without doors or windows, and pay a dollar a pound for butter or a dozen eggs. Incoming settlers created a boom in Oregon, where money and goods had always been scarce. Cookstoves were going for a hundred dollars, and girls aged thirteen were snapped up for wives—often in order to garner the additional land a wife could file on. There was no hope of hiring household help, and the pioneer women worked hard; even boys considered it "disgraceful" to be seen milking cows.

Eliza Spalding, forced to abandon her home and flee with her young children, heartbroken over the treatment of her ten-year-old daughter at the hands of her captors, never recovered her strength again. In the Willamette, the family settled in an unfinished house lent to them by a neighbor.

She wanted to teach again, especially since on the Oregon frontier "a female teacher gets the same wages in school as a man," but she was too weak. She "suffered very much with sickness" since they left "the Nez Perce country." The wet climate was "very unfavorable for diseased lungs" and she was resigned to the idea that she "would not long survive."[2] The shock over the Whitman's deaths at the hands of natives she thought so highly of, and the dismay at seeing her life's work dissolve crushed her optimism. She had given up; her new life was meaningless.

It was hard for any of them to accept that they had failed in an era when failure was attributed to sin. If they hadn't been sinners, the mission would have been successful—they had only themselves, on a very personal level—to blame.

Eliza died after a painful decline at age forty-three, regretting that her children were left motherless, the youngest aged four. Henry blamed her death on the fear, anxiety and fatigue of breaking up the Mission; he mourned her deeply. He wrote, "At this moment I seem to see her poor white hands, holding in one a golden harp whose angelic notes in harmony with united millions, floating upon the zephyrs of heaven, seem to call upon me to weep not for a wife dead, but to rejoice on account of a wife glorified."[3]

Henry's mind snapped after the massacre; Elkanah Walker judged him to be insane. His anger vented itself in the tombstone inscription he had made to place over Eliza's grave, on which he insisted the following be carved: "She always felt that the Jesuit Missionaries were the leading cause of the massacre." Years later, when both Henry and Eliza Spalding's bodies were reburied at Lapwai, the headstone was replaced with a less inflammatory inscription.

Elkanah Walker explained that, "Much might be said which led to this horrid massacre. Some doubtless attach too much blame to the Catholics. I am yet to be convinced that they had any direct agency in it . . . that they put the natives up to do the deed I do not believe . . ." To Eliza and Henry Spalding, blaming the Jesuits was easier than blaming the Indians for the massacre, something they could not accept emotionally or intellectually.

Eliza Spalding's efforts with the Nez Perces were the most successful of all the mission women, and working as a team with her husband, the two surpassed all other missionary efforts in the Pacific Northwest. The Nez Perce faction (not all the tribe responded to the Spalding's efforts) that worked with the Spaldings developed a peaceful, agrarian community which could not be driven from their rich farmland. They never went to war with the whites, and they were not exiled on reservations. Their introduction to Americans had been through the efforts towards literacy that the Spaldings had worked so hard to teach, and the Nez Perces so determined to achieve.

As historian Deborah Dawson reminds, "Eliza was not merely her husband's helpmate, nor was she someone who simply took care of the house and children while her husband took care of the mission. She has been quietly left in the background too long; it is time that Eliza Spalding received recognition for the important role she played in the history of the Oregon Mission and American frontier."[4] Her inner strength, and the belief that she was doing what was right provided her with the endurance to make the journey and build the ties—language, friendship, loyalty—that established the mission presence among the Nez Perce people. From their first meeting, it was Eliza who was the Indians' favorite.

In the last week of May, 1850, during the height of the exodus from Oregon Territory to California in the search for gold, the Whitman Massacre trial was held at Oregon City, the territorial capital. There were 9,000 white settlers in Oregon, the number increasing steadily with every autumn wagon train, the number shrinking with every party of men that headed south to California to dig their fortune in gold.

The settlers had been angry for the two and a half years since the residents of Waiilatpu had been killed. Now justice would be done in this wilderness settlement. There was no courtroom, it was held in a hotel saloon. The accused: Clokomas, Kiamasumkin, Isiaasheluckas, Tomahas (named The Murderer by the Cayuses years before the massacre), and Chief Telokite, had been surrendered to the white Oregon volunteer troops in April by the Cayuse band under Young Chief. They were represented by three defense lawyers and two interpreters.[5]

Lawyers for both sides argued vociferously, but after several days, and a jury deliberation of one hour and fifteen minutes the verdict of guilty, the sentence of death by hanging (there was no jail to hold the prisoners in to await an appeal—death was figured the only solution) was given out. After a public hanging before a thousand residents, the Cayuses were all but forgotten.

The Spaldings, Walkers, and Eells families were "destitute of almost every thing, no dwelling place . . . food or raiment to be found . . ." The worst was their "soul bleeding from many wounds."[6] They'd never been interested in claiming land for farming, or setting up lucrative trade posts; the men found work as teachers and preachers, the women began the task of creating new households one more time. Now they weren't missionaries, they weren't people with a chosen path or guiding light, they were just pioneers.

It was spring, 1849, a year after moving away from Tshimikain, that Mary "found [her] stuffed birds so full of moths" that she "burned them all up" because the moths were "consuming all the plumage." She had nothing left of her work at Tshimikain except a few precious mineral samples that no one was interested in.

Myra and Cushing Eells eventually returned to the Whitman's farm at Waiilatpu, lived there for several years, and spearheaded efforts to found an academy which grew into today's prestigious Whitman College in the town of Walla Walla, Washington.

Elkanah Walker couldn't settle down and farm, instead he left Mary and the children to run their little farm at Forest Grove while he itinerated at small churches. Mary became active in community life, founded a maternal society, and made a new life for herself. In her later years, she supported herself by taking in student boarders which provided her with the social and intellectual stimulation she always craved. Her donation of ten acres of land provided a site for Pacific University.

Groups of Spokane Indians made the trek to Forest Grove, trying to urge the missionaries to return and teach them, asking for "nothing but teachers."[7] But that was no longer possible. The Board had officially disbanded the Indian mission project.

Author's Photo

Tshimikain Mission site as it looks today.

The Inland Plateau Indians were swept up in warfare that lasted for years until they were finally settled on reservations, their cultural and economic systems nearly devastated by the settlement boom.

An 1853 entry in Mary Walker's diary seems an appropriate place to close:

> *I am 42 years old. On reviewing my life altho I see much to deplore I would not be willing to live it over lest I might do worse instead of better. When I undo a piece of work I never have the patience to do it as well the second time.*

Mary outlived Elkanah by twenty years. The last survivor of the mission band, she died in 1895. Her most precious possession, her mind, drifted away in her final years. She would sometimes take her old saddle out and perch it on a chair. She'd seat her fragile body upon it once more, drape her old cape over her shoulders and relive the past, when she was riding sidesaddle over the Rockies, hoping to change the world.

Notes on Chapter Eighteen

1 Dawson, *Laboring in My Savior's Vineyard*, p. 173.

2 Drury, *Henry Harmon Spalding*, p. 359.

3 Ibid, p. 361.

4 Dawson, *Laboring in My Savior's Vineyard*, p. 179.

5 Ronald B. Lansing, Juggernaut, *The Whitman Massacre Trial, 1850* (Oregon: Ninth Judicial Circuit Historical Society, 1993), p. 11.

6 *Whitman, Letters*, p. 230.

7 Drury, *Elkanah and Mary Walker*, p. 231.

Reflections

In 1873, following decades of warfare between the white military and native tribes, Reverend Henry Spalding journeyed back to the Nez Perce and Spokane villages, baptising hundreds into the Presbyterian Church.

Great changes occurred during the lifetimes of the missionaries. The Grays, Henry Spalding and the Walkers all made trips back to New England after the Union Pacific Railroad was completed in 1869. The Walkers surveyed the damages following the Chicago Fire, had photographs taken, and rode "steam cars"—Elkanah even lost his wallet to a pickpocket. Telegraph lines made it possible to communicate across the continent in minutes; mail delivery from the East now took weeks, not years. As historian Stephen Ambrose explains, "At the beginning of the 19th century, people thought nothing was possible. By the end of the century, people thought anything was possible. In many ways, that's more American than anything else—that sense that anything is possible."[1]

Certainly that attitude of possibility is what fortified and unified the women of the Oregon mission, and frontierswomen in general, enabling them to build homes and communities, and raise families, as they moved rapidly into an unknown future.

The spiritual aspect of the missionary women's lives was certainly their source of strength. They continually wrestled with what we call the "character issue" on a personal level and among themselves. Their lives were as difficult as one gets on the frontier, yet they continually refreshed themselves by honoring what they had been taught was right, for the best of reasons. They may have been too naive, too simplistic, too judgmental. But they were products of their time, and few women

Author's Photo

Whitman massacre burial site today.

today could do as well. Few would discount that they were brave, selfless, and stalwart in the face of adversity.

Above all else they were Christians, before Americans, women or teachers. They could criticize their own culture and note its flaws, but they did not alienate themselves from it (as the mountain men did). They were trying to reform society, at the same time they tried to give the best of it to less advantaged people. In the mission field, they found a complicated role for themselves, affirming a culture they were not completely satisfied with themselves.

Contrary to the Bible-thumping, prissy stereotype of missionaries bent on wreaking cultural disaster, research now reveals that missionaries themselves defied that image, and were instead, much the same sort of individuals who chose to serve in the Peace Corps a hundred and fifty years later.

Notes

[1] *USA Today*, "Technology moving too fast? Be glad it's not the 1840s," by Kevin Maney. January 30, 1997, p. 2B.

Bibliography

Allen, Opal Sweazea, *Narcissa Whitman*. Portland, Oregon: Binfords and Mort, 1959.

Armitage, Susan, and Elizabeth Jameson, Eds. *The Women's West*. Norman, Oklahoma: University of Oklahoma Press, 1987.

Beaver, R. Pierce. *American Protestant Women in World Mission: History of the First Feminist Movement in North America*. Grand Rapids, MI: William R. Eerdmans Publishing Company, 1980.

Blair, Karen J., Ed., *Women in Pacific Northwest History*. Seattle: University of Washington Press, 1988.

Brosnan, C.J., *Jason Lee, Prophet of the New Oregon*. New York: Macmillan, 1932.

Burns, Robert Ignatius, S.J., *The Jesuits and the Indian Wars of the Northwest*. Moscow: University of Idaho Press, 1966.

Cartwright, Frederick E. *Disease and History*. New York: Dorset Press, 1972.

Child, Mrs. *The American Frugal Housewife*. Twelfth Edition. Boston: Carter and Hendee, 1833. Reprinted by Chapman Billies, Inc., Bedford, Mass.

Cross, Whitney R., *The Burned-Over District: The Social and Intellectual History of Enthusiastic Religion in Western New York, 1800-1850*. New York: Harper and Row, 1950.

Dawson, Deborah Lynn. *Laboring in My Savior's Vinyard*. Unpublished dissertation. Ann Arbor, MI: University Microfilms, 1988.

DeVoto, Bernard, *Across the Wide Missouri*. Boston: Houghton Mifflin Company, 1947.

Drury, Clifford Merrill. *Diaries and Letters of Henry H. Spalding and Asa Bowen Smith Relating to the Nez Perce Mission, 1836-1842.* Glendale, CA: Arthur H. Clark Co., 1963.

Drury, Clifford Merrill. *Elkanah and Mary Walker: Pioneers Among the Spokanes.* Caldwell, Idaho: The Caxton Printers, Ltd., 1940.

Drury, Clifford Merrill. *First White Women Over the Rockies.* Glendale, CA: Arthur H. Clark, Co., 3 vols. 1963-1966.

Drury, Clifford Merrill. *Henry Harmon Spalding.* Caldwell, Idaho: The Caxton Printers, Ltd., 1936.

Drury, Clifford Merrill. *Marcus and Narcissa Whitman and the Opening of Old Oregon.* Seattle: Pacific Northwest National Parks and Forests Association, 2 vols. 1986.

Drury, Clifford Merrill. *Spalding and Smith On the Nez Perce Mission.* Glendale, California: Arthur H. Clark Company, 1958.

Dunn, J.P. *Massacres of the Mountains: A History of the Indian Wars of the Far West, 1815-1875.* New York: Archer House, 1886.

Dwight, Rev. Henry Otis, Rev. H. Allen Tupper, D.D., and Rev. Edwin Munsell Bliss, D.D. *The Encyclopedia of Missions.* 2nd edition. New York: Funk and Wagnalls, 1950.

Eells, Ida Myra. *Mother Eells, A Story of the Life of Myra Fairbank Eells.* Mimeograph. Wenatchee, Washington, 1947.

Fahey, John. *The Flathead Indians.* Norman: University of Oklahoma Press, 1974.

Garrison, Fielding H. *The History of Medicine.* Philadelphia: W.B. Saunders, Co., 1929.

Hafen, LeRoy R., editor, *Mountain Men and Fur Traders of the Far West.* Lincoln: University of Nebraska Press, 1982.

The Hymnal. Philadelphia: Presbyterian Board of Christian Education, 1949.

Hutchinson, William R. *Errand to the World: American Protestant Thought and Foreign Missions.* Chicago: University of Chicago Press, 1987.

Hymowitz, Carol, and Michaele Weissman. *A History of Women in America.* New York: Bantam Books, 1978.

Irving, Washington. *Astoria, or Anecdotes of an Enterprise Beyond the Rocky Mountains*. Philadelphia: J.B. Lippincott, 1961, reprint of 1836 edition.

Jeffrey, Julie Roy, *Converting the West: a Biography of Narcissa Whitman*. Norman: University of Oklahoma Press, 1991.

Johnson, Paul. *The Birth of the Modern: World Society 1815-1830*. New York: Harper Collins, 1991.

Johnson, Paul E. and Sean Wilentz. *The Kingdom of Mathias*. New York: Oxford University Press, 1994.

Lansing, Ronald B. *Juggernaut, The Whitman Massacre Trial, 1850*. Oregon: Ninth Judicial Circuit Historical Society, 1993.

Lavender, David. *Land of Giants: The Drive to the Pacific Northwest, 1750-1950*. Lincoln: University of Nebraska Press, 1956.

Luchetti, Cathy. *I Do! Courtship, Love and Marriage on the American Frontier*. New York: Crown Publishers, 1996.

McBeth, Kate. *The Nez Perces Since Lewis and Clark*. Moscow, Idaho: University of Idaho Press, 1993.

McKee, Ruth Karr. *Mary Richardson Walker: Her Book*. Caldwell, Idaho: The Caxton Printers, Ltd., 1945.

McWhorter, L.V., *Hear Me, My Chiefs: Nez Perce History and Legend*. Caldwell, Idaho: The Caxton Printers, Ltd.,1952, 1992.

Miller, Christopher L. *Prophetic Worlds: Indians and Whites on the Columbia Plateau*. New Jersey: Rutgers University Press, 1985.

Miyakawa, T. Scott. *Protestants and Pioneers: Individualism and Conformity on the American Frontier*. Chicago: University of Chicago Press, 1964.

Newman, Peter C. *Company of Adventurers: the Story of the Hudson's Bay Company*. New York: Penguin Books, 1985.

Parker, Samuel. *Journal of an Exploring Tour Beyond the Rocky Mountains*. Original, Ithaca, New York: Mack, Andrus, and Woodruff, 1842. Reprint, Moscow, Idaho: University of Idaho Press, 1990.

Riley, Glenda. *Women and Indians on the Frontier, 1825-1915*. Albuquerque: University of New Mexico Press, 1984.

Ruby, Robert H. and John A. Brown. *Indian Slavery in the Pacific Northwest*. Spokane, Wash.: Arthur H. Clark Company, 1993.

Ruby, Robert H. and John A. Brown. *The Spokane Indians: Children of the Sun*. Norman: University of Oklahoma Press, 1970.

Sager, Catherine, Elizabeth and Matilda. *The Whitman Massacre of 1847*. Fairfield, Wash.: Ye Galleon Press, 1986.

Schwantes, Carlos A. *The Pacific Northwest: An Interpretive History*. Lincoln: University of Nebraska Press, 1996.

Speer, Robert. *Presbyterian Foreign Missions*. Philadelphia: Presbyterian Board of Publications and Sabbath School Work, 1901.

Stewart, William Drummond. *Edward Warren*. Original, London: G. Walker, 1854. Reprint, Missoula: Mountain Press Publishing Company, 1986.

Szasz, Ferenc Morton. *The Protestant Clergy in the Great Plains and Mountain West, 1865-1915*. Albuquerque: University of New Mexico Press, 1988.

"Technology Moving Too Fast?" Kevin Maney, *USA Today*, January 30, 1997, p. 2B.

Utley, Robert M. *A Life Wild and Perilous: Mountain Men and the Paths to the Pacific*. New York: Henry Holt and Company, 1997.

Vernam, Glenn R. *Man on Horseback*. New York: Harper and Row, 1964.

Walker, Deward E., Jr. *Indians of Idaho*, Moscow: University Press of Idaho. 1978.

Warren, Eliza Spalding, *Memoirs of the West*, Portland, Oregon: Marsh Printing Company, 1916.

Wayland, Francis. *Memoir of the Life and Labors of the Rev. Adoniram Judson, D.D.*. Boston: Phillips, Sampson and Co., 1853. Two vols.

Whitman, Narcissa Prentiss. *The Letters of Narcissa Whitman*. Fairfield, Wash.: Ye Galleon Press, 1986.

Index

The Author:

Laurie Winn Carlson is the author of several successful books, including *More than Moccasins: A Kid's Activity Guide to Traditional North American Indian Life*, winner of the 1995 Museum Store Association Buyer's Choice Award. The book was also a finalist for the 1994 Western Writers of America Golden Spur Award. Laurie was named 1993 Idaho Writer of the Year by the Idaho Writers League. Her articles have been published in several magazines and newspapers.

She is a member of the Western Writers of America, Women Writing in the West and served on the Idaho Public Television advisory board.

Laurie is a Cheney, Washington resident.

Caxton Press
A brief history

In 1895, Albert E. Gipson moved his family from Colorado to Caldwell, Idaho, a small farming community located in the southwest corner that state. Gipson began publishing a horticultural magazine.

In 1907, Albert's son, James Herrick Gipson, joined the enterprise. The company reorganized as a commercial printer. The Gipsons called the new business, The Caxton Printers, Ltd., named for English printer William Caxton, considered the father of modern printing. They also adopted Caxton's unique logo.

In 1925, Caxton published its first trade book. By the 1930s, the company was releasing as many as thirty titles a year.

Several Caxton authors, including Vardis Fisher, Ayn Rand and Bill Gulick, have received national and international recognition. The company also has produced some of the best-known Western Americana books. *Yellow Wolf*, and *Hear Me, My Chiefs!*, by L.V. McWhorter, are considered foundation books for any study of the Nez Perce Indians.

Caxton still is owned and operated by members of the Gipson family. It is one of the oldest publishers west of Kansas City. It also is one of the oldest family-owned businesses in the Pacific Northwest.

Today *CAXTON PRESS*, a division of the Caxton Printers, Ltd., continues to publish the finest in Western Americana titles. It still adheres to the philosophy of its founders:

Books to us never can or will be primarily articles of merchandise to be produced as cheaply as possible and to be sold as slabs of bacon or packages of cereal over the counter. If there is anything that is really worthwhile in this mad jumble we call the twentieth century, it should be books. – J.H. Gipson

New Titles from
CAXTON PRESS

River Tales of Idaho
by Darcy Williamson
ISBN 0-87004-378-1 342 pages paper $17.95

The Cabin on Sawmill Creek
A Western Walden
by Mary Jo Churchwell
ISBN 0-87004-380-3 240 pages paper $12.95

Silver Creek: Idaho's Fly Fishing Paradise
by David Clark and David Glasscock
ISBN 0-87004-382-x 224 pages paper $18.95

Pioneers of the Colorado Parks
by Richard Barth
ISBN 0-87004-381-1 276 pages paper $17.95

Encyclopedia of Western Railroad History
Vol. IV   California
by Donald B. Robertson
ISBN 0-87004-385-4 cloth $42.95

For a free catalog of Caxton books write to:

CAXTON PRESS
312 Main Street
Caldwell, ID 83605-3299

or

Visit our Internet Website:

www.caxtonprinters.com

Caxton Press is a division of The CAXTON PRINTERS, Ltd.

WC